TEXTS AND CONTEXTS

Writing About Literature
with Critical Theory

TEXTS AND CONTEXTS

Writing About Literature
with Critical Theory

STEVEN LYNN
University of South Carolina

HarperCollins*CollegePublishers*

For Ben and Leora Lynn

Acquisitions Editor: Lisa Moore
Project Coordination and Text Design: Proof Positive/
    Farrowlyne Associates, Inc.
Cover Design: Kay Petronio
Production Manager: Kewal Sharma
Compositor: Proof Positive/Farrowlyne Associates, Inc.
Printer and Binder: Malloy Lithographing, Inc.
Cover Printer: Malloy Lithographing, Inc.

For permission to use copyrighted material, grateful acknowledgment is
made to the copyright holders on the following two pages,
which are hereby made part of this copyright page.

Texts and Contexts: Writing About Literature with Critical Theory,
First Edition

Library of Congress Cataloging-in-Publication Data

Lynn, Steven, 1952–
    Texts and contexts: writing about literature with critical
    theory / Steven Lynn.
        p. cm.
Includes bibliographical references and index.
ISBN 0-06-500099-4
1. English language—Rhetoric. 2. Literature—History and criticism—
Theory, etc. 3. Criticism—Authorship. 4. College readers. I. Title.
PE1479.C7L96 1994
808'.0668—dc20   93–30630
                                                           CIP

94 95 96 9 8 7 6 5 4 3 2

CREDITS

CONTENTS

PREFACE

This is a book born of excitement and frustration.

The excitement pervades the study of literature today, as a growing number of readers have discovered how various critical theories invigorate and enrich literary study. We understand better today than at any time in history how writing about literature is produced and the purposes it may serve. And we also understand more clearly how centrally important literary study is: every discipline depends on various assumptions about language, meaning, and knowledge; and every discipline involves applying these underlying theories to "texts" of various kinds. Every discipline involves reading and writing, in other words. Critical theory, which cuts across various fields (rhetoric, philosophy, composition, literary criticism, psychology, and others), most directly engages the questions of reading and writing—how are reading and writing motivated? What activities are involved in reading and writing? How are these activities taught, controlled, evaded? How can we read and write more effectively, more powerfully, more humanely?

Yet, despite the excitement and centrality of critical theories and practices, many students come to the study of literature with misgivings, forebodings, anxieties, yawns, and puzzlements. Even those students who love literature almost invariably are uneasy writing about it—uncertain how to proceed, wondering what the teacher "really wants," worried that their own experience or interpretation differs from their teacher's or classmates'. So, even in the best of classrooms, even when literary study is conducted with effort and imagination, there's still considerable frustration associated with writing about literature.

What is wrong with this picture? Why are we so often frustrated by what should be exciting and deeply meaningful? The problem (in large part anyway) is that something is missing from the study of literature. While the teaching of writing in general has been transformed by attending to the *process* of writing, writing about literature in particular *as an activity* has been relatively ignored. We've assumed, apparently, that the process of writing about literature is the same as writing about anything. Therefore, students primarily need to be given information about the concepts and terms used in literary criticism—the "elements" of literature, as they're usually called. But writing about literature, in addition to calling on general writing abilities, depends on some special strategies of invention and insight. While literary terms and concepts are often helpful, a clear understanding of what one is trying to accomplish and how to go about doing it is essential.

That's where critical theories come in. Whether we're aware of them or not, theories of some sort inevitably must guide our perceptions, our thinking, our behavior. By explaining and illustrating a variety of critical theories, *Texts and Contexts: Writing About Literature with Critical Theory* aims to take writing about literature out of the realm of mystery and intuition. It reveals the *process* of writing about literature, beginning in each chapter with an explanation of the purpose of a particular approach, then showing students how to put the assumptions to work, then illustrating how an essay is evolved from that particular theoretical stance, and finally offering some works to practice on, accompanied by guiding questions. The introductory chapter offers a preview of the theories treated here; and the last chapter discusses writing a research paper, while at the same time offering a review of various theories.

This book, in other words, promotes a very valuable ability—it explains a variety of different assumptions about texts, and it illustrates how to use those assumptions to explore and understand literature. It aims to make writing about literature more interesting, more satisfying, and less frustrating. There's really no reason why only literary scholars and teachers should have all the fun.

Acknowledgments

I will always be grateful to Gregory Jay and David Miller for organizing the theory discussion group at the University of Alabama. I also very much appreciate the generous, honest feedback my students have offered as the materials in this book have evolved in my classes. I especially want to thank the hundred or so high school teachers in the various Advanced Placement training courses that Karl Beason (and sometimes Ken Autry) and I have taught. Their enthusiastic and successful deployment of theoretical awareness in high school English classes has often inspired me. I thank the South Carolina State Department of Education for funding those AP Institutes. I also want to thank Valerie Winsemann and Todd Stebbins for their responses to various portions of the book.

For release time to work on this book, and for various other forms of support, I thank the English department of the University of South Carolina. I'm fortunate to be in a department inhabited by stimulating, intelligent, and colorful colleagues: I appreciate their conversation and interest. My assistant, Elizabeth Smith, and my research assistants, Jennie Ariail and Martha Thomas have provided invaluable and cheerful help.

At HarperCollins, I especially want to thank Lisa Moore for believing in this project, and Marisa L. L'Heureux for thoughtfully guiding its development. Laurie Brown of Proof Positive/Farrowlyne Associates, Inc., did an impressively careful and patient job of copyediting.

I also appreciate the good suggestions that the various reviewers offered. In particular, I acknowledge the extremely useful comments of the following people: Dana Beckelman, University of Wisconsin—Milwaukee; Donella Eberle, Mesa Community College; Peter Garrett, University of Illinois at Urbana-Champaign; John Glavin, Georgetown University; Julia Hamilton, Inver Hills Community College; David P. Haney, Auburn University; James Heldman, Western Kentucky University; Martha Kendall, San Jose City College; John Miller, Normandale Community College; Diane Quantic, Wichita State University; John Schilb, University of Maryland; Stephen Smolen, Saddleback College; and Isabel Stanley, East Tennessee State University.

I am always inspired by my wife, Annette Williams Lynn, and by the supposition that Lesley, Jacob, Laura, Hannah, Alicia, Danielle, and Callie may someday read some of my work. To the most important and constructive critics of my life, my parents, I dedicate this book.

Steven Lynn

INTRODUCTION
Textual Tours

*We should study literary crit-
icism and the theories of literature for the same reasons
we read literature—to forever
alter our perspectives, to
escape our own vanities, and
to extend the horizons of our
limitations.*

—Lynn Jordan Stidon
   (student)

Literary works are, in a way, like places we can visit. Some are foreign, mysterious, puzzling; others make us feel right at home. Some call us back again and again; others we feel obliged to experience, knowing they'll do us good even though we never quite enjoy them. Inhabiting a literary work, we can see how other people live; we can see, to a certain extent, through other people's eyes. We can momentarily transcend the boundaries of our lives.

Although wandering around is always an option, travelers who know what they're looking for and have a plan for getting there are more likely to have a satisfying, interesting visit. Literary criticism aims to bring such order and organization to our experience of literary works, focusing our attention on this, disregarding that, putting various parts together, making sense of what we see. When you write about literature, you serve as a kind of tour guide, leading your reader (and yourself) through the work. Readers can see what's in front of them, but they don't necessarily know what to make of it without some persuasive commentary.

Critical theories are like the different travel agencies through which the various tour guides generally work. Different agencies feature different kinds of tours: one specializes in cultural immersion, another in artistic appreciation, another in historical recollection, another in personal indulgence. The agencies provide the frameworks, the general guidelines for your performance as a tour guide. To write most successfully about a literary work, then, you need not only to have spent some time with the work, but also to have some clear idea of the kinds of tours available, and how they might be combined or adapted. You need, in other words, an understanding of various critical theories and practices.

But before we begin our tours, we should consider some basic questions often asked by students embarking on such investigations, and then address a bit more directly the purpose and plan of this book.

"Is there one correct interpretation of a literary work?"

Perhaps there are English teachers somewhere like the one in John Cheever's "Expelled," who tells students that her interpretation of *Hamlet* is the only one they need to know—it's "the one accepted on college-board papers," she says. But most teachers (and certainly your own if this book has been assigned) cherish variety and difference in literary criticism, encouraging students to think for themselves when they write about literature. Just as there is no one best place to view the Blue Ridge Mountains, so there is no one best reading of *Hamlet* or any work. Shift your vantage point a little, change your interests, or just let some time pass, and you'll see something new.

"So are all opinions about literature equally valid?"

Surely some opinions seem more convincing or satisfying than others. Endorsing variety doesn't necessarily mean that all opinions are equal, that any piece of literary criticism is just as good as any other. Just because we appreciate various views of the mountains, we need not also agree that all vantage points are equally satisfying to all people. If you construct a reading of *Hamlet* this week and a different interpretation next week, it's unlikely that you or your readers will value both of them equally, or even that everyone will agree on which one is superior. Some readings are arguably better than others, but to make such a determination, we need first to ask: Better for what? Better for whom? This book aims to address such questions, attempting not only to explain clearly and explicitly how to use various critical approaches, but also to consider what purposes different approaches are likely to serve (better for what), as well as what sort of audience is likely to be influenced and even created by different critical strategies (better for whom).

But don't such theoretical questions distract from the study of literature itself?

The focus in this text on the assumptions, strategies, and purposes shaping literary criticism—on critical theories in other words—is not a step away from literature or writing about literature; rather, such assumptions, strategies, and purposes make a deeply rewarding engagement with literature possible. Theory enables practice. Even the simplest acts of literary response, such as "This is boring," depend on a certain theoretical stance: in this case, the stance includes the assumption that the purpose of literature includes entertaining the reader, and that the critic's job includes identifying works that fail this test.

In fact, you already have a critical theory (at least one) that you use to make sense of literature, even if you're unaware of your theoretical stance. Some kind of principles guide you in determining what you expect a work to do, how you evaluate its performance, what you decide to say about it. (Even the absence of principles constitutes a theoretical position, as does the presence of contradictory principles.) The "elements" of literature, such as plot, character, point of view, are easy to understand; what is harder, and where more help is needed, is knowing what to say about such elements—how to approach them. In the following explanations and illustrations of the various critical approaches, you'll get to see the "elements" in action. You'll see, for instance, how New Criticism, psychological criticism, and deconstruction provide very different views of "character," giving you a wider range of purposes and strategies in writing about character.

To begin enhancing your awareness of literary criticism, take an inventory of what you already assume, asking yourself the following questions:

- What do I suppose is the function of literature? What do I look for in a literary work?
- What do I think is the function of writing about literature? What should literary criticism do?
- How do I believe the task of criticism is carried out? What strategies, routines, procedures, and activities do literary critics engage in?

As you try out the various approaches discussed here, you'll be able to compare your own starting assumptions with some of the various options available. At the least, you'll have a better understanding of the critical possibilities, allowing you to understand published criticism more readily; more likely, you'll find yourself incorporating new strategies or stances into your writing about literature, enriching and deepening your insights.

But isn't such theoretical study too abstract and difficult for a student at my level?

Such work is challenging at times, but it isn't beyond your abilities: college students can understand and use critical theories, and this book is intended to make such theory and practice clear and accessible. There are, to be sure, many controversies, variations, complexities, exceptions, and qualifications that are not treated here, and critical theory can be astonishingly difficult (and often just astonishing). After working through this book, you won't find the writings of Jacques Derrida or Annette Kolodny easy to understand—just as an introduction to physics wouldn't make the scientific papers of Steven Hawking or John Wheeler easy to comprehend. But an introduction can make the ideas of these specialists accessible: there's no reason you shouldn't be told about black holes or deconstruction simply because the theories, in all their specifics and intricacies, are difficult. Few people, if pressed, could explain even Isaac Newton's physics in detail; but just about anyone can understand in a useful way how momentum and gravity work.

This text offers a basic, working understanding of critical theory and practice, freely acknowledging that a more advanced understanding is possible. I have tried hard to clarify without distorting, but some matters have no doubt been represented to be simpler than they are. This is, after all, an introduction.

"So what's the plan here?"

Unfortunately, there's no way a reasonably sized textbook (one without wheels and a handle) can cover adequately all the different kinds of criticism that can be identified today— even if I understood them all. Nor can any one particular theory in all its mutations, combinations, and complexities be presented here. What I can do is provide a practical introduction to some of the most influential theories, leaving aside for the most part, with considerable regret, some of the most interesting and exciting for now. My goal is to put you in a position to develop and refine your understanding, to move into other critical arenas, to evolve your own readings and even theories.

The plan is simple. The first chapter briefly visits all the approaches discussed here by applying them to a single passage. Then each of the next six chapters inhabits a single theory in some detail, again applying the theories to various passages and evolving essays step-by-step from the various critical stances. The eighth chapter deals with writing research papers.

CHAPTER
1

CRITICAL WORLDS
A Selective Tour

"The question is," said
Alice, "whether you can
make words mean so
many things."
"The question is," said
Humpty Dumpty, "which is
to be master—that's all."
—Lewis Carroll

This chapter begins to show you how critical theories work. The various approaches treated in this book are introduced here, and when you finish this chapter you should expect to have a fairly good idea of each theory's most basic assumptions and strategies. To allow you to compare and contrast the various theories, I apply each one to the same passage from Brendan Gill's *Here at The New Yorker*.

It's entirely possible that you are encountering critical theories for the first time, and your prior experience with literature may be limited; don't be dismayed if some of the terms and ideas are unfamiliar and a bit challenging. In subsequent chapters each approach and its use in the process of writing about literature will be explained in more detail. The brief excursions in this chapter are a preview, intended to raise questions as much as provide answers. You may well want to use this chapter as a review also, returning to it after you've read the other chapters.

NEW CRITICISM

New Criticism (which is now decades "old") focuses attention on the work itself, not the reader or the author. New Critics are not allergic to talking about the responses of readers or the intentions of authors, but they believe that the work itself ultimately must stand on its own. Talk of readers and authors is of secondary importance. The purpose of giving attention to the work itself is, first, to expose the work's unity. In a unified work, every element works together toward a theme. Every element is essential. In addition, the "close reading" (a phrase popularized by New Critics) of a literary work reveals its complexity. Great literature, New Critics assume, contains oppositions, ambiguities, ironies, tensions; these are unified by the work—if it is successful by the standards of New Criticism.

So how does one do New Criticism? Begin by reading closely. Since everything should contribute to the work's artistic unity—figures of speech, point of view, diction, imagery, recurrent ideas or events, and so forth—then careful analysis of any aspect of the work should be revealing. Look for oppositions, tensions, ambiguities. These add complexity to the work's unity. A mediocre work might be unified but have little complexity; or it might be complex but never really come together. The New Critic, finally, shows how the various elements of a great work unify it.

Let's see how New Criticism can be applied to a particular passage from *Here at The New Yorker* by Brendan Gill. The passage will be used to illustrate the other theories covered in this chapter, so you'll want to read it carefully, becoming familiar with it. Here's the passage:

> When I started at *The New Yorker,* I felt an unshakable confidence in my talent and intelligence. I revelled in them openly, like a dolphin diving skyward out of the sea. After almost forty years, my assurance is less than it was; the revellings, such as they are, take place in becoming seclusion. This steady progress downward in the amount of one's confidence is a commonplace at the magazine—one might almost call it a tradition. Again and again, some writer who has made a name for himself in the world will begin to write for us and will discover as if for the first time how difficult writing is. The

machinery of benign skepticism that surrounds and besets him in the form of editors, copy editors, and checkers, to say nothing of fellow-writers, digs a yawning pit an inch or so beyond his desk. He hears it repeated as gospel that there are not three people in all America who can set down a simple declarative sentence correctly; what are the odds against his being one of this tiny elect?

In some cases, the pressure of all those doubting eyes upon his copy is more than the writer can bear. When the galleys of a piece are placed in front of him, covered with scores, perhaps hundreds, of pencilled hen-tracks of inquiry, suggestion, and correction, he may sense not the glory of creation but the threat of being stung to death by an army of gnats. Upon which he may think of nothing better to do than lower his head onto his blotter and burst into tears. Thanks to the hen-tracks and their consequences, the piece will be much improved, but the author of it will be pitched into a state of graver self-doubt than ever. Poor devil, he will type out his name on a sheet of paper and stare at it long and long, with dumb uncertainty. It looks—oh, Christ!—his name looks as if it could stand some working on.

As I was writing the above, Gardner Botsford, the editor who, among other duties, handles the copy for "Theatre," came into my office with the galleys of my latest play review in his hand. Wearing an expression of solemnity, he said, "I am obliged to inform you that Miss Gould has found a buried dangling modifier in one of your sentences." Miss Gould is our head copy editor and unquestionably knows as much about English grammar as anyone alive. Gerunds, predicate nominatives, and passive periphrastic conjugations are mother's milk to her, as they are not to me. Nevertheless, I boldly challenged her allegation. My prose was surely correct in every way. Botsford placed the galleys before me and indicated the offending sentence, which ran, "I am told that in her ninth decade this beautiful woman's only complaint in respect to her role is that she doesn't have enough work to do."

I glared blankly at the galleys. Humiliating enough to have buried a dangling modifier unawares; still more humiliating not to be able to disinter it. Botsford came to my rescue. "Miss Gould points out that as the sentence is written, the meaning is that the complaint is in its ninth decade and has, moreover, suddenly and unaccountably assumed the female gender." I said that in my opinion the sentence could only be made worse by being corrected—it was plain that "The only complaint of this beautiful woman in her ninth decade . . ."

would hang on the page as heavy as a sash-weight. "Quite so," said Botsford. "There are times when to be right is wrong, and this is one of them. The sentence stands." (7–8)

My New Critical reading of this passage was developed by reading carefully, marking up the text, asking myself questions, drafting answers to the questions, brainstorming and freewriting, and putting my ideas together. Although this reading didn't just pop out of my head, it wasn't a frustrating struggle because I knew what I was trying to do, and I was confident that my assumptions and strategies would produce something interesting. Specifically, I knew that a New Critical reading would identify some tension (or irony, or opposition) in the text, and some tensions in the story do seem pretty clear:

> editor vs. writer
> the world vs. *The New Yorker*
> grammar vs. style
> confidence vs. doubt
> right vs. wrong.

I also knew that such tensions must somehow be resolved if the text succeeds (by New Critical standards). Therefore, it's especially important from a New Critical perspective how the text ends.

New Critics might have some trouble with the idea of an "ending" here, because the "work" I've chosen is not really a work, but rather an excerpt from a work. But for the purposes of demonstration, let's imagine this passage stands alone, entitled "Writing a Wrong." And since endings are crucial, I decided to focus on the reconciliation at the end, when Botsford pronounces "right is wrong," which is reflected in the (hypothetical) title. As a New Critic, I then had to consider, "How does this idea—'right is wrong'—unify or resolve the work in a complex or ambiguous way?" In other words, what conflicting ideas are at work in the passage that are brought into balance and harmony by this theme?

You'll benefit most, I think, if you try to sketch out a New Critical reading of your own before (and perhaps after) you read mine.

THE PARADOXICAL UNITY OF "WRITING A WRONG"

In Brendan Gill's story of a dangling modifier, "Writing a Wrong," the editor Botsford solves the conflict between Miss Gould's rules and Gill's taste. He does so by offering a paradox that unifies Gill's story: sometimes "right is wrong," Botsford says. It turns out that Miss Gould was right to spot the error, but Gill was right to have written the sentence as he did. The irony of this solution is reinforced by various paradoxical images in the story.

For example, the dolphin in the second sentence is "diving skyward." This action simultaneously suggests a downward movement ("diving") and an upward motion ("skyward"). The description thus embodies the same sort of logic as a wrong rightness. Likewise, the "progress downward" of the writer, and even his "becoming seclusion" ("becoming"—attractive and appealing to others; "seclusion"—unknown to others), convey the same kind of image. In larger terms, the writer's "unshakable confidence" quickly becomes a "dumb uncertainty"—which again suggests the kind of reversal that resolves the story.

In such an upside-down world we would expect to find imagery of struggle and violence, and we do encounter a "yawning pit" and an "army of gnats." Such tension is harmonized by Gill's brilliant conclusion: in writing, conducted properly, the demands of correctness and style are unified by the writer's poetic instincts. Similarly, the story itself is resolved by the notion of a correct error.

READER-RESPONSE CRITICISM

Reader-response criticism starts from the idea that the critic's interest ultimately ought to be focused on the reader, rather than the text itself or the author. Without readers, it seems safe to say, there would be little reason to talk about literature; it is the reader who brings the text to life, who gives it meaning. Otherwise, it's just black marks on a white page.

The reader-response critic focuses on the reader's activity in one of two ways: by describing how readers *should* respond to the text, or by giving the critic's own personal response. That is, the reader-response critic either is claiming to be describing what is "normal," or conventional, or ideal, or implied by the text; or the critic is expressing that which is personal, subjective, perhaps even eccentric. One could argue that reader-response critics are always engaging in subjective response, even when they think they're objectively describing "the" response. In any event, reader-response critics tend to deal with works eliciting responses that are somehow note-worthy.

How does one do reader-response criticism? If the goal is to offer a personal, subjective response, one simply reads the text and responds. As you can imagine, such a strategy has been especially popular because it really liberates the reader. It's difficult to see how any response could be wrong: who could say, No, that isn't your response? Some responses may seem richer than others; some responses may seem to deal more fully with the text; some responses may seem more authentic and honest than others. But any particular response may well help another reader to a more interesting or satisfying experience of the work.

If the idea is to describe how a reader *ought* to respond, which might better be called "reader-reception" criticism, then you'll need to try to suppress whatever is personal in your response, and offer instead an "ideal" response, one that is (or rather ought to be) shared by all attentive and intelligent readers. Describing in careful detail the slow-motion progress of a hypothetical reader through the text, such "objective" or receptive reader-response criticism may consider these kinds of questions: What expectations does the text create? What happens to those expectations? (Are they met, undermined, exploited, transformed, denied?) What literary conventions does the text employ to affect the reader? How, in other words, does the text shape the reader's response?

Although I'm presenting these two versions of reader-response criticism as oppositions, flip sides of a single coin, it may be more accurate and helpful to see them in terms of a progression. Reader-response critics unavoidably must use their own personal responses as a starting point for talking about how the ideal, or implied, or common reader responds; but the close examination of such "ideal" responses would seem inevitably to reveal some personal and subjective features. (No one, I would suggest, not even the author, can be *the* ideal reader.)

At this point, before we get any deeper into the question of whether reader-response criticism is unavoidably subjective, let's see how the theory applies to our passage.

The following essay tries to present a record of my movement through this passage. It was fairly easy and fun to write because I simply read through the passage slowly and asked myself, "Okay, how am I responding now? What does this make me think? What am I expecting next?" Although I decided that the passage was continually surprising me, I would not argue that surprise is the only or the correct response: I might have focused on the passage's humor, on a pervading sense of doom, or something else. That's the beauty of reader-response criticism: different responses. As a piece of reader-response criticism, this essay strives to be neither rabidly subjective nor dogmatically objective. I focus on my personal response, but I also try to play the reader's role that I believe Gill has imagined. I quote the text repeatedly, trying to show my reader exactly what I'm responding to.

THE READER'S SURPRISE IN AN EXCERPT FROM
HERE AT THE NEW YORKER

Beginning with its first sentence, the story of the buried dangling modifier in Brendan Gill's *Here at The New Yorker* is continually surprising, setting up expectations and then knocking them down. Gill begins the first sentence with "When I started at *The New Yorker*," and I naturally expect him to talk about how nervous and insecure he was starting off at one of the largest and most famous magazines in the world.

Instead, Gill refers to his "unshakable confidence."
The third sentence begins with "After almost forty
years," leading me to expect some explanation of how
his joy at the magazine has grown. But forty years of
experience, it turns out, have not developed Gill's
confidence and happiness. Instead, his "assurance is
less than it was." How, I must wonder, has he managed
to be there for forty years and yet grow less confident?

Expecting Gill to explain the oddity of his deteriorating confidence, I find, surprisingly, that such an
effect "is a commonplace at the magazine," a "tradition" even. Since the loss of confidence occurs for
everyone, we might then expect that *The New Yorker*
staff sticks together, sharing insecurities and supporting each other. Such is hardly the case, as Gill
continues to surprise me by tracing one imaginary
writer's loss of confidence to the point of what
appears to be a nervous breakdown. The writer, who is
said to have "made a name for himself in the world,"
is reduced to weeping on his blotter and trying to
revise his name. Such is not what I expect from a
famous writer.

Given this tradition of disaster, it seems clear to
me that Gardner Botsford is appearing in the third
paragraph to star in the story of Gill's own downfall.
Botsford points to a major error Gill has made, and
Gill's assertion that he "boldly challenged" the allegation seems to set him up for a major humiliation.
"Unshakable" confidence and bold challenges certainly
seem unwarranted in the atmosphere of *The New Yorker*.
But, once more, Gill crosses me up and provides a
story of triumph. Rather than undermining his confidence, which is what everything in the story suggests
will happen, Botsford becomes Gill's champion. "The
sentence stands," he says, as the last reversal provides a happy ending.

DECONSTRUCTIVE CRITICISM

Think, for starters, of deconstructive criticism as the mirror image of New Criticism: whereas New Criticism aims to reveal the coherence and unity of the work, deconstruction aims to expose the gaps, the incoherences, the contradictions of the text. Deconstructive critics assume these gaps are present because of what they assume about the nature of language. Specifically, they notice that language makes meaning by oppositions: we know what "good" means because it is the opposite of "bad"; "tired" means something to us because it is the opposite of "rested." So words make sense because of their relationship *to other words,* not because of any "natural" grounding in reality. Although we may like to think "bad" and "rested" refer to something solid and real, they don't. "Bad" has come to mean in certain contexts "good." It could come to mean "blue," or "hungry," or anything. "Rested" with regard to a fighter pilot during combat may mean "having had three hours sleep in the last twenty-four." Meaning is relative and relational.

Deconstruction aims (among other things) to remind us of the arbitrary and unstable nature of language by taking texts apart—undoing them until we see how a text inevitably contradicts itself, containing traces of its opposite or "other." Any effort to explain deconstruction is therefore doomed according to the theory itself. Any effort to say *anything,* in fact, must go astray. Such an assumption could be dismaying, but many deconstructive critics have chosen to adopt a mischievously comic and even shocking stance. Although deconstructive criticism can be very difficult to read (perhaps as an illustration of how language eventually fails?), it can also be very amusing and engaging.

Thus, deconstructing a text calls for careful reading and a bit of creativity, but it's often revealing and even fun. One way to think of your goal as a deconstructive critic is that you're trying to turn the text against itself. For instance, Botsford's concluding decision, "The sentence stands," may appear to be reassuring. Here is a case where a writer makes a mistake, but the mistake turns out to be okay. If we were to press this reading, however, asking if the text might say something other than what it appears to say, we may begin to move into the realm of deconstruction. If you are a student in a writing-about-literature class, I suspect that Gill's passage is only superficially comforting. If a writer at *The New Yorker* can't always tell whether a sentence is right or wrong—if in fact the rules of writing are so complex that not even three people in America "can set down a simple declarative sentence correctly"—then how is a college student to feel? If a grown man and an established writer is weeping onto his desk blotter and considering revising his name, then how can the ordinary student hope to write an error-free paper—especially when the rules seem to apply in one case and not in another, and the rules for determining such exceptions don't seem to exist but are instead invented and applied by those who happen to be in charge? Writing seems to be a nightmare.

In fact, Botsford's "reassuring" vindication is deceptive, for he does not actually say that sometimes right is wrong and wrong is right. He only says that sometimes "right is wrong." Isn't wrong also usually wrong? But Botsford's apparent reversal of the dismantling of authors at *The New Yorker* is finally ambiguous, since we never know if the writer is ever correct, no matter what he does: "The sentence stands" indeed, but it stands with its error intact, a monument to Gill's inability to correct it and to the inevitable errors of writing. A monument to the way language masters us.

Although deconstructive critics may well deal with obviously major features of a text, like its ending, they may also choose some marginal element of the text and vigorously explore its oppositions, reversals, and ambiguities. In fact, for some critics, deconstruction is simply a name for "close reading" of an especially rigorous kind. The deconstructive critic, for example, might well decide to concentrate on the assertion that because of the editors' merciless correction, "the piece will be much improved." A New Critic, I think, would not be very likely to consider this assertion central, the key to the passage. But a deconstructive critic might. Here is what happened when I turned around the idea that "the piece will be much improved" and questioned it.

"THE SENTENCE STANDS" TRIUMPHANT:
A DECONSTRUCTIVE READING

Gill's anecdote clearly sets the world's writers against the editors, and the latter control the game. The editors and their accomplices, the checkers and copyeditors, get to say what is wrong. They get to dig the "yawning pit" in front of the helpless writer's desk; they determine the "tiny elect" who can write correctly; they make the scores and hundreds of "hen-tracks" on the writer's manuscript, which serve as testimony to the incompetence of writers, the near-impossibility of writing, and the arbitrary power of the editor.

To be sure, it is acknowledged that these editorial assaults upon the writer serve their purpose, for "Thanks to the hen-tracks and their consequences, the piece will be much improved." But the cost is terri-ble. Not only is the writer unable to write his own name with any confidence; he has become a "Poor devil," outside "the elect." In delivering his writing over to the editors, conceding their dominance, the writer inevitably places his own identity, perhaps even his very soul, in jeopardy. Thus, the cry "oh Christ!" comes to be an invocation to the only power who can save the writer from the devil and the edi-tor's destructive forces.

In fact, this story of the errors of writing actu-ally reveals that the kingdom of editors is based upon a lie: it simply is not true, despite the beleaguered writer's admission under torture, that "the piece will be much improved" by editorial intervention. Miss Gould's enormous grammatical lore does not improve the piece at all; her effort nearly made it "worse." And Botsford's contribution involves simply leaving the piece as it was written—a strange method of improve-ment. This instance, in other words, suggests that the writer need not approach falling apart in order to compose his writing.

At the same time, Gill can never again become like
the gill-less dolphin of the first paragraph, confi-
dently "diving skyward," because the dangling modifier
remains: it is a part of the sea of language the
author cannot leave. In the end, both writer and editor are defeated by their inability to control their
language. The status of the writer at *The New Yorker*
becomes a paradigm for the alarming status of writing
itself: deceptive, mute, and intractable, "The sentence stands," neither improved nor made worse, standing really for nothing.

BIOGRAPHICAL, HISTORICAL, AND NEW HISTORICAL CRITICISM

Biographical and historical critics begin from the com-
monsensical notion that there is certainly something "outside
the text," and that these biographical and historical facts help
us to make sense of literature. Biographical and historical
critics have at least two compelling reasons to exist. First,
such criticism is often fascinating. We want to know what
authors were like as persons, what kinds of lives they led,
even if such information doesn't directly help us understand
their works—although often it does. And second, we cannot
take for granted that we know what authors might reasonably
expect their initial audiences to know. By reconstructing the
past, understanding the historical context of a work, we're
able to see more clearly through the lens of the author's time.

Biographical and historical criticism thus seek rather
direct connections between authors and works, between historical events and works: this happened, which affected this,
which affected that. New Historical criticism starts from a
different (a new) view of history, one much more compatible
with Jacques Derrida's assertion that "there is nothing outside
the text" (158). Historical events, new historicists observe, are
nothing more than texts now. Any event has meaning because
of its place within a system of meaning. Rather than moving
through time, showing us how one thing led to another, new
historicists are more likely to take a slice of time and analyze

it as a system, studying the relationship of one thing to another. If you think of history as a movie, biographical and historical critics watch the movie in the usual fashion, trying to figure out the plot, keeping track of the characters. A new historical critic may select one frame of the film, carefully analyzing minute details, and then compare that frame to another one ten minutes later, showing the radical differences between the two. Whereas traditional historians see connections, new historians see ruptures and revolutions.

I'll illustrate briefly the way that history can be used to write about literature by employing a biographical stance.

ON BRENDAN GILL'S CAREER AND AN EXCERPT FROM
HERE AT THE NEW YORKER

This passage from Brendan Gill's *Here at The New Yorker* is a kind of meditation on his own career. Gill begins with confidence yet seems to deteriorate, like everyone else who writes at the magazine, into profound self-doubt. According to the entry on Gill in *Contemporary Authors*, he started his career at *The New Yorker* in 1936—"almost forty years ago," as he says in the passage, published in 1975. Thus, his "unshakable" optimism seems even more remarkable for arising in the midst of the Depression, with failure and fear of failure rampant all around him.

When Gill begins to tell in detail how his "assurance is less than it was," he shifts to third person, seemingly illustrating his own fortunes at the same time that he shows us everyone else's. It is not, however, Gill who has his head on the blotter in the second paragraph, but the hypothetical writer. Some investigation into Gill's life suggests, in fact, that this hypothetical writer does not stand for Gill, even though that may seem at first to be the case. Gill only says "my assurance is less than it was"; he doesn't say "I was reduced to tears."

Elsewhere in *Here at The New Yorker*, Gill writes, "I am always so ready to take a favorable view of my powers, that even when I am caught out and made a fool

of, I manage to twist this circumstance about until it
becomes a proof of how exceptional I am" (62). This
statement fits the story of the dangling modifier
nicely. Although Gill says he is humiliated by his
error, such a reaction seems unreasonable and unlikely. He does manage to twist his error around to be "a
proof" of his "exceptional" ability: his error is an
exception, a correct error. Gill's use of "humiliating" thus appears, especially in light of this other
statement, to be an exaggeration for comic effect.

Another comment by Gill, reflecting on his career,
further suggests that his story of profound self-doubt
and humiliation is not to be taken literally: "I
started out at the place where I wanted most to be and
with much pleasure and very little labor have remained
here since." The writer with "hundreds" of "hen-tracks
of inquiry," endlessly revising even his name, does
not seem to be experiencing "much pleasure" or "very
little labor." Gill's autobiographical "Foreward" to *A
New York Life* also indicates that his troubles in the
passage under consideration are largely for effect.
For one thing, Gill explains in the "Foreward" how the
metaphorical nature of language so delighted him as a
child that he perceived at age "five or six" that he
would be a writer. He was thrilled to find, he says,
that the "ladyfingers" his mother served weren't really lady's fingers. Gill's real outlook, as he presents
it, seems more like that of the dolphin in his opening
paragraph than that of the poor anxiety-driven writer.
Reference to Gill's life thus emphasizes for us the
hypothetical (not historical) and comic (not tragic)
nature of the writer's struggles in the passage.

PSYCHOLOGICAL CRITICISM

Anyone whose writing is evaluated will be intrigued, I
think, by what Gill's passage implies about the psychological
effects of criticism. You too may have felt at some point the
discomfort of "pencilled hen-tracks of inquiry, suggestion,

and correction." The passage provides a good opportunity to consider how such feelings arise and what purpose, if any, they serve. You don't, in other words, have to be a psychologist in order to do psychological criticism. Common sense and an interest in human thinking and behavior are the only essentials.

Still, psychological concepts can be valuable and stimulating in writing about literature. Take, for instance, the idea put forward by Sigmund Freud that creative writing is like dreaming: both allow wishes or fears to be fulfilled that would otherwise be suppressed. A desire or a fear too powerful to be confronted directly can be disguised by the unconscious and expressed by the author or dreamer, Freud said. One possible task of the psychological critic, then, like the psychologist, would be to decode what is being disguised. The critic may make educated guesses about what has been repressed and transformed by the author, or by characters, or even by other readers.

Another useful psychological concept is the idea that there are basic patterns of human development, even though everyone's formative history is different in particulars. One of the most famous and controversial of these developmental concepts is Freud's idea of the Oedipus complex. In Greek myth, Oedipus was the man who unknowingly murdered his father and married his mother. For Freud, this myth depicted the infantile desire experienced by all little boys, who want to see the mother as the principal object of their affections, and resent sharing her with the father. The Oedipus complex comes about when this sensual desire for the mother is not suppressed. And the vehicle for this suppression, Freud argued, is the young boy's recognition that the father is more powerful. Rather than lose his capability for pleasure, the boy pulls back from his focus on the mother and eventually turns his desires elsewhere. At its most instinctual level, Freud maintained, the threat to the boy's sexuality is perceived as a threat to that which determines his sex: it is ultimately a fear of castration that motivates the boy's withdrawal.

Although many of Freud's ideas, including the Oedipus complex, have been vigorously challenged or revised, his work did form the basis for modern psychology. Many of his ideas are so well-known that any educated person can be expected to be familiar with them. It would be difficult to go very far toward understanding psychology or psychological criticism today without some awareness of Freud, who relied heavily on literature in developing his ideas. By no means, however, should you infer that psychological criticism means Freudian criticism. Other approaches are welcome. But since an introduction to psychology isn't practical here, I've elected to indicate simply how psychological concepts can be applied by using Freud, who is arguably the most important single figure. If you can apply Freud, you can apply Abraham Maslow or Carl Rogers or whomever.

The following essay was developed primarily by applying Freud's central theory of the Oedipus complex to Gill's passage.

A PSYCHOLOGICAL READING OF GILL'S PASSAGE

Writers are brought into the world by editors, and Brendan Gill is thus in a sense the product of Miss Gould and Gardner Botsford's union. Gardner Botsford imposes the grammatical law in a fatherly enough way, but his counterpart, Miss Gould, functions only as a kind of uncreating anti-mother: she is a "Miss," and her notion of "mother's milk" is truly indigestible— "Gerunds, predicate nominatives, and passive periphrastic conjugations." She nurtures neither writing nor writer.

But, at the same time, the well-being of the writers at *The New Yorker* depends on her approval because, like Gill, they have accepted the criterion of correctness as the law of the father. Miss Gould imposes that law to the letter, undermining the writer's self-esteem until finally his very identity is threatened, plunging him into such "self-doubt" that his name is called into question. He may then become an orphan; his work may be abandoned.

In fact, the source of the writer's neurotic breakdown seems to be the linking of self to writing. Although the many corrections are imprinted upon the paper, Gill shifts them to the writer and transforms them from "pencilled hen-tracks" into stings. It is not, as we might suppose, the particular work that may be attacked so much that it dies, but rather *the writer* who may be "stung to death by an army of gnats." Gnats do not, so far as I know anyway, have stingers; they bite. The displacement here, one might argue, is the result of the writer's sense of personal vulnerability, making the threat more plausible since being bitten to death by gnats sounds absurd, while being stung is more ominous.

The more serious threat to Gill's identity is posed by Botsford, his editor and symbolic father. Botsford enters the scene with Gill's review "in his hand." Part of the review has been illegally "buried," and may subsequently be removed. This threat to Gill's writing is a disguised fear of castration because the writer identifies with his writing. The writer's identity, his name, is crucial to his potency. His name is the key to his ability to reproduce and promulgate himself. Yet his name "looks as if it could stand some working on."

Gill recognizes then that his editorial parent may correct and improve his "piece," but the cost may be terrible for the piece may be taken over by the authorities who control the emissions of his pen. Gill's image for what he has lost, the dolphin, thus becomes a rather blatant phallic symbol, reemerging as the pen (the grammatical penis) that the "dumb" writer loses. In other words, the writer must give up his "piece" to be published, to survive as a writer, but he is no longer the writer.

We now may see the psychological fittingness of the error Miss Gould finds: it is a structure that is "dangling." The writer may see his own fate in the sentence that sticks out, for it has suddenly "assumed the female gender." The writer's castration anxiety emerges here: he has desired to please Miss Gould, but focusing on grammar and correctness will render him

impotent and emasculated. Thus, Gill's story works to
resolve his Oedipus complex by pointing out the advan-
tages of accepting the values of the father (Botsford)
and shifting his desire from Miss Gould to a more
appropriate object: the reader. Gill evades symbolic
castration. "The sentence stands," the father says,
saving the writer's pen(is).

FEMINIST CRITICISM

Feminist criticism generally assumes, like reader-
response criticism, that a literary work is shaped by our reading of it, and this reading is influenced by our own status,
which includes significantly gender, or our attitude toward
gender. But, as feminists point out, since the production and
reception of literature has been controlled largely by men, the
role of gender in reading and writing has been slighted. The
interests and achievements of half of the human race have
been neglected—or appreciated largely from only one sex's
point of view.

You don't have to consider yourself a feminist to benefit
from feminist criticism. Simply taking gender into account,
regardless of your social and political views, is likely to open
your eyes to important works, authors, and issues you would
have missed otherwise.

Although it is difficult to generalize, given the diversity
and development of feminist criticism in recent decades,
there are some basic strategies you can adopt. You'll want to
consider the significance of the gender of the author and the
characters. You'll want to observe how sexual stereotypes
might be reinforced or undermined in the work. How does
the work reflect or alter the place of women (and men) in
society? Perhaps most powerful, imagine yourself reading the
work as a woman. If you happen to be female, this last suggestion may seem easy enough; but feminist critics point out
that women have long been taught to read like men, or to
ignore their own gender. So, reading as a woman, even if you
are a woman, may be easier said than done.

I developed the following feminist reading of Gill's passage by noticing references to gender and paying attention to any potential stereotypes.

A FEMINIST READING OF THE GILL PASSAGE

We know not all the writers at *The New Yorker* were men, even during the period Brendan Gill discusses in this passage from *Here at The New Yorker*. When he speaks of "some writer who has made a name for himself in the world," and about the editorial "machinery" that besets "him," Gill is of course referring to writers in the generic sense. One may still assert today, although with less assurance than in 1975, that "himself" and "him" in this passage include "herself" and "her."

Such a claim, that one sexual marker includes its opposite, may seem absurd—as if "white" included "black," or "communist" included "democratic." But the motivations for such a claim are suggested even in this brief passage, for Gill's story not only contains this obvious bias in pronouns, still accepted by some editors and writers; the story also conveys more subtle messages about sexuality and sexual roles.

For example, Miss Gould functions as a familiar stereotype: the finicky spinster, a Grammar Granny, who has devoted her life to "English grammar" and its enforcement. She is a copyeditor, subservient to the male editor and writer, and her lack of imagination and taste, as Gill presents them, seem to testify to the wisdom of this power structure.

This division of labor—male/creative, female/menial—is subtly reinforced by the reference to the "hen-tracks" that cover the writer's galley. Petty correction is the realm of the hen, the feminine. But these *"hen*-tracks" (they could not be rooster tracks) are more than an aggravating correction; they come to threaten the writer's very identity. In attempting to

produce "his copy," the writer is in a sense attempting to reproduce himself. The "glory of creation" is
his literary procreation, and thus Miss Gould's effort
to remove a particular sentence is a symbolic threat
to cut off some more essential part of the writer. It
is, after all, a "dangling modifier" that she has
located; and this dangling structure is in danger of
being fed to the "yawning pit," symbolic of the feminine editing and its excising dangers. Thus, men
should fear women, the passage suggests. Do not give
women power.

Because Gill's initial image for the writer starting out at the magazine, the dolphin in the sea,
derives some of its power from the well-established
association of the ocean and the womb, the images of
the "yawning" pit, not to mention the poisonous "mother's milk," become more telling. Even the error itself
is subtly connected to the feminine, for the problem
with the sentence is that part of it has "assumed the
female gender." That part, in the context of nagging
copyeditors who chop up one's prose, can only be a
"complaint."

The nonagenarian's complaint itself seems significant: in the mode of feminine busybodies like Miss
Gould, she laments not having "enough work to do."
Miss Gould, similarly overzealous, has herself done
more work than is reasonable, and Botsford's pro-
nouncement that "The sentence stands" returns her to
her place, negating her feminine fussiness.

OTHER APPROACHES

To give you some sense of just how rich and varied the
critical universe is, let me mention just a few other approaches not treated substantially here.

There could have been a chapter here on criticism that
focuses on the economic and class structures involved in literature (sometimes called "Marxist" criticism). The feminist

reading above does include some interest in money, class, and power, but these features could conceivably be brought to the forefront. The various forms of historical criticism are also necessarily concerned to some extent with class and power.

There might have been a chapter covering ethical criticism. I think it is easy to see how Gill's passage could spark substantive ethical analysis. It may be seen, for instance, to raise the issue of the cultural implications of determining that right is sometimes wrong, or the ethical consequences of setting up a standard that virtually no one can meet.

A critic interested in religious issues might wonder if the reference to "this tiny elect" in Gill's passage signals the importance of religious values or their trivialization. Likewise, what does the reference to "oh, Christ!" tell us? Is Botsford a Christ figure, forgiving Gill for his sins?

African-American criticism of this passage might start from the question of the role race plays in this passage and indeed in *The New Yorker* of the time. Do any *New Yorker* advertisements from the 1970s feature African-Americans? Do we assume that any of the characters in Gill's tale are black? Do we even assume that any of them *might* be black? What difference does our assumption make? In this respect, one might suggest, the passage reads *us*, showing us perhaps some of our racially motivated assumptions. If you were to do a reader-response criticism of the passage, would your racial or ethnic status play any part in your reading?

These and other approaches have vitalized the study of literature in the past few decades. In an ideal world, an introduction to writing about literature would include every identifiable approach. The goal of this introduction is necessarily more limited: using a sampling of the most visible approaches, it aims to show you how theory shapes practice—how assumptions stimulate and guide the process of developing critical essays. This goal is still an ambitious one, but well worth your effort, providing a powerful passport to the various ways meaning is made, preparing you for these and other kinds of literary excursions.

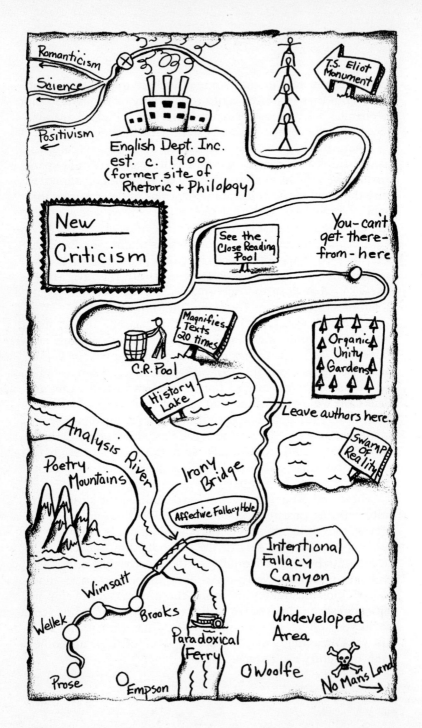

CHAPTER

2

UNIFYING THE WORK
New Criticism

The study of literature means the study of literature, *not of biography nor of literary history (incidentally of vast importance), not of grammar, not of etymology, not of anything except the works themselves, viewed as their creators wrote them, viewed as art, as transcripts of humanity— not as logic, not as psychology, not as ethics.*

—Martin Wright Sampson

THE PURPOSE OF NEW CRITICISM

For much of this century, "traditional" criticism has in large part been synonymous with what has become known as "New Criticism." This way of looking at literature began to emerge clearly in the 1920s and dominated literary criticism from the late 1930s into the 1960s. In 1941 John Crowe Ransom's *The New Criticism* gave this movement its name (even though the point of Ransom's book, ironically, is that *the* New Critic had not appeared). Its effects continue even to the present day, when it might better be called "the old New Criticism." Although those who have been called "New Critics" have not agreed in every respect, and some have even rejected the title, it is possible to identify a number of fundamental assumptions shared by an enormous number of critics and teachers, and their students. The odds in fact are excellent that your English teachers were trained in the methods of New Criticism, even if they never heard the term; and in surprisingly many classrooms today, even in the midst of a cornucopia of critical options, New Criticism is still essentially the only approach on the menu, its principles so pervasive that they seem natural and obvious—and therefore remain, often enough, unarticulated.

Basic Principles Reflected

One way to get at these principles, and begin to see why they have remained so appealing, might be to look at a famous poem written about the time that New Criticism was emerging as a critical force. This poem is of particular interest because it is about poetry, attempting to define it, advising us how to view it. Thus it seeks to provide a kind of guide for criticism: "Here is what poetry ought to be," the poem says; "read it with these standards in mind." Widely anthologized in introduction-to-literature texts since its appearance, the poem not only reflects the ideas of a nascent New Criticism, but it also probably helped to promote those ideas over several generations. Read it through carefully a few times, noting any questions or confusions that arise. It will be discussed in detail below.

Ars Poetica (1926)
   Archibald MacLeish

A poem should be palpable and mute
As a globed fruit,

Dumb
As old medallions to the thumb,

Silent as the sleeve-worn stone   5
Of casement ledges where the moss has grown—

A poem should be wordless
As the flight of birds.

A poem should be motionless in time
As the moon climbs,   10

Leaving, as the moon releases
Twig by twig the night-entangled trees,

Leaving, as the moon behind the winter leaves,
Memory by memory the mind—

A poem should be motionless in time   15
As the moon climbs.

A poem should be equal to:
Not true.

For all the history of grief
An empty doorway and a maple leaf.   20

For love
The leaning grasses and two lights above the sea—

A poem should not mean
But be.

The poem is startling from its opening lines, asserting
that a poem should be "palpable and mute." How can a poem
possibly be "palpable," or "capable of being handled, touched,
or felt" (*American Heritage Dictionary*)? Whether we think of a
poem as an idea, or a group of ideas, or the writing on a piece
of a paper, or a group of spoken words, none of these seems
to be the sort of thing we can handle. And how can a poem be
"mute"? Isn't a poem made of words? Don't we at least imagine a voice speaking the words? Suggesting that a poem be
mute seems a bit like suggesting that a movie be invisible, or
a song be inaudible, or a sculpture be without shape.

But MacLeish reiterates these ideas in subsequent lines,
saying explicitly that a poem should be "Dumb," "Silent," and
(most amazingly) "wordless" (lines 3, 5, and 7). He uses com-

parisons that reinforce particularly the idea of being "palpable." In comparing the poem to a "fruit," for instance, MacLeish suggests that the poem should be a real thing, having substance. The idea that it should be "globed" (a "globed fruit") emphasizes the three-dimensionality that MacLeish desires: like a globe, the poem should have more extension in time and space than a map or a picture. Not just a depiction of a fruit, it should *be* a *globed* fruit. Likewise, "old medallions to the thumb" and "the sleeve-worn stone / Of casement ledges where the moss has grown" are both not only "silent" or "dumb," but they also have an enduring solidity, a tangible reality. These images of fruit, old medallions, and worn ledges may also seem a bit mysterious, like "the flight of birds" (line 8), which in some "wordless," seemingly magical way is organized and orchestrated—as anyone knows who's ever seen a flock of birds rise together and move as one, silently.

From lines 1–8, then, we draw our first principle of New Criticism:

1. A poem should be seen as an object—an object of an extraordinary and somewhat mysterious kind, a silent object which is not equal to the words printed on a page.

Lines 9–16 articulate another idea, that "A poem should be motionless in time." This idea seems easy enough to understand: MacLeish believes that poems shouldn't change. Aren't Shakespeare's sonnets the same today as they were when he wrote them? ("So long as men can breathe or eyes can see, / So long lives this, and this gives life to thee," as Sonnet 18 says.) But MacLeish's comparison, "As the moon climbs," is not so easy to grasp: how can the moon be "climbing" through the sky, yet "motionless in time"? Perhaps the answer lies in the repeated idea that the moon, like the poem, should be "Leaving, as the moon releases / Twig by twig the night-entangled trees" (11–12); it should be "Leaving, as the moon behind the winter leaves / Memory by memory the mind" (13–14). Something that is "leaving" is neither fully here nor fully gone; it is caught in time and space, in an in-between contradictory timespace. We do not notice a memory deteriorating: it is there, unchanging; then it is only partly there; then it may be gone. The moon climbing in the sky does seem like this: it appears to sit there, motionless in time, yet it is leaving and will "release" the trees. MacLeish repeats lines 9–10 in lines 15–16, as if his own poem is motionless, continuing on but remaining in the same place it was.

This paradox adds to the mystery of the earlier lines, and also suggests a second principle:

> 2. The poem as silent object is unchanging, existing some-
> how both within and outside of time, "leaving" yet
> "motionless."

Lines 17–18 offer a third surprising idea: "A poem should be equal to: / Not true." It's difficult to believe that MacLeish is saying that poems should lie. But what is he saying? Lines 19–22 appear to explain his point, but these lines seem particularly difficult. What can these lines possibly mean—ignoring for the moment the concluding assertion of lines 23–24, which seems to be that poems ought not have meanings? The lines are obscure basically because the verbs are missing, so our task of making sense must include imagining what has been left out.

First MacLeish says, "For all the history of grief / An empty doorway and a maple leaf" (19–20). If we look closely at this statement, its form is familiar and clear enough: "For X, Y." Or, adding a verb, "For X, substitute Y." Thus, I take these lines to mean simply that instead of recounting "all the history of grief," the poet should present instead "An empty doorway and a maple leaf." An empty doorway can speak to us of someone departed, conveying an emptiness and an absence that may be more compressed and intense than an entire history of grief. A maple leaf, perhaps lying on the ground, bursting with fall colors inevitably turning to brown and crumbling, may tell us something about loss more directly and powerfully and concisely than any history book.

The next two lines are similarly structured: "For love / The leaning grasses and two lights above the sea." That is, "For love," an abstraction, impossible to grasp, the poet should present something concrete: "The leaning grasses and two lights above the sea." Although I can't say precisely how the grasses and lights here stand for love, somehow as images they do seem romantic, mysterious, moving to me. This principle of selecting something concrete to stand for an abstraction had already been advocated by T. S. Eliot in 1919, in what turned out to be an extremely influential opinion for the formation of New Criticism: "The only way of expressing emotion in the form of art," Eliot said, "is by finding an 'objective correlative'; in other words, a set of objects, a situation, a chain of events which shall be the formula of that *particular* emotion" (124–25). Not surprisingly, throughout its history New Criticism has been especially concerned with analyzing the imagery of particular works, noticing how a poem's "objective correlatives" structure its ideas.

It is not then that the poem should lie, but rather that it does not strive to tell the truth in any literal or historical or prosaic way. Poetry, MacLeish is saying, should speak metaphorically, substituting evocative images for the description of emotions, or historical details, or vague ideas. Instead of telling us about an idea or emotion, literature confronts us with *something* that may spark emotions or ideas. A poem is an experience, not a discussion of an experience.

The final two lines summarize this point in a startling way: "A poem should not mean / But be." Ordinarily we assume that words are supposed to convey a meaning, transferring ideas from an author to a reader. But the images that MacLeish's poem has given us—the globed fruit, the old medallions, the casement ledges, the flight of birds, the moon climbing, the empty doorway and the maple leaf, the leaning grasses and the two lights—these do not "mean" anything in a literal, historical, scientific way. What is the meaning, for example, of a flight of birds? Of a casement ledge where some moss has grown? These things just *are*. They are suggestive and even moving, but their meaning is something we impose on them; they simply exist, and we experience their being more powerfully than any abstract idea. It would be a mistake to think an empty doorway is somehow a *translation* of all the history of grief.

In much the same way, poems (MacLeish is asserting) do not mean, but rather have an existence—which takes us to the third principle:

3. Poems as unchanging objects represent an organized entity, not a meaning. In this way, poems are therefore fundamentally different from prose: prose strives to convey meaning; but poems cannot be perfectly translated or summarized for they offer a being, an existence, an experience perhaps—not a meaning.

Radicals in Tweed Jackets

What was the appeal of these principles? Why did New Criticism, a radically new way of reading, become so popular on college campuses?

In the landmark study that did much to solidify the academic prestige of the New Criticism, Wellek and Warren's *Theory of Literature* (1949), René Wellek declares, "The work of art is an object of knowledge" (156). Because the literary work has an "objective" status, Wellek says, critical statements about a work are not merely opinions of taste. "It will always be possible," Wellek maintains, "to determine which point of view grasps the subject most thoroughly and deeply" (156). Thus, "All relativism is ultimately defeated."

Although this assumption that the poem exists like an object, like fruit, like medallions, allows New Critics to think of literary criticism as a discipline just as rigorous and prestigious as a science, it is clear that for New Critics poems are in an important way also not like the objects studied by science. Poems, as MacLeish puts it, are "motionless in time"; they embody, as Marianne Moore says, "imaginary gardens with real toads in them." Thus, a poem is an entity somehow transcending time, existing in a realm different from that of science, the realm of the literary, of the imagination.

The implications of this second crucial assumption, that poems exist outside of time, can already be seen in the criticism of T. S. Eliot, whose ideas influenced the New Critics. In

"Tradition and the Individual Talent," Eliot's famous essay of 1919, poetry is said to be "not the expression of personality, but an escape from personality" (10). The New Critics are aware of course that poems have authors, and they will some-times refer to biographical information, but it is not the focus of their attention. Close reading of the work itself should reveal what the reader needs to know. Historical and bio-graphical information, to be sure, may sometimes be helpful, but it should not be essential.

This exclusion of authors and their contexts is taken to what might appear to be its logical extreme in Wimsatt and Beardsley's influential essay on "The Intentional Fallacy." Even when biographical and historical information is meticu-lously and voluminously gathered, as in the case of Lowes' work on Coleridge and *Kubla Khan*, Wimsatt and Beardsley question its value for reading the work. Even Coleridge's own account of how the poem came to him (in a dream, supposed-ly), Wimsatt and Beardsley say, does not tell us anything about how to read the poem itself—even if we can be sure that Coleridge is telling the truth. Only the poem can tell us how to read the poem.

By the same token, Wimsatt and Beardsley question the importance of the individual reader's response in "The Affective Fallacy." The groundwork for their position had already been worked out in the 1920s by I. A. Richards. Richards conducted a series of close-reading experiments with his students at Cambridge. He began with the assump-tion that students should be able to read poems richly simply by applying careful scrutiny to the works themselves. To focus students' attention on the work itself, Richards would often remove the distraction of authors' names, dates, even titles. In 1929, when he reported his results in *Practical Criticism*, two things appeared to be clear.

First, his students seemed not to be very good at reading texts carefully. Richards thought, and many people agreed, that students obviously needed much more training in "close reading." They needed to learn how to look carefully at a text, suppressing their own variable and subjective responses, as

Wimsatt and Beardsley would later persuasively argue. How a work affects a particular reader, Wimsatt and Beardsley assert, is not critically significant. Whereas "the Intentional Fallacy," they say, "is a confusion between the poem and its origins," the "Affective Fallacy is a confusion between the poem and its *results*" (21). Biographers may want to speculate on the poet's intention, and psychologists may want to theorize about a poem's effects, but literary critics should study the poem itself.

The second thing made evident by Richards' "experiments" was that such close reading was not only possible but very rewarding, as Richards himself was able to read these isolated works in revealing and stimulating ways, exposing unsuspected complexities and subtleties in the works he examined. Even in the following description of the creative process of poets, taken from Cleanth Brooks and Robert Penn Warren's New Critical textbook, *Understanding Poetry* (1938), the author's intention is of little enduring interest:

> At the same time that he [the poet] is trying to envisage the poem as a whole, he is trying to relate the individual items to that whole. He cannot assemble them in a merely arbitrary fashion; they must bear some relation to each other. So he develops his sense of the whole, the anticipation of the finished poem, as he works with the parts, and moves from one part to another. Then as the sense of the whole develops, it modifies the process by which the poet selects and relates the parts, the words, images, rhythms, local ideas, events, etc. . . . It is an infinitely complicated process of establishing interrelations. (527)

Implicit in this description of how a poet works are the directions for what a critic should do: most obviously, the critic will want to recover the idea, or principle, or theme, that holds the poem's parts together, and thereby reveal how the parts relate to each other and to the whole. (Such a careful unfolding of the poem's parts and their relationships is often called an "explication.") Although speculation about the poet's actual process of creating the poem may be entertaining, it is finally irrelevant, for the critic's real interest is in the finished poem, not how it was finished. We can tell what the poet was working toward, the poem as a whole, the "interrelations" of its parts, simply by looking at the poem, as a whole.

HOW TO DO NEW CRITICISM

You may already have a pretty good idea how to apply New Criticism, but to make sure the process is clear in your mind, let's think of it in three steps:

1. What complexities (or tensions, ironies, paradoxes, oppositions, ambiguities) can you find in the work?
2. What idea unifies the work, resolving these ambiguities?
3. What details or images support this resolution (that is, connect the parts to the whole)?

Let's examine each step.

1. The first step assumes that great works are complex, even when they appear to be simple. Literature does not imitate life in any literal way, according to the New Critics; instead, poems (and other works) create concrete realities of their own, transforming and ordering our experience. A poem, as Coleridge says, in a quotation often cited by New Critics, is an act of the imagination, "that synthetic and magical power"—an act that "reveals itself in the balance or reconciliation of opposites or discordant qualities" (11). Poems have the power "of reducing multitude into unity of effect." And, for the New Critics, the richer and more compelling the "multitude" of ideas or "discordant qualities," the greater the poem's power. The sort of complexity that New Critics particularly value is captured in Keats' concept of "negative capability," which is often cited by New Critics: it is the capability "of being in uncertainties, mysteries, doubts, without any irritable reaching after fact and reason" (1:193).

When New Critics identify a poem's complexities (the first step here), they use a number of closely related terms, especially "irony," "ambiguity," "paradox," and "tension."

Although these terms mean slightly different things, they all point to the idea of complexity—that the poem says one thing and means another, or says two things at once, or seems to say opposing things, or strains against its apparent meaning. For instance, in "The Language of Paradox," a celebrated essay from *The Well-Wrought Urn* (1947), Cleanth Brooks shows how Donne's famous poem, "The Canonization" (included in many anthologies), sets up a dilemma:

> Either: Donne does not take love seriously; here he is merely sharpening his wit as a sort of mechanical exercise. Or: Donne does not take sainthood seriously; here he is merely indulging in a cynical and bawdy parody. (11)

2. The second step assumes that great works do have a unifying idea, a theme. It's much more useful to think of this theme in terms of a complete thought or a sentence rather than a phrase. For instance, to say that the theme of Donne's "Canonization" is "love and religion" really doesn't tell us much about how Donne solves the dilemma of sainthood versus love. Here's what Brooks tells his readers:

> Neither account [that Donne doesn't take love seriously, or that he doesn't take religion seriously] is true; a reading of the poem will show that Donne takes both love and religion seriously; it will show, further, that the paradox is here his inevitable instrument. (11)

A cynical reader might observe (with some justification) that paradox is Donne's "inevitable" instrument because the New Critics inevitably find something like paradox in every great poem. But Brooks' point, of course, is that paradox is inevitable because Donne, with the imagination of a great poet, sets up the problem in such a way that only paradox will resolve it.

3. The third step unfolds or explicates the poem, indicating how the parts work together. This description of the poem is no substitute for the poem itself, but it should enrich our experience of it. Oftentimes, as in the case of Brooks' essay on "The Canonization," the critic will move through the work carefully from beginning to end, dividing the work into parts, and then suggesting how every aspect of the parts relates to our sense of the whole. Following Aristotle's ancient ideas, New Critics have talked about the "organic unity" of works, as if the poem were a creature, a living being, with every part playing an essential role.

Here is a sample of Brooks' explication:

> In this last stanza, the theme receives a final complication. The lovers in rejecting life actually win the most intense life. This paradox has been hinted at earlier in the phoenix metaphor. Here it receives a powerful dramatization. (15)

In this passage, notice how Brooks identifies a paradox related to the theme, and then connects that paradox to an earlier image. These are both characteristic moves for New Critics.

These steps won't read the poem for you, nor will they supply the sort of imagination, creativity, and attention you'll need to read literature closely. They will help to structure your process of reading and writing. To give you a better idea of how to use these principles, I work through the process of writing a sample New Critical essay in the next section.

THE WRITING PROCESS: A SAMPLE ESSAY

Literary works are often charming, uplifting, amusing; but they are also often troubling and challenging, confronting difficult and disturbing issues, stimulating our thought. The following poem will probably haunt you. It is a powerful and moving engagement with one of the most controversial and emotional topics of our day. Read it carefully, writing down any questions or comments that occur, looking particularly for tensions or oppositions or ambiguities.

The Mother (1945)
   Gwendolyn Brooks

Abortions will not let you forget.
You remember the children you got that you did not get,
The damp small pulps with a little or no hair,

The singers and workers that never handled the air.
You will never neglect or beat   5
Them, or silence or buy with a sweet.
You will never wind up the sucking-thumb
Or scuttle off ghosts that come.
You will never leave them, controlling your luscious sigh,
Return for a snack of them, with gobbling mother eye.   10

I have heard in the voices of the wind the voices of my dim
    killed children.
I have contracted. I have eased
My dim dears at the breasts they could never suck.
I have said, Sweets, if I sinned, if I seized
Your luck   15
And your lives from your unfinished reach,
If I stole your births and your names,
Your straight baby tears and your games,
Your stilted or lovely loves, your tumults, your marriages,
    aches and your deaths,
If I poisoned the beginnings of your breaths,   20
Believe that even in my deliberateness I was not deliberate.
Though why should I whine,
Whine that the crime was other than mine?—
Since anyhow you are dead.
Or rather, or instead,   25
You were never made.

But that too, I am afraid,
Is faulty: of, what shall I say, how is the truth to be said?
You were born, you had body, you died.
It is just that you never giggled or planned or cried.   30

Believe me, I loved you all.
Believe me, I knew you, though faintly, and I loved, I loved you
All.

Preparing to Write

Compare what you've written in your brainstorming to
the following list of observations:

(a) The speaker says "Abortions will not let you forget," as if abortions could actively do something. I know what the speaker means, but an abortion is a medical procedure; it can't make "you" remember or keep you from forgetting. Assuming that this phrasing is significant, why doesn't the speaker just say "You can't forget about your abortion"? This question raises another one: why does the speaker say "you" rather than "me," especially since the second section reveals that she has had abortions?

(b) The second line is contradictory, referring to children "you got that you did not get"? Either you got them or you didn't, it would seem.

(c) Why is the poem called "The Mother" if she has had abortions? Does this refer to her other children, or to the abortions? This is probably an important tension: it is, after all, the title.

(d) Lines 3 and 4 offer conflicting views. In line 3 "the children" are simply "damp small pulps with a little or with no hair." A "pulp" isn't alive, isn't a person, so removing a hairless (or nearly hairless) pulp isn't a big deal. But line 4 refers to the abortions in a strikingly different way, as "singers and workers that never handled the air." As singers and workers, the children are real, and their loss is tragic: they did not even get a chance to handle the air—which is a wonderful and surprising description of living. We are all, as singers and workers, handling the air.

(e) Another opposition shapes the next few lines. Lines 5-6 suggest that the abortions were in some respects a good thing: "You will never neglect or beat/ Them." The next image, never "silence or buy with a sweet," is perhaps faintly negative or even neutral: it doesn't sound good to think of silencing or buying children, and giving them "a sweet" probably

isn't the greatest thing to do, but every parent
resorts to such strategies. And the next image moves
into the realm of tenderness: to wind up "the sucking
thumb" or "scuttle off ghosts that come"—these are
acts of kindness. So the lines move from abuse, which
places the abortions in a more positive light, to
parental care, which makes the abortions seem more
tragic.

(f) I notice that the speaker seems to be talking
about more than one abortion. But the pain revealed in
the poem won't let us easily conclude that the speaker
is callous, readily aborting babies without a thought.

(g) The idea of eating up the children in line 10
is strange ("a snack of them, with gobbling mother-
eye").

It's fine if your ideas aren't similar to those above. In fact,
it's great because we'd certainly be bored if everyone thought
the same things. But you may find it useful to notice the level
of detail involved above and the kind of attention being paid.
This kind of preparation will make writing about the poem
much easier.

As you think about the poem, putting your ideas on
paper, you might reasonably wonder how much you need to
know about 1945, when the poem was published; about the
history of the debate over abortion; about Gwendolyn
Brooks's life; about her career as a poet and about her other
poems; and on and on. All these things would be good to
know, but you could end up spending a semester on this
poem. Further, adopting a New Critical stance, you will
assume that the poem itself will reveal whatever it is essential
for you to know.

Of course, once you decide to limit your attention to the
poem itself as an object, you need some principles to guide
your reading. It isn't really that helpful just to say,
"Concentrate on the poem itself and read it closely." So,
remind yourself specifically what a New Critical reading

attempts to expose: unity and complexity. Great works confront us with a unified ambiguity; second-rate works see things simply or fragmentarily.

Shaping

What would you say is the unifying idea of "The Mother"? What holds it together? Those questions are crucial to a New Critical reading because they lead to your thesis, which will shape and control the development of your essay. Even in the few notes I've reproduced above here, it seems clear that the title points us toward the poem's complexity: the speaker, as the title identifies her, is "The Mother," and yet she speaks only of the children she does not have, the children who have been aborted. So how can she be a mother without any children? How can she love her children, or have destroyed them, if they don't exist? That, it seems to me, is one way of saying what the poem struggles through. The theme or unifying idea, holding together the ambiguous status of the speaker, can be stated in any number of ways, and you might try out your own way of expressing it. Here's one way to put it:

> Although her children do not exist, and may have never existed, the speaker is a mother because she loves her "children."

In articulating this theme, I've given emphasis to the way the poem ends. Generally that's where the oppositions are resolved. In this case, I would argue, the ambiguity between the speaker as mother and non-mother is resolved at the end of the poem with her declaration of her love. She could not love the children if they did not have some kind of existence, and if they exist in some way, then she is some kind of "mother." But her status is by no means simple. Likewise, she "knew" them, she says, even if it was "faintly"; and, again, it would seem she could not know them if they did not exist, if they were not her children.

The strategy of a New Critical reading, then, would involve showing how the details of the poem support and elaborate this complex or ironic unity. Your structure involves arranging this evidence in a coherent way, grouping kinds of details perhaps, or moving logically through the poem. That is, throughout the poem, a New Critical reading would find oppositions reinforcing and supporting in some way the poem's central ambiguity. For instance, line 21 would be seen as a reflection of the central opposition. The speaker says, "even in my deliberateness I was not deliberate." Just as the children who are aborted are not children; just as the woman who gives up her motherhood by having an abortion nonetheless retains her claim to the name of "mother"; by the same token, the speaker's "deliberateness is not deliberate."

In other words, her decision to have the abortion was made with "deliberateness," and for such decisions we are more accountable, by some measures anyway, than for impulsive decisions. Pre-meditated murder, for instance, is in theory a more serious crime than a spontaneous crime of passion. But the mother's culpability is qualified by the rest of the sentence which says that the deliberateness was not "deliberate." She carefully decided something she did not carefully decide, so it seems.

Drafting

After you've worked your way through the poem, noting oppositions, tensions, ambiguities, paradoxes, and considering how these relate to the poem's unity, then it's time for a draft. Here is a first draft developed out of the annotations above; it's been polished up a bit, and there are annotations in the margin to help you see what is going on.

THE MOTHER WITHOUT CHILDREN:
A READING OF GWENDOLYN BROOKS'S
"THE MOTHER"

Gwendolyn Brooks's "The Mother" points to a paradox with its first word, "Abortions." Although the speaker is called "the mother" in the title, she quickly reveals that

From (c) in the notes: this tension seemed to unify to poem.

The intro has set up
the essay's form:
mother vs. not-mother

"the children" have actually been
aborted. How can she be a mother if
her children never existed? Her
opening line asserts that "Abortions will not let you forget," but
what is there for her to remember?
The rest of the poem shows the
"mother's" struggle with this problem: how to remember "the children
that you did not get" (2).

This paragraph elabo-
rates on the two possi-
bilities: children or
not.

On the one hand, the speaker
realizes the children are nothing
more than "damp small pulps with a
litle or with no hair" (3), but the
rest of this sentence sees them as
"singers and workers that never handled the air" (4). If they can be
called "singers and workers," then
they must have some existence. But
if they never "handled the air,"
they did not work and sing, and so
their status as workers and singers
is problematic, to say the least.
This question is what is distressing the "mother," because if these
fetuses were children, then her
statement in line 17 is accurate: "I
stole your births and your names."
But the line begins with an "If,"

The two possibilities
come together in the
uncertainty.

and it is this uncertainty that provides the speaker with some comfort.

The comfort takes two forms. The
mother first eases her pain by
pointing to the uncertainty of her
decision to have the abortions:
"even in my deliberations I was not
deliberate" (21). Since she is

This explains how the uncertainty comforts the mother.

uncertain about the status of what is being aborted, she decided without knowing what she was deciding. In truth, she still does not know what her decision means: no one can say with authority when life begins, or when fetuses become persons and when they are still unviable tissue masses, or "pulps" (3).

This point began to emerge in (f): the mother's pain suggests her love, which is explicitly declared later on.

More importantly, the speaker is also comforted in the end by declaring her love, even though this expression paradoxically sustains her pain and mourning. She clings to the idea of her "dim killed children" (11), refusing to let them become "pulps," because she can love them only if they actually existed. So she must say that she "knew" them, even while admitting it was only "faintly" (32). She does claim her status as "the mother," as the title says, even though it causes her pain. As she says in the opening line, "Abortions will not let you forget," but perhaps only if you continue to see yourself as a mother, even though you have no children. Thus, the poem balances the speaker's two visions of herself, as murderer and as mother; and it resolves this conflict in the final lines, as the mother is able to atone for her decision, in some measure, by suffering with her memory always, saying "I loved you, I loved you / All" (32–33).

Still relying on the opposition: mother/not; children/not.

From (a) above.

Resolving the problem set up in the intro.

In the preceding essay I obviously didn't explicate every detail that supports my thesis. Rather, I tried to bring forth enough evidence to be persuasive. How much evidence you need to present to make a close reading convincing will vary depending on the work and your thesis. Follow your common sense and the guidance of your teacher.

Finally, as you apply New Criticism on your own, notice how two factors helped the sample essay develop smoothly.

1. Thorough preparation. The essay, for the most part, arranges and connects the extensive notes on the poem. When I came to write my essay, I had already written a great deal. I had much more material than I could use in my essay, and so I was able to pick and choose which ideas to use. This process, of selecting from an abundance of ideas, is a whole lot more pleasant than struggling for something to say.

2. Theoretical awareness. Since I knew what kind of approach I wanted to take, I knew to look for certain things in the poem: ideas or images in opposition; complexity or ambiguity; the unifying idea or theme. Likewise, I knew what my essay was going to set out to do. I didn't have to worry about whether Brooks might have intended to say this or that; nor did I have to worry about my own attitude toward abortion, or even my own reaction to the poem. My job was to focus on the text itself, exposing its complexity and unity. By being aware of the theoretical stance you are evolving or adopting, you clarify for yourself what you're doing and how to do it.

PRACTICING NEW CRITICISM

It's highly unlikely that one example will make New Criticism crystal clear for you. You'll need to practice it for yourself, see other examples, and (ideally) discuss its workings with your teacher and classmates.

To get you started, I offer here two poems and some sample questions.

forgiving my father (1969)
Lucille Clifton

it is friday. we have come
to the paying of the bills.
all week you have stood in my dreams
like a ghost, asking for more time
but today is payday, payday old man,   5
my mother's hand opens in her early grave
and i hold it out like a good daughter.

there is no more time for you. there will
never be time enough daddy daddy old lecher
old liar. i wish you were rich so i could take it all   10
and give the lady what she was due
but you were the son of a needy father,
the father of a needy son,
you gave her all you had
which was nothing. you have already given her   15
all you had.

you are the pocket that was going to open
and come up empty any friday.
you were each other's bad bargain, not mine.
daddy old pauper   old prisoner,   old dead man   20
what am i doing here collecting?
you lie side by side in debtor's boxes
and no accounting will open them up.

Questions

1. How does the title relate to the poem? (That is, how is
   the title at odds with what the poem says?) List the
   statements in the poem that do not sound "forgiving."

2. What is the significance of "collecting" in line 21? How
   is this word like "accounting" and "open" in line 23? In
   what sense is the speaker "collecting"?

3. What reasons does the poem offer for forgiving the
   father?

4. How is the poem's conflict resolved? Is the phrase "forgiving a debt" relevant to this poem?
5. How would you state the theme of this poem in one sentence? (Try a two-part sentence: "Although x, y.")

My Father's Martial Art   (1982)
Stephen Shu-ning Liu

When he came home Mother said he looked
like a monk and stank of green fungus.
At the fireside he told us about life
at the monastery: his rock pillow,
his cold bath, his steel-bar lifting   5
and his wood-chopping. He didn't see
a woman for three winters, on Mountain O Mei.

"My Master was both light and heavy.
He skipped over treetops like a squirrel.
Once he stood on a chair, one foot tied   10
to a rope. We four pulled; we couldn't
move him a bit. His kicks could split
a cedar's trunk."

I saw Father break into a pumpkin
with his fingers. I saw him drop a hawk   15
with bamboo arrows. He rose before dawn, filled
our backyard with a harsh sound *hah, hah, hah:*
there was his Black Dragon Sweep, his Crane Stand,
his Mantis Walk, his Tiger Leap, his Cobra Coil . . .
Infrequently he taught me tricks and made me   20
fight the best of all the village boys.

From a busy street I brood over high cliffs
on O Mei, where my father and his Master sit:
shadows spread across their faces as the smog
between us deepens into a funeral pyre.   25

But don't retreat into night, my father.
Come down from the cliffs. Come
with a single Black Dragon Sweep and hush
this oncoming traffic with your *hah, hah, hah.*

Questions

1. Where is the poem's speaker located? How does this location relate to what he remembers?

2. What has happened to his father? What does line 25 suggest? Why does it seem especially appropriate that the "smog" comes between them?

3. What do you make of the name of the mountain? What might the oncoming traffic symbolize?

4. In each of the following pairs, which quality is embodied in the poem?

   Closeness, distance
   Presence, absence
   Power, impotence
   Light, heavy
   Spiritual, mundane

5. Do you think the word "Infrequently" in line 20 is significant? How does it contribute to the poem? (Does it simplify things? Make them more complex?)

6. What is the speaker struggling against in the poem? How is the struggle resolved? How is the resolution ambiguous and complex?

CHAPTER 3

CREATING THE TEXT
Reader-Response Criticism

*Unless there is a response on
the part of somebody, there is
no significance, no meaning.*

—Morse Peckham

THE PURPOSE OF READER-RESPONSE CRITICISM

New Criticism as the Old Criticism

Reader-response criticism can be seen as a reaction in part to some problems and limitations perceived in New Criticism. New Criticism did not suddenly fail to function: it remains an effective critical strategy for illuminating the complex unity of certain literary works. But some works don't seem to respond very well to New Criticism's "close reading." Much of eighteenth-century literature, for instance, has generally not been shown to have the sort of paradoxical language or formal unity that New Critics have found in, say, much of Donne or Keats. And New Critics appear to see pretty much the same thing in whatever work they happen to read: "this work has unified complexity"; "so does this one"; "yep, this one too."

Further, if the work is indeed a stable object, about which careful readers can make objective statements, then why hasn't there been an emerging consensus in criticism? Instead, the history of criticism seems to be one of diversity and change, as successive critics provide innovatively different readings of the same work. Even in the sciences, the idea of an objective point of view has been increasingly questioned. Facts, as Thomas Kuhn has argued, emerge because of a certain system of belief, or paradigm. Scientific revolutions occur not simply when new facts are discovered, but when a new paradigm allows these "facts" to be noticed and accepted.

Such ideas about the conceptual nature of knowledge, even scientific knowledge, call a fundamental assumption of New Criticism into question. In positing the objective reality of the literary work, New Criticism was arguably emulating the sciences; but in the wake of Einstein's theory of relativity, Heisenberg's uncertainty principle, Gödel's mathematics, and much else, it seems clear that the perceiver plays an active role in the making of any meaning, and that literary works in particular have a *subjective* status.

In addition, by striving to show how great works balance opposing ideas, New Criticism has seemed to some to encourage the divorce of literature from life and politics, indirectly reinforcing the status quo. By the standards of New Criticism, any literary work that takes a strong position ought somehow to acknowledge the opposing point of view, and criticism ought to point to that complexity and balance. Further, by assuming that literary language is fundamentally different from ordinary language, New Criticism may further tend to support the idea that literary study has little or no practical value, but stands apart from real life (a poem should not mean but be, MacLeish says). New Criticism sometimes seems, especially to unsympathetic eyes, like an intellectual exercise.

The perception of these shortcomings of New Criticism—its limited applicability and sameness of results, the questionable assumption of a stable object of inquiry, and the separation of literature from other discourses—no doubt helped open the door for reader-response criticism (and other approaches). But reader-response criticism has its own substantial appeals, as we shall see.

The Reader Emerges

In 1938, while future New Critics were formulating ideas of the text as a freestanding object, Louise Rosenblatt prophetically called for criticism that involved a "personal sense of literature" (60), "an unself-conscious, spontaneous, and honest reaction" (67). *Literature as Exploration* was ahead of its day, but by the time Rosenblatt published *The Reader, the Text, the Poem* in 1978, much of the critical world had caught up with where she was forty years before. For instance, the creative power of readers was championed by David Bleich's *Readings and Feelings* in 1975, and by *Subjective Criticism* in 1978. Because "the object of observation appears changed by the act of observation," as Bleich puts it, "knowledge is made by people and not found" (*Criticism* 17, 18).

This insight leads Bleich to embrace subjectivity, even calling his approach "subjective criticism." Writing about literature, he believes, should not involve suppressing readers' individual concerns, anxieties, passions, enthusiasms. "Each person's most urgent motivations are to understand himself," Bleich says, and a response to a literary work always helps us find out something about ourselves (297). Bleich thus encourages introspection and spontaneity, and he is not at all worried that different readers will see different things in a text. Every act of response, he says, reflects the shifting motivations and perceptions of the reader at the moment. Even the most idiosyncratic response to a text should be shared, in Bleich's view, and heard sympathetically.

It is easy to imagine that many students have found such an approach liberating and even intoxicating, and that some teachers have contemplated it with horror. "There's no right or wrong," as one teacher said to me; "students can say *anything*." But Bleich actually does not imagine that the student's engagement with literature will *end* with a purely individual, purely self-oriented response; rather, he expects that students will share their responses, and in *Subjective Criticism* he describes the process of "negotiation" that occurs as a community examines together their individual responses, seeking common ground while learning from each person's unique response.

An especially striking illustration of the benefits of Bleich's orientation appears in an essay by Robert Crosman. Crosman recounts a student's response to Faulkner's famous "A Rose for Emily" that is so eccentric, so obviously "wrong" (if it were possible to be wrong within this approach), that one must begin to wonder if the student really read the story with any attentiveness. The student's response seems in fact to expose the absurdity of letting students say whatever comes into their heads, for she writes that Emily, the mad recluse who apparently poisons and then sleeps with her suitor, reminds her of her kindly grandmother. Crosman's student ignores the horrible ending of the story, which implies that Emily has recently slept with the much-decayed remains of her murdered lover; instead, the student writes about the qualities of her grandmother—"endurance, faith, love"—that she also sees in Emily (360). The student finds that her grandmother and Emily both inhabit houses that are closed up with "relics and momentos of the past"; both her grandmother and Emily seem to think of past events and people as being "more real" than "the world of the present."

The value of this student's response emerges in the way Crosman uses it to modify his own reading. He comes to see that his interpretation, which is much more typical of experienced readers, actually "suppresses a good deal of evidence" (361). Crosman has perceived Emily to be a kind of monster, but he is led by his student to see that such is not entirely the case. Confronting the heroic aspects of Emily's character, Crosman notices that she triumphs, in a sense, over the men (father, lover, townfathers) who are, Crosman says, "ultimately responsible for Emily's pitiful condition" (361). By the same token, just as Crosman is able to see the positive aspects of Emily's character, making her human rather than monstrous, so is his student, by considering Crosman's response, placed in a position to see more than her grandmother's goodness in Emily.

Whereas Bleich sees the reader's response evolving by such "negotiation" within a community of readers, Rosenblatt focuses on the "transaction" between the text and the reader. While she accepts multiple interpretations, as readers actively make different works out of the text, she also considers some readings to be incorrect or inappropriate because they are unsupportable by the text. So the "unself-conscious, spontaneous, and honest reaction" that Rosenblatt encourages ought to be checked against the text and modified in a continuing process, or "transaction": a poem is made by the text and the reader interacting.

The various reader-response critics all share the sense of reading as a process, an activity; their differences stem from this question of how meaning is controlled. Who's in charge? The reader? A community of readers? The text? The case of Stanley Fish is especially interesting in this regard because over his career Fish has taken just about every position. Fish's early work emphasizes how the text controls the reader's experience; the task of criticism is to describe this experience, and Fish's readings seem much like watching a movie in super-slow motion as it is being analyzed by an imaginative film critic. Fish moves through a few words or phrases, and then considers in brilliant and clever detail what "the reader" makes of it. Fish repeatedly finds that admirable texts continually surprise us, evading our expectations, exposing us to "strains," "ambivalences," "complexity" (*Artifacts* 136, 425). These values, as Jane Tompkins has suggested, are very similar to the values of New Criticism. But the way they are discovered in texts is quite different.

In *Surprised by Sin,* for instance, Fish argues that the reader "in" *Paradise Lost* experiences temptations and disorientations that parallel those of Adam and Eve. Thus, the critics who have thought Satan more appealing than God have not spotted a flaw in Milton's achievement; they have simply succumbed to the temptation Milton meant for them to experience. Likewise, in *Self-Consuming Artifacts* Fish shows how the process of reading certain seventeenth-century texts involves creating expectations that are thwarted, complicated, reversed, transformed as the reader goes on.

In his later work, in *Is There a Text in This Class?* and *Doing What Comes Naturally,* Fish moves away from the idea of an ideal reader who finds his or her activity marked out, implied, in the text, and he moves toward the idea of a reader who creates a reading of the text using certain interpretive strategies. These strategies may be shared by other readers, and the critic's job is to persuade his or her interpretive community to accept a particular reading. Neither the text's implied activity nor the community's shared reading strategies can be said to determine interpretation; for even when readers inhabit the same interpretive community, they must struggle to persuade one another of the "facts" regarding a particular text. Such persuasion may include information about the author, or the author's audience, or the initial reception of the work, or the history of its reception, or the text itself, or the conventions of interpretation the text draws upon. But the continuing process of discussion begins with the response of the person persuading.

That's why reader-response criticism is so valuable: it authorizes and encourages readers to begin where, really, readers always must begin: with an individual response. It is always possible to evolve that response based on interaction with a community, or further reference to the text, or the employment of a particular political or aesthetic theory, or some other impetus. But you must, it seems to me, start with a response.

Let's move to a more specific discussion of responding.

HOW TO DO READER-RESPONSE CRITICISM

Preparing to Respond

Imagine that you've been asked to write about the following poem, drawing on audience-oriented criticism. You'll want to read the poem carefully, thinking in terms of the following possible questions:

1. How do I respond to this work?
2. How does the text shape my response?
3. How might other readers respond?

Love Poem #1 (1987)
Sandra Cisneros

a red flag
woman I am
all copper
chemical
and you an ax   5
and a bruised
thumb.

unlikely
pas de deux
but just let   10
us wax
it's nitro
egypt
snake
museum   15
zoo

we are
connoisseurs
and commandoes
we are rowdy   20
as a drum
not shy like
Narcissus
nor pale as plum

then it is I want to hymn   25
and halleluja

sing sweet sweet jubilee
you my religion
and I a wicked nun

What can you say about this poem? How can audience-oriented criticism help you to understand and appreciate it?

Making Sense

My own response to this poem began when I started to annotate it. I underlined some words that I thought might be especially important or unclear, and then, on a separate sheet, I speculated on their meanings. With any approach, you may need to look up some words. If you're a little hazy on who "Narcissus" is (line 23), for instance, a dictionary definition may be all you need: "A youth who, having spurned the love of Echo, pined away in love for his own image in a pool of water and was transformed into the flower that bears his name" (*American Heritage Dictionary*). Dictionary definitions aren't always sufficient, and (it probably goes without saying) the more you know, the more experience you have as a reader, then the richer and more informed your response is likely to be. Responding to a poem always involves you in creating a context in which the sequence of words makes sense: you must ask, "who is speaking to whom?" "Under what circumstances would someone say these things?"

Still, all responses are potentially worthwhile. You may want to underline some important or puzzling words and speculate on their meanings before you look at my annotations below. And you may want to share your responses with another reader.

```
a red flag woman— What does this mean? A red flag
   means something to watch out for, dangerous, a
   warning. For instance, "The temperature reading
   should have been a red flag." So she is dangerous?

all copper— Why copper? Because it's cold? Because it
   turns green?! No, I don't think so. Copper is a
```

great conductor of electrical current and heat. She's
hot; she's electrified. That is, she's passionate,
emotional, responsive?

chemical— Like a chemical reaction?

an ax and a bruised thumb—— Is he clumsy? He does
things aggressively, in an imprecise way. He breaks
or splits things like an ax, but he isn't always
careful (the bruised thumb).

pas de deux— A ballet dance for two, according to
Webster. The sort of grace and coordination we'd
expect from a ballet is indeed unlikely for these
two together, a live wire and a wild man.

nitro etc.— This is a neat list of unexpected things,
each one giving a different aspect of their relationship. Nitro = explosive?; egypt = foreign,
exotic, mysterious, enduring (like the pyramids)?;
snake = something wicked? a phallic symbol? the
garden of Eden? Are "egypt" and "snake" related?
"Museum" and "zoo" point us to public institutions.
"Museum" suggests their love is rare, valuable,
enduring, worth showing off; "zoo" suggests perhaps
they're animals?

connoisseurs and commandoes— They again appear to be
radical opposites: connoisseurs are refined, tasting carefully; commandoes are reckless and go wild.

you my religion— This is about as involved in another
person as you can get. There's something troubling
about such devotion to another person. No human
being should worship another one. But am I taking
this line too seriously?

wicked nun— This image continues the religious reference. Being a wicked nun seems especially exciting,
combining suggestions of the forbidden and the
delayed.

Subjective Response

Thinking about the words, you're already unavoidably beginning to think about the poem as a whole and your own response to it. The next step might be to freewrite about the poem. Just focus on the poem and write quickly whatever occurs to you. Don't worry about grammar, and don't stop writing. If you can't think of anything to say, say whatever is most obvious. The important thing is to keep the pen or keyboard moving. As a last resort, write "I can't think of anything to say" until you think of something. If that fails, then read the poem again and then try once more. Set yourself a time limit for this free response; ten minutes is about right for most people. There's no way to do this exercise incorrectly: just read carefully and respond, being as honest and involved as you can.

Here is my freewriting response:

> This poem reminds me of Carol and Bob's relation-
> ship. They are about as unlikely and mismatched a cou-
> ple as this pair, an "unlikely pas de deux." But
> instead of "copper" and "chemical," Carol is more like
> plutonium and nuclear. She's incredibly energetic,
> especially when you compare her to Bob. He could fit
> "an ax / and a bruised / thumb," but I suspect the
> result would be an amputated thumb in his case. They
> are amazing, like the couple in the poem.
>
> Are Carol and Bob "nitro" together, like this cou-
> ple? I don't know. There seems to me to be a good bit
> of energy in their marriage. I don't see Carol wanting
> "to hymn / and halleluja," perhaps, but I'm really in
> no position to judge, am I. I don't know what happens
> when they "wax," whatever that means. Certainly, the
> two people in Cisneros' poem are not living a dull
> life, and I think the constrast is also stimulating to
> Carol and Bob. There is power in conflict or differ-
> ence. Opposites not only attract; they make sparks.

Many people find this kind of freewriting exercise very useful: it generates material that you may be able to use in an essay, and it is likely to stimulate your thinking about the work. Just to give you an idea of how individualistic and personal such responses can be, here is another one:

> This poem seems to talk about an exciting relationship: she says "it's nitro." That suggests the relationship is great, but I think it's really doomed. I think this relationship, the first time it is shaken, will probably explode, just like nitro. She is emotional; he is rough and clumsy. Where's the long-term interest and compatibility in this set-up? Opposites attract, sure, but when they're so totally opposite, so far apart the attraction may be volatile. This is after all only "Love Poem #1." I am wondering if there will be #2 and #3 once the relationship matures and cools off.
>
> I think the speaker's comparison of herself to "a wicked nun" is revealing. The comparison supports my feeling that the relationship, despite its current heat, isn't going to make it. I notice that she does not see herself as a nun who has decided to give up her habit. She is just "wicked," doing something wrong and enjoying the extra excitement that doing the forbidden gives her. If her love feels that way to her, then won't that eventually put a strain on the relationship? Will she decide to give up her old life, her old religion, and become devoted to her new religion, her lover? Or will her prior life win out?
>
> In my experience, relationships built on excitement are treacherous and fragile. I bet the nun will reform.

Which of these responses is correct? Both are. Both are responses to the text. Taken together, these two different responses may suggest a third one that tries to determine whether the poem really does evoke some skepticism on the reader's part, or if it is simply a joyous celebration. Are there some elements that would qualify the poem's enthusiasm for most readers?

After engaging the text in a personal way, you can begin to ask such questions about your own response in the context of other readers' responses. Let's see what happens when the reading process is slowed down and an effort is made to imagine how the reader is supposed to respond moving through the poem.

Receptive Response

First, obviously, every reader encounters the title. What response does the title elicit? The poem announces itself as a love poem. What sort of title do we expect from such a thing? Most readers no doubt expect a love poem to have a more romantic or imaginative title than "Love Poem #1," and the reader's initial reaction is to wonder if the poem is in truth a love poem. If it is, then why is the title so bluntly direct? The numbering also creates certain possibilities: will the poem reflect the intensity of love in its first bloom? Will it deflate or satirize infatuation? At this point, the reader cannot know, but the firstness of the poem is perceived to be an important feature, to be taken into account as the poem unfolds.

The first line seems to open further the possibility that the poem is not a love poem in the usual sense: "a red flag" signals a warning, a danger, and seems more appropriate to a poem announcing the end of a love affair. So perhaps the first is the last, and the unimaginative title is ironic? The second line, "woman I am," seems to be an affirmation of the speaker's individuality and her sisterhood. In other words:

Line 1: "a red flag" = Watch out! There's something dangerous here.

Line 2: "woman I am" = The reason you should watch out: a red flag (look out!), I am woman.

But as the reader begins to wonder about these two statements—"a red flag" and "woman I am"—the possibility arises, reading backwards, that these two lines go together in a different way, as a single statement: "a red flag" becomes a modifier of "woman"—I am a red-flag woman.

Without punctuation, the reader cannot decide for sure which syntax is correct, and so both readings continue on: "watch out, I'm a woman"; and "I'm a dangerous kind of woman." Do the next two lines support the suggestion of an unromantic, even threatening self-portrait of the speaker? Most readers will think of electrical wiring and plumbing when they read "all copper," which appears to refer back to the speaker; likewise, things that are "chemical" are perceived by most readers as dangerously reactive. Only experts should fool around with plumbing, wiring, chemistry: pipes explode, wires spark, chemicals blow up.

There is of course an element of surprise at finding the speaker describe herself in this way. "All copper" and "chemical" are not part of the usual vocabulary of love poetry, are they? The reader will find the next three lines equally disorienting, as the speaker's love is described in the decidedly unromantic terms of "an ax / and a bruised / thumb." He or she is potentially destructive and apparently dangerous. (Although some readers may assume the speaker's lover is male, the poem doesn't prescribe that response, does it?) An ax usually isn't used to build things, but rather to cut them, kill them, chop them down. Such wrecking sometimes results, especially if the worker is clumsy, in a bruised thumb, or worse. As a love poem, this one seems to be going nowhere, and the reader may well not be surprised that it is #1. How can there be any more?

Thus, I would argue that the opening of the second group of lines confirms the attentive reader's assessment: they are indeed an "unlikely / pas de deux." This admission also sets the reader up, however, for a turn. By saying they are unlikely as a pair, Cisneros implies that they *may be* nonetheless a couple, somehow. The rest of the poem vigorously fulfills that implication, reversing the reader's inferences, which he or she may have suspected would be reversed. Still, the explanation of their relationship is startling, as the reader encounters a list of unexpected and even puzzling comparisons:

nitro—This one is easy. They are explosive together.
But since nitroglycerine is used to blow things up

(as well as to prevent heart attacks), an element
of danger remains.

egypt—How can the lovers be "egypt"? Perhaps the reference means they are exotic together? Hot, like
the deserts? Mysterious, like the pyramids?
Alluring, like Cleopatra? Fertile, like the Nile?
By not saying how the lovers are like Egypt,
Cisneros opens up a space in which the reader can
supply all sorts of qualities.

snake—This comparison is as tantalizing and amazing,
at least, as "egypt." A snake is of course often
considered a phallic symbol, and the reader may
think of the lovers' conjunction as a kind of living version of that symbol. But it may also remind
us, in the context of a couple, of Adam and Eve,
suggesting that they are somehow participating in a
return to Eden together; but this time, the lovers
are not ruined by the serpent, but rather become
one themselves? Or, is the snake, in the context of
"egypt," supposed to suggest some sort of ancient
fertility cult that involved the handling of
snakes? We don't know, but the attentive reader
will consider these and other possible responses to
this rich and startling image.

museum—Another strange and disorienting comparison.
How can the lovers be like a museum? Perhaps they
create, in their lovemaking, something of enduring
value, something so wonderful that future generations would want to preserve it, as in a museum.

zoo—This reference is perhaps the easiest for the
reader to respond to: it suggests obviously that
they are animals together—a collection in fact of
all sorts of exotic and wondrous animals.

The rest of the poem continues to celebrate the lovers in
unexpected ways, even though certain ideas reappear. The
speaker calls them "connoisseurs and commandoes," which

repeats to some degree the oppositions already set up. The reader may connect "connoisseurs" to the cultured reaction of museum goers, but at the same time the lovers are wild "commandoes," which the reader may link to "nitro," or an "ax." The difference in this third section of the poem is that instead of each lover having distinctly different qualities, they are together "connoisseurs and commandoes," unifying opposing features in their relationships.

If the reader believes, however, that the rest of the poem will fit some sort of pattern set up thus far, the next lines seem designed to thwart that expectation. The lovers are "rowdy / as a drum," which suggests, I suppose, the rowdiness of someone beating a drum. Perhaps this simile reinforces the earlier suggestions of wildness, but it is certainly difficult to see how a drum in itself is "rowdy," or what this comparison is supposed to accomplish. The reader next learns the lovers are "not shy like Narcissus," an allusion that means obviously that they are not self-absorbed, that they don't hold back from love. But is there any deeper significance to this allusion? Why bring in Narcissus and shyness? Would any reader suspect at this point that they *are* shy—these commandoes, who are "nitro"? The next line seems even more elusive, as if the lovers are slowly becoming incomprehensible to the reader: "nor pale as plum"? Perhaps this comparison refers to the color plum, and tells us in another way that they are not shy—although the reader surely must hesitate to call "plum" a "pale" color.

But "plum" serves another function beyond befuddling the reader, as it becomes clear at this point, if not before, that a recurrent rhyme is appearing, unobtrusively: "thumb," "museum," "drum," and "plum." And with the appearance of this music, the poem moves to its climactic ending, comparing the speaker's feelings to a religious ecstasy:

> then it is I want to hymn   25
> and halleluja
> sing sweet sweet jubilee
> you my religion
> and I a wicked nun

The reader may hear the assertion that she wants "to hymn" as a pun on "him," as if her lover has become an activity in which she can engage, or as if the male role is one the speaker longs to adopt. The associations of "hymn" continue for the reader, as singing halleluja, and enjoying the "jubilee" appear. Immediately these religious comparisons are carried beyond the reader's expectations (which may be, at this point, what the reader does expect), as the speaker declares her lover to be her religion. For most readers, such sacrilege is an exaggeration at the edges of propriety: most readers are all in favor of love, but to make another person one's religion is perhaps troubling. The experienced reader probably sees this assertion as exaggeration (hyperbole), but it is nonetheless worrisome in its implications.

But the final line takes even a further step, as the speaker names herself "a wicked nun." This final move completes the effort to convey the excitement of the forbidden, the impossible, the dangerous in the relationship, leaving the reader shaken and stunned—like the speaker herself, it seems—by the power of their love. Their love is itself vigorously direct, like the poem's title; their love is also apparently unadulterated and uncompromised, pure and explosive at its very beginning.

It is quite likely that your own thinking about the reader's reception of this poem is different from mine—perhaps radically different. That's fine with me. Although we could argue over which one of us is insufficiently attentive to the poem's cues, in the context of reader-response criticism it makes more sense to try to learn from each other. For me, even when I'm trying to play the role of the implied reader, I'm continually aware that I'm making choices, filling in blanks and gaps, interpreting in one particular way when several other ways (some of which aren't occurring to me) are feasible. I say "the reader," and I am trying to think of an ideal or implied response, but I'm aware at several points that "the reader" may be only me. Still, it seems helpful to *try* to think of how other readers will respond. The real beauty of audience-oriented criticism, after all, is that the focus is on our activity: we make the text say whatever it's going to say, and then try to persuade others to accept our reading.

Let's take another example and this time develop an essay.

THE WRITING PROCESS: A SAMPLE ESSAY

Preparing to Respond

Here is a very short story by Ernest Hemingway, "A Very Short Story," which is actually part of a sequence of stories (for the whole sequence, see *Ernest Hemingway: The Short Stories*).

A Very Short Story (1925)
Ernest Hemingway

1   One hot evening in Padua they carried him up onto the roof and he could look out over the top of the town. There were chimney swifts in the sky. After a while it got dark and the searchlights came out. The others went down and took the bottles with them. He and Luz could hear them below on the balcony. Luz sat on the bed. She was cool and fresh in the hot night.

2   Luz stayed on night duty for three months. They were glad to let her. When they operated on him she prepared him for the operating table; and they had a joke about friend or enema. He went under the anaesthetic holding tight on to himself so he would not blab about anything during the silly, talky time. After he got on crutches he used to take the temperatures so Luz would not have to get up from the bed. There were only a few patients, and they all knew about it. They all liked Luz. As he walked back along the halls he thought of Luz in his bed.

3   Before he went back to the front they went into the Duomo and prayed. It was dim and quiet, and there were other people praying. They wanted to get married, but there was not enough time for the banns, and neither of them had birth certificates. They felt as though

they were married, but they wanted every one to know about it, and to make it so they could not lose it.

4   Luz wrote him many letters that he never got until after the armistice. Fifteen came in a bunch to the front and he sorted them by the dates and read them all straight through. They were all about the hospital, and how much she loved him and how it was impossible to get along without him and how terrible it was missing him at night.

5   After the armistice they agreed he should go home to get a job so they might be married. Luz would not come home until he had a good job and could come to New York to meet her. It was understood he would not drink, and he did not want to see his friends or any one in the States. Only to get a job and be married. On the train from Padua to Milan they quarrelled about her not being willing to come home at once. When they had to say good-bye, in the station at Milan, they kissed good-bye, but were not finished with the quarrel. He felt sick about saying good-bye like that.

6   He went to America on a boat from Genoa. Luz went back to Pordenone to open a hospital. It was lonely and rainy there, and there was a battalion of arditi quartered in the town. Living in the muddy, rainy town in the winter, the major of the battalion made love to Luz, and she had never known Italians before, and finally wrote to the States that theirs had been only a boy and girl affair. She was sorry, and she knew he would probably not be able to understand, but might some day forgive her, and be grateful to her, and she expected, absolutely unexpectedly, to be married in the spring. She loved him as always, but she realized now it was only a boy and girl love. She hoped he would have a great career, and believed in him absolutely. She knew it was for the best.

7   The major did not marry her in the spring, or any other time. Luz never got an answer to the letter to Chicago about it. A short time after he contracted gonorrhea from a sales girl in a loop department store while riding in a taxicab through Lincoln Park.

How this story shapes the reader's response has already been suggested by Robert Scholes in *Semiotics and Interpre-*

tation. As Scholes observes, the point of view in the story is technically third person (if it were first-person narration, it would read this way: "One hot evening in Padua they carried me up on the roof . . ."). But the viewpoint, Scholes says, seems to be closer to the unnamed man than to Luz (116-17). If the narrator were equally distanced from both characters, they would both have names. But "he" apparently doesn't need a name. The reader is told in the first and second sentences what "he" could see. Also, as Scholes notes, the assertion "She was cool and fresh in the hot night" really makes sense only from his perspective: *to him,* she seemed cool and fresh. This point of view plays an important role in the reader's response, and I would like to elaborate on Scholes' view of the story by tracing out in some detail "the reader's" experience.

For starters, we might consider how the reader responds to Hemingway's opening paragraph. Our response must be problematic at that point because we know so little: important information is being left out. But we do know something. We know "he" is in Padua, but we don't know what he is doing there or who he is. We learn that "they" carried him to the roof, but we don't know who "they" are or why he has to be carried: is he sick or injured? Does he have a handicap? The reference to searchlights in the third sentence probably suggests to most readers that the story may be taking place during wartime: these are searchlights looking for attacking planes. If that's the case, then perhaps he is being carried because he is wounded. We also learn that he and Luz are somehow close: "they" leave them alone on the roof, and Luz sits on his bed, appearing "cool and fresh."

In this second paragraph, the implied point of view is made clearer, and additional clues are offered. The notion that he is in a hospital is confirmed here. Luz is on night duty, so she would seem to be a nurse—an inference further supported by her preparation of him for the operating table. The reader may notice, as Scholes points out, that the male character's reticence is much like the story's own restraint (119). He doesn't want to blab, and neither apparently does the story's narrator, telling us only the minimum. Letting go is the enemy, and the enema; as Scholes puts it, "Logorrhea and diarrhea are equally embarrassing" (119).

Even if the reader finds the male character's fear of talking about anything problematic, the embodiment of a dumb macho stereotype, the strong silent man, we must be softened by his kindness in taking the temperatures. Here he is on crutches, and yet he gets up so Luz won't have to. What is not said by the narrator is what Luz is doing in his bed, but this is a blank that the reader easily fills in. The reader can easily discern that the "it" that the few patients "all knew about" must be an affair "he" and Luz are having. Why else would the narrator present the revelation that "they all knew about it" as if it were a kind of secret?

Recognizing what "it" is, most readers will probably acknowledge that a nurse sleeping with her patient probably does not represent the highest ethical standards. And recognizing this response perhaps makes clear why Hemingway has the narrator immediately tell us "They all liked Luz": their affection for Luz is designed to qualify the reader's disapproval. With the paragraph's final sentence, the reader must also realize, as "he" thinks of Luz in his bed, that she apparently means a lot to a recovering man, perhaps a wounded soldier. Having immersed ourselves in "his" point of view, readers may not notice, without some consideration, that we do not know what Luz is thinking.

In the third paragraph we learn that he is in fact a soldier because he goes back to the front. We learn that he and Luz pray together in church, and the narrator tells us that they wish they could be married, and feel as if they are married. If this feeling really is mutual, the reader may wonder about their plan. Why doesn't Luz return with him rather than waiting on his "good job"? Doesn't this condition make her seem a bit mercenary? Also, why are the restrictions on him seemingly so severe? Perhaps it makes sense that he will not drink, especially if he has a problem with drinking. But why does he not want to see his friends? In fact, he doesn't want to see anyone at all, according to their understanding. Does Luz not trust him? Does he not trust himself? The reader cannot be sure, the way this understanding is phrased, whether Luz imposes these conditions or he volunteers them; but since they restrict his behavior, the reader may assume the rules are Luz's idea.

Such subtle shaping of the reader's response prepares us for the bombshell in the sixth paragraph: she dumps him. In thinking about the reader's response here, we might consider (among other things) the effect of the information that "she had never known Italians before." The passage seems to offer this fact as a kind of explanation of her behavior, but it is an excuse that makes Luz seem worse, as if she wants to try Italians the way one might try a new flavor of ice cream. Hemingway does not say this excuse is disgustingly inadequate, but he sets up the story so that the reader easily comes to such a conclusion. Her letter is not quoted, but is filtered through his perspective; from that vantage point, it seems reasonable to assume that Luz has shamefully betrayed him.

There are in fact aspects of the letter, as it is reported, that seem so unfeeling they appear to be cruel. It is difficult for any reader to imagine what could more devastating than saying what he thought was the love of his life was actually "only a boy and girl affair." To say "she loved him as always" similarly demeans their relationship. "I thought we were in love," she is in effect saying, "but now that I've been with this Italian, I see we were just playing like children." Her love hasn't changed, just her understanding of what that love was. Finally, to say she "believed in him absolutely" after refusing to come to America before he had a "good" job seems the height of hypocrisy and coldness.

How do we respond to the conclusion? Hemingway has led the reader, it may seem, to see Luz's own jilting by the major as just what she deserves. He adds "or any other time" to prevent the reader from assuming that Luz and the Italian had some problems but worked them out. The affair that *she said* she thought was the real thing, in comparison to their boy and girl thing, does not turn out to be real after all. But did she really believe that the Italian was different? Is Luz a "loose" woman? Is that the significance of her name?

By telling us that Luz never got an answer to her letter, Hemingway conveys indirectly the soldier's pain. The reader can imagine he is so hurt, and so thoroughly disgusted, that he can't even respond to her. The final sentence further deepens the reader's perception of his pain. As Scholes points out, first Luz wounds his heart; then the salesgirl wounds him in a different place. The reader will naturally assume that he wouldn't have been in that taxicab, fooling around recklessly and decadently, in public in Lincoln Park, if it had not been for Luz. The narrator does not say it is Luz's fault that he gets gonorrhea, but that clearly is the implication: when he loses Luz, he loses everything. "A short time after" here implies some connection. First the war wound; then Luz's; then the salesgirl's.

In moving through the story, I am carrying out and elaborating on the reading Scholes suggests. About the reader's response to this story—that is, the implied response that Hemingway marks out—Scholes says the following:

> Most male students sympathize with the protagonist and are very critical of Luz—as indeed [the story] asks them to be. Many female students try to read the story as sympathetic to Luz, blaming events on the "weakness" of the young man or the state of the world. This is a possible interpretation, but it is not well supported by the text. Thus the female student must either "misread" the work (that is, she must offer the more weakly supported of two interpretations) or accept one more blow to her self-esteem as a woman. Faced with this story in a competitive classroom, women are put at a disadvantage. They are, in fact, in a double bind. (120-21)

I have thus far essentially agreed with this analysis of the implied reader's response. The text, in Scholes' opinion, makes the case against Luz. Although taking Luz's side is "a possible interpretation," Scholes says, it seems more difficult to him, a misreading. Scholes does, to be sure, place "misread" inside quotation marks, indicating his awareness of alternatives. But in truth, Scholes sees the reader—the male reader anyway—as being pulled toward one best response.

Not only does Scholes implicitly assume the text is a stable structure, marking out a particular response, he also assumes that "most" males will naturally take the soldier's side, and females will naturally try to take Luz's side. But one of the beauties of reader-response criticism is that it takes advantage of the diversity of readers in the world, reminding us of the treacherousness of generalizations about them. Reader-response criticism—by bringing the personal, the individual, even the eccentric responses to our attention—can revitalize texts that we think we have already learned how to read. Having processed the story with considerable care, attempting to play the role of a passive reader, we're ready now to take a more active part as a responding reader, entering into a debate within a community of readers.

Preparing to Write

What seems more difficult to Scholes (that is, taking Luz's side) seems to me in fact more compelling. I felt the first time I read this story that Luz was getting a raw deal, both from the soldier and from the narrator. Does that mean that I am responding from a woman's point of view? And is that point of view necessarily "at a disadvantage"? Even if we assume that women tend to side with Luz, and that the evidence for doing so is weaker than the evidence against Luz, we should still note that what is most obvious is oftentimes not very interesting in literary criticism. Making the case for Luz against the soldier is generally a more interesting endeavor than showing how Luz is cruel to the soldier.

Thus, I argue that Hemingway creates such apparent bias against Luz in order to expose it: that is, the soldier is so obviously being made into a martyr, and Luz into a villain, that the reader's response ought to resist this bias and look more carefully at the text, seeing past the narrator's obscuring point of view.

To give you an idea how I developed this response into an essay, I present below my notes and then the essay that resulted from them. Before examining these documents, you might want to sketch out your own response to Hemingway's story. What does it say to you?

> Make clear that the narrator clearly takes his side: Hemingway is reminding us to consider the source. You can't let the player's coach call the balls in or out, and the narrator in this case is on the soldier's team.
>
> I could make Hemingway into the villain who tries to cover for the soldier, making Luz into an Eve figure. Or, I could argue that Hemingway has the narrator make those moves, thus exposing him. I think the latter would be more fun.
>
> What is the absolute worst evidence against Luz? Probably the reason she gives for the break-up. Focus on that reason: "theirs had been only a boy and girl affair." The reader assumes, in the context created by the soldier's spokesman, that this excuse is cruel and cold. But maybe it isn't a rationalization, a way of getting her Italian major. Consider the possibility that Luz is right: they are immature; it is a boy/girl affair. Any evidence?
>
> - The soldier does reveal his immaturity after Luz breaks it off: having sex in a taxicab, getting an S.T.D.—now that's really mature.
>
> - We also must wonder about his decision not to respond to Luz's last letter. If he really loved Luz, wouldn't he consider forgiving her? Doesn't everyone make mistakes? Isn't it possible that Luz just got confused and mistook infatuation with the major for love? At such a distance from the soldier, in such bleak circumstances, she simply erred. But the soldier is such an immature hothead that the idea of forgiving her never occurs to him.
>
> - What is after all the basis of the soldier's relationship with Luz? If she is wrong, if it is more

than a boy/girl affair, what evidence is there in
the story of his maturity and the depth of his
love? The story in fact tells us nothing that suggests any great passion on his part. He seems perfectly willing to leave her behind while he goes to
the United States to get a job. What does he think
of Luz? We know only two things, really: She was
"cool and fresh" and "he thought of Luz in his
bed." So far as we can tell, the relationship is
based on sex, which isn't the strongest foundation
for marriage.

- What is the evidence that Luz is a bad person? She
does have sex with the soldier while he's a
patient. She sleeps in his bed. She lets him get up
and take the temperatures. But none of this makes
her evil. He is a wounded soldier in a foreign
country about to go back to the front. She is comforting him. She offers him love and affection. She
is the nurse every wounded soldier no doubt dreams
of. In letting the soldier get up and take the temperatures, Luz is arguably letting him act as her
protector, strengthening his ego, which is likely
to be fragile after his injury.

- Why is there an understanding that he won't drink
and won't hang around with his friends? Is Luz
being mean? Hemingway leaves this meaningful gap in
the story, when he could have easily filled it in.
Perhaps the soldier has a drinking problem. Early
in the story other people do take away the bottles.
The story doesn't say that Luz imposed this "no
drinking" policy on him; perhaps he imposed it on
himself to indicate his seriousness and trustwor-
thiness to Luz.

- What does it mean when Luz breaks it off? Had there
been a formal proposal, an acceptance, a ring, an
engagement? All the reader knows is that the two
are sleeping together, and that they come to view

each other as married—at least from the soldier's
perspective. Hemingway says the understanding is
that "he should go home so they might be married."
What does "might" mean here? If they wanted to get
married before he went back to the front, why
didn't they arrange it when he returned? Such unex-
plained gaps must lead the reader to wonder about
the facts. Has the soldier come to assume something
that just isn't the case: he assumes, because they
are sleeping together, they're going to get married; and poor Luz, feeling sorry for his wounds
and his inevitable return to danger doesn't have
the heart to tell him it just isn't that serious.

- If they really were in love, why might Luz fall for
  the Italian major? The reader isn't told anything
  about what things look like from her perspective.
  Does he write letters? Does he get a job? Does he
  follow through on his "no drinking" pledge? If he
  does get a job, then why hasn't Luz already come
  over? It seems likely, in fact, the more one thinks
  about it, that something is seriously wrong on his
  end. Hemingway, by withholding vital information,
  allows the reader to jump to conclusions—conclusions that the careful reader must eventually withdraw. The reader leaps to conclusions, much like
  the soldier.

Shaping

Based on these notes, which meditated on the possibility
that Luz is being set up, and that the reader ought to see
through this unfair treatment, I sketched out a draft of the
main points I might want to make in articulating my
response. Here's what I wrote:

Main point:
    Luz is right. It was a boy and girl affair.

Evidence:

1. Their relationship is apparently based on sex;
   plus, some questionable ethics are involved in
   their affair.

2. The soldier appears to be unreliable: Luz is afraid
   he won't get a job, but will just drink and run
   around. Since she doesn't come to the United
   States, it appears that she may have been right.

3. Luz obviously wasn't ready to get married, or she
   would have married him when he returned to the
   front, before he returned to the States. She just
   couldn't break his heart so soon after the war.

4. He doesn't respond to her last letter; he doesn't
   try to win her back. Instead he responds with
   reckless indulgence. Our first impulse is to feel
   sorry for him; our more reasoned response is to
   fault him.

Problems:

- If Luz has no intention of marrying him, it is only
  momentarily kind to string him along.

- If Luz aims to get him to the States, where he'll
  slowly forget about her, then why do they have this
  understanding about his drinking and socializing?

Drafting

At this point, I feel ready to write a draft. After several
tries, and some rewriting and rethinking, here is the essay I
produced.

THE LONGER VIEW OF HEMINGWAY'S "A
VERY SHORT STORY"

The obvious response
described: the set-up.

Most readers of Hemingway's "A
Very Short Story" will naturally
pity the poor nameless soldier. He
is wounded in the war, and then his

fiancée breaks off their relationship when she falls for an Italian
major. Her name, Luz, which might be
pronounced like "lose," points to
his fate: where women are involved,
he will lose. As a final indignity
and injury, another woman gives him
gonorrhea, emphasizing his status as
a victim and a loser—because of
women. Although the main villain is
Luz, his experience with the salesgirl, who wounds him in a different
way, suggests quite simply that
women are untrustworthy, evil, dangerous—as bad as the war, it seems.

But this immediate reaction of
pity is the effect of our point of
view. Although the story is told in
third-person, Hemingway actually
gives us, as Robert Scholes points
out, what is essentially the soldier's point of view. Repeatedly in
the brief story, we are told what he
experiences and what he is thinking.
In the opening, for instance, we are
told that "he could look out over
the top of the town." We learn that
Luz "was cool and fresh in the hot
night"—a perception that clearly is
his. We know his motivation for trying not to talk under anaesthetic
(he does not want to "blab"), and we
know how many letters he received
and what was in them. We never know,
however, what Luz is really thinking, and we learn the content of her
letters from his perspective, when

**Why this response
occurs (point of view):
more set-up for an
alternative response.**

**How third-person
seems like first.**

he reads them. The real context of their writing is hidden from the reader.

Transition to a different response, one that looks beyond the point of view.

But Hemingway gives the careful reader plenty of clues that suggest we should look closer, overcoming the limitations of the narrative's point of view. Is Luz in fact entirely the villain, and the soldier purely the innocent victim?

This focuses on the crucial factor in our response to Luz: she betrays him.

Our opinion of Luz is of course influenced by the fact that in falling for the Italian major, she betrays the American soldier. There is little question that Luz made a mistake, but it is also clear that she pays for her mistake, for "The major did not marry her in the spring, or any other time." And when Luz writes to the soldier about the major's departure, she is perhaps attempting to resurrect her relationship with the soldier, but he fails to respond. The soldier cannot forgive her, apparently.

The letter is most important in shaping this negative response to Luz.

Nor, it seems, can many readers. The most important reason, I believe, is Luz's letter breaking off her relationship with the soldier. Specifically, her assertion that "theirs had been only a boy and girl affair" seems especially thoughtless and cruel. It is bad enough to be dumped for an Italian stallion, but it is even worse to

learn that your own relationship
was, in your partner's view, immature and superficial. But before we
damn Luz's insensitivity, we ought
to consider the possible validity of
her remark. In other words, is she
possibly right? Was their relationship only a boy and girl affair?

My response, contrast-
ing the obvious
response: Luz may be
right.

What in fact is the basis of
their relationship? It appears to be
only physical. All we know of his
view of Luz is that she is "cool and
fresh." She sounds more like a soft
drink or a vegetable than a partner
for life. Luz is after all sleeping
in the hospital with one of her
patients, and another pronunciation
of her name, as "loose," may also be
appropriate. When she says their
relationship was immature, perhaps
she accurately assesses her own
behavior. The conditions, to be
sure, were extraordinary: it is
wartime, and the wounded soldier is
returning to the front. I can under-

I see Luz's immaturity
easily.

stand Luz's looseness, but I can
also agree that she is immature.

I also see the soldier's
immaturity.

Her assessment of the soldier's
maturity also seems accurate to me.
Just look at his response to her
last letter. He goes from hospital-
bed sex to taxi-cab sex. Hemingway
provides the tawdry details to
emphasize his poor judgment: "A
short time after [her letter] he
contracted gonorrhea from a sales

girl in a loop department store while riding in a taxicab through Lincoln Park." The poor soldier is wounded again in "combat," but surely this problem is his own fault. It is not Luz's fault, nor even the salesgirl's fault, is it? Even if we grant that mature and thoughtful people might contract a sexually transmitted disease, and that things were much different back then, the circumstances here still do not suggest responsible behavior. In fact, it is hard for me to imagine how he could be more immature, unless perhaps he had sex on the sidewalk with a prostitute.

Most immature: his response to Luz's break-up.

I also notice the soldier's promise not to drink, nor to see "his friends or anyone." Given the reference early in the story to drinking on the roof, I have to wonder if he has a drinking problem. I wonder why they did not marry when he returned from the front. There was not sufficient time before he left, but surely there is enough time when he gets back. It seems fair to suspect that the lack of time was just a convenient excuse. Likewise, why does he go ahead and leave Luz if he is unhappy with the arrangement? How long does it take him to get a job? Does he in fact get one? If so, then why is Luz still overseas? We are not told many things we need to know to evaluate

How I respond to earlier evidence of his immaturity.

I think Luz is right: I can see her side.

his responsibility, but what is left out, together with what we do know, does suggest to me that Luz's view may not be thoughtless or cruel, but simply accurate. Theirs was indeed a boy and girl affair. At least Luz is perceptive enough to see it.

PRACTICING READER-RESPONSE CRITICISM

I offer here two works along with some questions intended to stimulate your response, helping you to develop a reader-response essay. These are just sample questions; other ones will probably occur to you. The important thing is to generate materials that allow you to articulate your response. Without you, there is no response.

Since There's No Help (1619)
Michael Drayton

Since there's no help, come, let us kiss and part,—
Nay, I have done, you get no more from me;
And I am glad, yea glad with all my heart,
That thus so cleanly I myself can free;
Shake hands for ever, cancel all our vows,   5
And when we meet at any time again,
Be it not seen in either of our brows
That we one jot of former love retain.
Now at the last gasp of Love's latest breath,
When his pulse failing, Passion speechless lies,   10
When Faith is kneeling by his bed of death,
And Innocence is closing up his eyes,—
    Now if thou would'st, when all have given him over,
    From death to life thou migh'st him yet recover.

Questions

1. As you read the first line, what scene do you imagine taking place? At the end of the first line, what tone do

you imagine the speaker is using?

2. How do the next three lines (2-4) affect your perception of the speaker's tone? What do the words "cleanly" and "free" suggest about the speaker's tone?

3. The speaker says about ten times (depending on how you count them) that the lovers should break it off. Why all the repetition? And why the extreme declaration that not "one jot of former love" should remain?

4. Imagine yourself as the person being addressed in this poem. How would you feel after line 8?

5. How does your view of the relationship change in the last six lines? How does presenting "Love" as a dying person affect your response?

6. The poem speaks to "you." Who is this "you"? What clues does the poem give us about the character of "you"?

7. Sometime around 1591 Michael Drayton fell totally in love with Anne Goodere (he said he lost his mind over her). This sonnet was probably written shortly after that, even though it was not published until 1619. Anne Goodere married Sir Henry Rainsford in 1596; Drayton never married. But he did spend every summer at Clifford Hall, the country home of Anne and Henry, his passion apparently turning into a deep friendship. How does this information affect your response to the poem?

Killing the Bear (1991)
Judith Minty

1   She has strung the hammock between two birch trees at the edge of the clearing. Now she drifts in and out of the light there and drowsily studies the pattern made by the rope's weaving and the flickering leaves.

2   When she had the dog, he stretched out beneath the hammock. Hackles raised, growling and nipping at flies, he'd meant to save her

from shadows. In truth, he startled at noises, even at shifts in the wind, and she ended up more his protector than the other way around.

　　　　　　　　　　　　　　　　　　　෨

3　　There were wolves at the little zoo when she was a child. She heard them howling from her aunt's kitchen and went to see them up close.

4　　And a bear.

5　　Three times she visited, slowly circling the bear pen, but he was always sleeping. He looked like a bundle of clothes by the dead tree. His fence was electrified and posted with signs, and she was afraid to touch the iron bars.

6　　The wolves set off a chorus of neighborhood dogs. Their calling floated back and forth all that summer vacation.

　　　　　　　　　　　　　　　　　　　෨

7　　She lies in the hammock every afternoon, her life in the rhythm of the woods. Up at dawn to the shrill pitch of bluejays. Logs tossed into the stove, match lit, breath steaming in the cabin's chill. Trip to the outhouse, coffee perking, bucket of water from the river. The rest of the morning, ping of nails driven into boards. Her porch is nearly done. One room and another room. Something inside and something out.

8　　The afternoon silence and the sway of the hammock lull her and when she hears a low guttural, she thinks, at first, it is the dog. Then she remembers the dog is gone.

9　　She struggles to sit up and makes the hammock sway crazily.

10　　A bear stands beyond the pines—small jets of eyes, heavy black coat. He snuffles, then drops on all fours and weaves into the forest.

11　　Her hands lift to cover her breasts.

　　　　　　　　　　　　　　　　　　　෨

12   Her favorite doll was a stuffed animal and she slept with it close to her heart. She was nine when her mother said, "Give me your bear for three months. Let's see if you can stop sucking your thumb."

13   She tried very hard to stop, and when the time was up, she asked for the bear again.

14   Her mother said, "Another month."

15   One day, as she sat in the kitchen watching a cake being stirred and poured into the pan and then put into the oven, it came to her that her bear was gone, that it had been thrown down the incinerator.

16   Only a few years ago, her mother told her, misspeaking even then, "I'm sorry for burning the animal in you."

᠉

17   Her hammer has stopped its thump and echo. The roof is laid. The porch smells of fresh paint. She has hauled the old sofa out and can sit there in the evenings, if she wants.

18   When the bear understood that she was alone, he came closer. The first time, she was reading in the hammock and heard something like a sigh. She knew it was him, even before she caught a glimpse of black gliding through the woods. The next time, he was so close she smelled him—a terrible, rancid odor. Without looking, she swung out of the hammock and walked to the cabin. Two days later, he stood next to the birch tree, breath rattling his throat. If she'd turned, she could have touched the bristles on his shoulder.

᠉

19   The Gilyak tribe honored him. They put his head on a stake outside their doors and made offerings to it. On Yezo Island, the Ainus thought he was a man trapped inside the body of a bear. If a hunter found a cub, he brought it to his wife who suckled it.

20   In Lapland he was King of Beasts. The men lived alone, purifying themselves, for three days after the hunt. At the funeral, after they had feasted, they put his bones back together in the ground.

21   Once she spent an evening with two Swedes. At dinner, their wineglasses held the tint of leaves. Ole, the painter, said, "You live in green light." Gunnar told magic tales. "When a woman meets a bear in the woods, she must lift her skirt. Then he will let her pass."

ɞ

22   In the travelogue about Alaska, the Kodiak caught a salmon, his claws stretched out like fingers. When the second bear approached, he reared up. He looked soft and gentle, as if he were greeting a friend, until, with a sweep of his paw, he split open the head of the other.

23   In college, a classmate told about the summer he'd worked at Yellowstone and got too close. He never felt the nick, only knew when blood trickled down his forehead.

24   There was also the news story about the woman dragged from her tent in the middle of the night, crying, "He's killing me. Oh God, he's killing me." The bear carried the woman away, his claws tangled in her hair, ripping at her arm.

ɞ

25   When she drove to town for supplies, she bought a secondhand rifle. She keeps it loaded now, propped against the doorjamb inside the cabin.

26   The clerk at the hardware store showed her how to fire it, how to aim along the sights. He winked and told her she could get a man with it at twenty yards. She said she didn't need a man, just wanted to do some hunting.

27   She misses the dog. She carries the gun awkwardly over her shoulder when she goes to the woodpile, or to the river.

ɞ

28   Her calendar hangs on the cabin wall, each day of summer marked with an X, the rest of the year clean and open. She turns up the wick on the lamp and starts to brush her hair, staring at her reflection in the windowpane.

29   She is thinking about leaving. She is thinking about driving out of the clearing.

30   When the scream begins, it breaks against the walls. It shudders in a moan, then rises. Everything, even the wind, holds its breath.

31   It is over so quickly she almost believes it didn't happen and raises the brush again, and barely recognizes herself in the glass. She runs to the lamp and blows out the flame, then to the window, hoping she will not see what must be there.

∂●

32   She did not shoot cleanly the first time. When he ripped the screen and tore the siding loose, she stood on the porch, gun leveled.

33   "Go away."

34   He was no more than ten feet from her when she fired. He spun around and fell to the ground, then raised himself up.

35   When she realized she had only wounded him, she ran into the cabin and turned the lock and leaned against the door. She could hear him thrashing and bellowing in the bushes and against the trees.

36   She knew she would have to step onto the porch again, go to the ripped screen, with nothing but night air between them. She would have to take aim and shoot again. And if that didn't stop him, she would have to slip the bolt and reload the rifle and stand there and shoot him again until he stopped bawling and weeping and falling down and getting up and lurching against the trees.

37   When they began this, she never thought she would have to kill him so slow. She never dreamed she would have to hurt him so much.

∂●

38   It is nearly dawn when he dies, when she gets up from her chair, when his groans stop pricking her skin. She takes the flashlight and goes out on the porch. She shines the beam around in the gray light and sees the blood dried on the new screen and on the fresh-painted sill and spattered on the leaves around the cabin. She sees the tram-

pled bushes and broken branches and where he crawled into the weeds.

39   She shines the arc out, light bouncing on tree and log, until it lands on a black heap, huddled in the middle of the clearing.

40   As soon as the sun rises, she begins to dig, and by midafternoon she is through with it—the rope tied to him, the car backed up to the hole, the rifle and box of ammunition remembered and dropped in next to him, the musty soil put back, and branches over that.

41   Then she bathes with the last of the water from the river and sweeps the cabin floor, thinking that rain will wash away the blood and that, soon enough, snow will fall and cover it all.

≥≈

42   It is dark when she gets to the state line. Next summer, she will dig him up to take the claws.

Questions

1. What associations do the first two paragraphs bring to your mind? Can you imagine yourself in a similar scene? How would you feel? How do you react to the suggestion that "she" ended up more the dog's protector "than the other way around"?

2. Do paragraphs 3–6 alter the mood created by the first two paragraphs? What contrasting moods are created by the third section?

3. What is your response to the following sentence? "Her hands lift to cover her breasts." For instance, what expectations does the statement create for you?

4. How do paragraphs 12–16 affect the reader's understanding of her attitude toward bears?

5. How does her construction of a porch, and the movement of her sofa onto the porch, affect your response to the bear's appearance? What does the bear's smell contribute to your response? How about the bear's sex? (The bear is a "him," not an "it.")

6. Paragraphs 19–21 observe how various cultures have honored bears, but it also has its ominous aspects. Explain how the reader's sense of danger builds in the seventh section.

7. Why are the summer days marked with an X? Does that have anything to do with bears?

8. Describe your reaction to the paragraphs 32–41.

9. Is the final sentence surprising? Why, or why not?

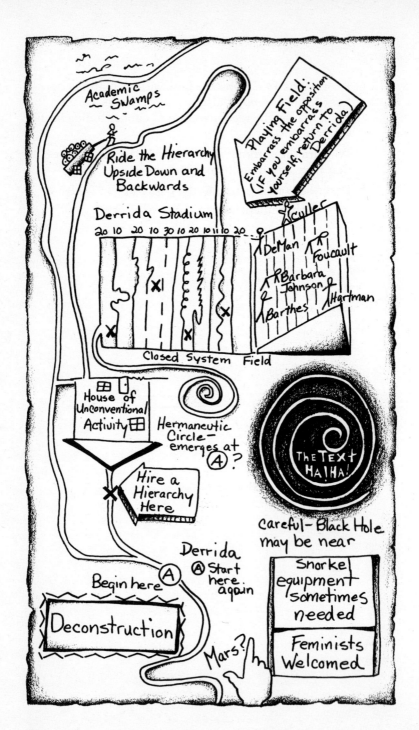

OPENING UP THE TEXT
Deconstructive Criticism

*Imagine being the first to
say, with confidence:*
uncertainty.

—Michael Blumenthal

THE PURPOSE OF DECONSTRUCTION

Not so long ago, "deconstruct" and "deconstruction" were used only in what was perceived as radical criticism (or in attacks on such criticism). Now the terms and ideas of deconstruction have passed into the general critical vocabulary and pervade fields as diverse as architecture and theology, appearing in both specialized journals and in *Time* and *Newsweek*. But any effort to explain what deconstruction is and why its ideas have been so appealing immediately runs into two problems.

First, "deconstruction" has been used in so many different ways and contexts that it is hard to say what it means. As Gregory Jay puts it, "deconstruction has now become an indeterminate nominative" (xi): a name without a reference. Second, if the assumptions of deconstruction are correct, it always was an uncertain term: for deconstruction's assumption that all terms are unstable must apply to itself. Few efforts would appear to be more ironic, perhaps even comical, than attempting to define and explain a philosophical position that assumes the inevitability of error and misreading, the impossibility of explaining and defining in any stable way.

There are, however, at least three reasons to attempt to explain deconstruction anyway:

1. The alternative to explaining what in the final analysis cannot be explained is silence. We explain deconstruction, and we practice it, even though something is always left undone, unstated, unclear, unthought of. Another explanation can supplement this one, and then another one can supplement it. Such is the case with any term.

2. Deconstruction makes no effort to suppress its own irony or absurdity; instead, deconstructive critics have generally indulged a playfulness that from the perspective of traditional criticism seems at times unprofessional; in the merciless punning of some of the most prominent deconstructive critics, it has seemed occasionally almost juvenile. (I am thinking for instance of Paul de Man's comparison of Archie Bunker [the television character] to "a de-bunker of the arche [or origin], an archie De-Bunker such as Nietzsche or Jacques Derrida"[9].)

3. Deconstruction can be learned by students, and it often stimulates a wonderfully imaginative playfulness and scrutiny. In fact, rather than being an esoteric, foreign, abstract, discouraging approach, deconstruction for most students, in my experience, makes tremendous sense: it articulates precisely what they have in fact already assumed in a vague way.

So, here we go. If the room starts spinning, or you find yourself getting dizzy, take a deep breath; or put the book on the floor so you can read with your head between your legs. Seriously, the next little stretch is a bit theoretical and even strange, but you'll see several illustrations later on. Just hang in there, and it will get clearer.

The most important figure for deconstruction is without question Jacques Derrida, a Frenchman who has relentlessly and astonishingly exposed the uncertainties of using language. Derrida starts from the recognition that the signifier (the word) and the signified (its reference) are not a unified entity, but rather an arbitrary and constantly shifting relationship. A dictionary seems to stabilize a language, but what we actually find in a dictionary is the postponement or deferment of meaning: words have multiple definitions, and these definitions require us to seek the meaning of other words, which are themselves defined in the same way.

Even if it were possible to construct instantaneously a dictionary that would be perfectly up-to-date, we would still find ambiguity, multiplicity, slippage pervading the language. The reason is nicely captured in Derrida's most famous statement, which is translated as "There is nothing outside the text," and as "There is no outside to the text" (this uncertainty regarding translation in itself tells us something important about language). Meaning cannot get outside of language, to reality. Therefore, words always refer to other words. Different languages divide up reality differently because the relationship between words and things is arbitrary; it's made up. And it can therefore be unmade.

Deconstruction reveals the arbitrariness of language most strikingly by exposing the contradictions in a discourse, thereby showing how a text undermines itself. As Barbara Johnson puts it, deconstruction proceeds by "the careful teasing out of warring forces of signification within the text itself" (5). Or, as Jonathan Culler says, "to deconstruct a discourse is to show how it undermines the philosophy it asserts, or the hierarchical oppositions on which it relies" (*Deconstruction* 86). This exposure of a text's self-contradictions is possible, deconstruction assumes, because words cannot stabilize meaning: if we choose to say one thing, we are leaving out another thing. And there is always a gap, a space in the text, that the reader cannot ultimately fill in.

Deconstruction is therefore particularly valuable because of its power to open up a text that we may have seen as limited or closed. Popularly, "to deconstruct" seems to be used to mean "to dismantle" or "to destroy," as if "deconstruction" were a fancier form of "destruction." But for most informed critics, deconstruction is not so much a way to obliterate the meaning of a text, as it is a way to multiply meaning infinitely. Deconstruction thus encourages us to resist a complacent acceptance of anything, and to question our positions and statements in a particularly rigorous way, even reading texts against themselves.

For instance, let's take a very simple text, one appearing beside an elevator: "Seeing Eye Dogs Only." A deconstructive reading of this text might point out that although it appears to extend assistance to the visually impaired, it literally should force them to walk up the stairs, for the sign literally appears to say, "This elevator is reserved for Seeing Eye dogs. No other animals or persons can ride it." Or, we might argue that the text shifts attention and power to a certain kind of dog, while ignoring the owners of the dogs. Here's a text ostensibly put up to help blind persons, and it actually ignores them. A blind person with a Seeing Eye monkey, presumably, must not ride. Plus, blind persons obviously cannot read the sign, which suggests that some other intention does motivate it. Perhaps the sign is intended to make sure that someone who is fully sighted and has a retired Seeing Eye dog as a pet, can take such a dog on the elevator? Isn't that what it says? What *is* the point of this sign? Does it subvert its own purpose?

Although such undoing of a text may seem at first glance a bit silly, it actually has enormous practical value. Imagining all the things a text *might* be saying, including even the opposite of what it may appear to say, will help us to become more creative and careful readers and writers. Some colleagues of mine recently wrote a policy statement that told students "You will fail your Freshman English course if you miss more than three scheduled tutoring sessions." One student read this statement as a prediction rather than a rule, and he elected to skip all his tutoring sessions in order to prove the prediction wrong. As he told me later, appealing his failing grade, "I knew I was smart enough to pass the course without any help, and I resented them telling me I couldn't do it."

But a deconstructive stance not only may help us anticipate some of the ways that even simple texts can be misread, it may also help us see what is being excluded or suppressed in a text. For instance, the J. Peterman Company advertises a reproduction of "Hemingway's Cap." The point of the advertisement is, of course, that Ernest Hemingway picked out a tough, distinctive, very masculine hat to wear; and now you can have the same. The ad conveys this message by telling us that Hemingway probably bought the cap "on the road to Ketchum," which is where Hemingway's Idaho ranch was located, the scene of hunting, fishing, and other outdoor activities; that he found it "among the beef jerky wrapped in cellophane," which also helps create a rustic, macho atmosphere (isn't beef jerky primarily eaten by guys in a duck blind or deer stand—or wishing they were?); that the bill is longer than average, longer in fact than the advertiser has ever seen, and "impervious" to rainstorms; that the cap is the color of "scalding expresso"—a drink for tough men who need a tough cap; that there's an elastic band "to keep this treasure from blowing off your head and into the trees;" and much else. Thus, the advertisement celebrates masculine toughness, durability, endurance, sensibility, using these values to sell the product.

But a deconstructive stance encourages an acute alertness to rhetorical strategies and even the assumptions these strategies depend upon. Although the cap appears to promote and depend upon a masculine toughness, deconstruction tells us that it also unavoidably promotes and depends upon masculine insecurity. Why would anyone want the longest bill anyone ever saw? For the same reason one might want the fastest car anyone ever saw. Or the biggest ranch. Made of "deerskin," this longest bill becomes a symbol of its owner's power and potency. It may be too much to claim that the bill is a phallic substitute, although it is pretty clear what part of their skin many men would consider most "dear." Certainly, Hemingway was fascinated by potency and its lack: in *The Sun Also Rises*, for instance, Jake Barnes has been emasculated by a wartime injury and loses Brett, Lady Ashley, to a young bullfighter and then to another aristocrat.

Likewise, the idea that Hemingway may have bought his cap "on the road to Ketchum" conjures up scenes of hunting

and fishing. But Ketchum is also where Hemingway committed suicide. Seriously ill for some time, he put a shotgun in
his mouth and pulled the trigger. Denied the sort of active,
impervious masculinity embodied in the cap, Hemingway
apparently could not face life in a compromised manner.

How the cap relates to this weakness or insecurity is most
startlingly seen in an especially revealing (or especially unfor-
tunate) phrase, referring to the "elastic at back to keep this
treasure from blowing off your head." In asserting that the
cap is a "treasure," the ad unavoidably raises the danger—the
inevitability really—of losing it. This sentence is meant to
reassure potential owners, but it also points out how only the
elastic (which must age and wear out) stands between the
owner and loss of his manly treasure. The advertisement thus
helps to foster an insecurity that the cap covers over; but in
such a value system, depending on potency and toughness,
the danger of something "blowing off your head" is very real,
as Hemingway's case reveals.

Is such a mischievous, even outrageous, allusion intended
in "blowing off your head"? Although I've had students who
insist that the phrase is a wickedly clever joke, that the ad's
author must have been aware of the implications of "blowing
off your head" in the context of Hemingway, the issue is really undecidable, and from a deconstructive point of view irrelevant because other conflicting and contradictory meanings
are always available to the attentive, creative reader. There
will always be a trace of "don't buy this hat" left in any urging
to "buy this hat."

Let's turn now to some other examples and to the practical matter of how deconstruction works on more complex
texts, which often even more readily lend themselves to opening up.

HOW TO DO DECONSTRUCTION

In an essay designed to question and criticize, Lawrence
Lipking shows how deconstruction would deal with W. B.

Yeats's famous poem "Sailing to Byzantium." Since deconstruction turns a text against itself, multiplying its meanings, it seems only appropriate that Lipking's attack on deconstruction should provide a convenient illustration of deconstruction's value.

Here is Yeats's poem.

Sailing to Byzantium [1]   (1927)
William Butler Yeats

I

That is no country for old men.° The young
In one another's arms, birds in the trees
—Those dying generations—at their song,
The salmon-falls, the mackerel-crowded seas
Fish, flesh, or fowl, commend all summer long   5
Whatever is begotten, born and dies.
Caught in that sensual music all neglect
Monuments of unaging intellect.

II

An aged man is but a paltry thing,
A tattered coat upon a stick, unless   10
Soul clap its hands and sing, and louder sing
For every tatter in its mortal dress,
Nor is there singing school but studying
Monuments of its own magnificence;
And therefore I have sailed the seas and come   15
To the holy city of Byzantium.

III

O sages standing in God's holy fire
As in the gold mosaic of a wall,
Come from the holy fire, perne in a gyre,°
And be the singing-masters of my soul.   20
Consume my heart away; sick with desire
And fastened to a dying animal
It knows not what it is; and gather me
Into the artifice of eternity.

IV
Once out of nature I shall never take   25
My bodily form from any natural thing,
But such a form as Grecian goldsmiths make
Of hammered gold and gold enameling
To keep a drowsy Emperor awake;°
Or set upon a golden bough° to sing   30
To lords and ladies of Byzantium
Of what is past, or passing, or to come.

Deconstruction requires a norm or a convention to work
against. If we don't assume a text is logically coherent, then
exposing its incoherence and self-difference is hardly remarkable. In a way, then, a deconstructive reading is like an extension of a New Critical reading: setting aside authorial intention and the reader's response, one first identifies the unity
that appears to be present in the text, and then divides and
dispels it.

A classic New Critical reading of Yeats's poem is offered
by Cleanth Brooks in *The Well-Wrought Urn* (1947). As we
would expect, Brooks finds in the poem certain tensions or
oppositions, which include for instance "nature versus art."
By this opposition, Brooks means (among other things) that
the first two stanzas talk about "fish, flesh, or fowl" and about
aging—aspects of nature. The second two stanzas talk about
"gold mosaic," "artifice," "hammered gold"—works of art.

---

[1]*Byzantium:* Old name for the modern city of Istanbul, capital of
the Eastern Roman Empire, ancient artistic and intellectual center.
Yeats uses Byzantium as a symbol for "artificial" (and therefore death-
less) art and beauty, as opposed to the beauty of the natural world,
which is bound to time and death. 1 *That...men:* Ireland, part of the
time-bound world. 19 *perne in a gyre:* Bobbin making a spiral pattern.
27–29 *such...awake:* "I have read somewhere that in the Emperor's
palace at Byzantium was a tree made of gold and silver, and artificial
birds that sang" (Yeats's note). 30 *golden bough:* In Greek legend, Aeneas
had to pluck a golden bough from a tree in order to descend into Hades.
As soon as the bough was plucked, another grew in its place.

Brooks discusses other oppositions:

becoming	vs.	being
sensual	vs.	intellectual
here	vs.	Byzantium
aging	vs.	timelessness

To unify these oppositions, Brooks focuses on the speaker's "prayer," which begins in the third stanza and asks the "sages" to "come from the holy fire"; and he makes the word "artifice" the crux of the poem:

> The word "artifice" fits the prayer at one level after another: the fact that he is to be taken *out of nature;* that his body is to be an artifice hammered out of gold; that it will not age but will have the finality of a work of art. (188)

Yeats seems, Brooks says, to favor the second elements in the list above. "Artifice," however, complicates matters:

> But "artifice" unquestionably carries an ironic qualification too. The prayer, for all its passion, is a modest one. He does not ask that he be gathered into eternity—it will be enough if he is gathered into the "artifice of eternity." The qualification does not turn the prayer into mockery, but it is all-important: it limits as well as defines the power of the sages to whom the poet appeals. (189)

This move, as I pointed out in the chapter on New Criticism, is typical, as Brooks finds an ironic center that unifies the poem. Here is Brooks's thesis, as it is stated early in the essay, responding to the question of "which world" Yeats commits himself to:

> To which world is Yeats committed? Which does he choose?
>
> The question is idle—as idle as the question which the earnest schoolmarm puts to the little girl reading for the first time "L'Allegro—Il Penseroso": which does Milton *really* prefer, mirth or melancholy. . . .
>
> Yeats chooses both and neither. (187)

More directly, Brooks articulates his position this way near the end of his essay:

> The irony [of the poem] is directed, it seems to me, not at our yearning to transcend the world of nature, but at the human situation itself in which supernatural and natural are intermixed—the human situation which is inevitably caught between the claims of both natural and supernatural. The golden bird whose bodily form the speaker will take in Byzantium will be withdrawn from the flux of the world of becoming. But so withdrawn, it will sing of the world of becoming—"Of what is past, or passing, or to come." (189-90)

This "intermixture" that Brooks finds is the force unifying for him the poem's complex oppositions, thereby making possible the poem's greatness.

A deconstructive reading observes the text's oppositions, as Brooks has done; and it notices how the text appears to resolve its oppositions. But it goes further and shows how this resolution falls apart. Brooks claims that Yeats chooses both art and nature. But is that really true? In the final stanza, the speaker says, "Once out of nature I shall never take / My bodily form from any natural thing." If he escapes nature and becomes a golden work of art, then he has certainly chosen one member of the opposition. Brooks tries to cover this problem by saying the bird, outside of nature and time, will sing of the world of becoming—"Of what is past, or passing, or to come." But surely singing of something is not the same thing as being in it. Yeats *does choose*—art over nature, being over becoming, the intellectual over the sensual.

Or does he? The final step of deconstruction (after finding oppositions, noticing their resolution, and questioning that resolution) is to call the reversal into question, placing the text in uncertainty. Lipking, employing a deconstructive stance, repeatedly shows how the poem fails to resolve its meaning. He asks for instance why should soul "louder sing / For every tatter in its mortal dress"? Is it singing to distract itself or us from the tatters of its mortal dress? Then the singing is opposed to the tatters, as the soul sings in spite of physical ailments. Or is it singing in celebration of these tatters, because the body's deterioration brings the soul closer to separation from the body? Lipking ponders these alternatives and concludes that "the line does not make sense, if by sense we understand a single unequivocal meaning or even the Aristotelian logic that asserts that nothing can be itself and not itself at the same time. Language goes its own way" (431).

Likewise, Lipking raises the question of whether, in the third stanza, there is a singing school. If "Nor is there singing school" means there isn't one, then how come the speaker wants some singing masters in the next verse? Perhaps the speaker says there is no singing school *unless* it consists of studying monuments of the soul's magnificence. But such activity hardly sounds like a singing school, and it seems unlikely that such soul singing is learned in an academic way. In the final analysis, Lipking suggests that the poem, through a deconstructive lens anyway, is confusing.

Similarly, Lipking asks if the artifice of eternity is "something permanent (an eternal artifice) or something evanescent (an illusion without any substance)" (432). He confesses he can't decide. He also points even to the uncertain syntax of the opening "That" (which, Lipking points out, "Yeats himself said was the worst syntax he ever wrote"). In sum Lipking finds that "The elementary polarities that seem to provide its [the poem's] frame—the dialectic of 'that country' and Byzantium, of young and old, of time and timelessness, of body and soul, above all of nature and art—do not hold up under a careful reading" (432). Thus, "Whatever is begotten, born, and dies" only appears to parallel "what is past, or passing, or to come." The word "lives" would parallel "born" better than "passing"; and "begotten" does not clearly relate to "past." Even the word "dies" is not entirely satisfactory because the birds' "song" is one that lives on from generation to generation.

These points may seem rather minor to you. But there is one internal contradiction, as Lipking amusingly says, "so important and obvious that it is noticed by a great many students, and even some critics":

> When the speaker claims that "Once out of nature I shall never take / My bodily form from any natural thing," he seems to ignore the

blatant fact that every bodily form must be taken from nature,
whether the form of a bird or simply the golden form embodied by an
artist. (432-33)

In a famous letter, Sturge Moore did write to Yeats that "a
goldsmith's bird is as much nature as a man's body, especially
if it only sings like Homer and Shakespeare of what is past or
passing or to come to Lords and Ladies" (qtd. Lipking 433).
In fact, art seems already to be present in the world of nature
that is described so artfully in the first verse. "That" country
and Byzantium, Lipking says, "are equally unreal; they
acquire significance only by being contrasted with each
other" (433). "That" country never appears in the poem; it is
always absent. Nor does the poet arrive at Byzantium, as
Lipking reminds us: he is only "Sailing to" it. And the problem, deconstruction tells us, is that we "swim in a sea of language," where enduring "presence" is impossible: we never
arrive where we're going, linguistically. Instead, we find only
oppositions and differences that defer meaning.

In making this case, Lipking is depending on, I would
argue, the following assumptions:

1. Meaning is made by binary oppositions, *but* one item is
   unavoidably favored (or "privileged") over the other.

2. This hierarchy is arbitrary and can be exposed and
   reversed.

3. Further, the text's oppositions and hierarchy can be
   called into question because texts contain within themselves unavoidable contradictions, gaps, spaces, and
   absences that defeat closure and determinate meaning.
   All reading is misreading.

These assumptions lead Lipking to the following strategies:

1. Identify the oppositions in the text.

2. Determine which member appears to be favored and
   look for evidence that contradicts that favoring.

3. Expose the text's indeterminacy.

In its effects, deconstruction is quite comparable to other developments in twentieth-century thought. In mathematics, Kurt Gödel has shown how any mathematical system will contain at least one crucial axiom that cannot be proved within the system itself. There is always, in any interpretation, a loose end; an assumption that cannot be proven; a statement that is called into question by some other statement. Similarly, in physics, Heisenberg's uncertainty principle stipulates the indeterminacy of certain fundamental variables, like the position and momentum of a particle.

Still, we must remember that Lipking explains deconstruction only to attack it. He and some other critics find deconstruction disturbing and even dangerous, but many others find it invigorating. The most damning charge against deconstruction is that it allows a text to mean anything at all—or, as Lipking sees it, ultimately nothing. But deconstruction's supporters, both in Europe and America (which have somewhat different conceptions of the matter), believe that texts *always already* were unavoidably open to interpretation. Deconstruction, in this case, really changes nothing except our awareness of the complexity and "otherness" of our discourse. A text (of any sort) means ultimately whatever the entity with the most power says it means, unless of course other readers continue to read it otherwise.

We turn now to a closer look at the process of writing deconstructive criticism, leaving Yeats' golden bird for one of another metal.

THE WRITING PROCESS: A SAMPLE ESSAY

Here's a recent poem by Amy Clampitt, published on April 12, 1993, in *The New Yorker*.

Discovery (1993)
Amy Clampitt

The week the latest rocket went   1
up, a pod (if that's the word)
of manatees, come upriver

to Blue Spring, where it's
always warm, could be seen   5
lolling, jacketed, elephantine,
on the weedy borderline
between drowsing and waking,
breathing and drowning.
As they came up for air,   10
one by one, they seemed numb,
torpid, quite incurious. No
imagining these sirenians
dangerously singing. Or
gazing up yearningly: so much   15
for the Little Mermaid. True,
the long-lashed little ones
could have been trademarked
"Cute" by the likes of Walt Disney.
His world's over that way,   20

suitably for a peninsula where
the cozy mythologies we've
swindled ourselves with, on
taking things easy, might even
come true: sun-kissed nakedness   25
on the beach, year-round, guilt-free
hibiscus and oranges, fountains
welling up through the limestone,
the rumor of Ponce de León, having
found the one he was looking for,   30

living at ease in, some say
Boca Raton, others Cádiz. A last
bedtime placebo? Still, we keep
looking up. That clear morning,
just warm enough for a liftoff,   35
the fabulous itself could be seen
unwieldily, jacket by jacket,
in the act of shedding, as
a snake does its husk, or
a celebrant his vestments: 40

the fiery, the arrowy tip of it,
of the actual going invisible,
trailing its vaporous, ribboning
frond as from a kelp bed,
the umbilical roar of it   45
stumbling behind, while up in
the belly of it, out of their
element, jacketed, lolling
and treading, the discoverers
soar, clumsy in space suits.   50

What are we anyhow, we warmth-
hungry, breast-seeking animals?
At Blue Spring, a day or so later,
one of the manatees, edging
toward discovery, nudged a canoe,   55
and from across the wet, warm,
dimly imaginable tightrope,
let itself be touched.

Preparing to Write

What does this poem describe? What does it most clearly
and obviously say? Do any oppositions or tensions seem to be
involved?

It might be helpful to sketch out an initial response to the
poem, to show you as fully as possible how a deconstructive
essay might be developed. So, I'm going to divide the poem
into pieces and try to say what went through my mind as I
tried to make sense of it. I'd encourage you to write your own
notes before you look through mine.

Discovery

The week the latest rocket
went up,   (1-2)

Is the speaker referring to a fictional rocket
or a real one? Perhaps the speaker is referring to

> NASA's space shuttles (they aren't rockets, of
> course, but they're launched by rockets). Everyone
> knows one of the shuttles is called "Discovery";
> does the title refer to it?

a pod (if that's the word)
of manatees, come upriver
to Blue Spring, where it's
always warm, could be seen
lolling, jacketed, elephantine,
on the weedy borderline
between drowsing and waking,
breathing and drowning.   (2-9)

> Well, perhaps the poem isn't about the space
> shuttle or "the latest rocket." Maybe that's just
> the time frame. I saw manatees when I lived in
> Florida, and "elephantine" is right—they do seem
> like armless and legless elephants floating in the
> water. And they don't seem to swim: "lolling" is a
> good word for what they do. The idea that they are
> "between drowsing and waking" also seems just
> right. But how are they between "breathing and
> drowning"? And how are they "jacketed"? What does
> that mean?

As they came up for air,
one by one, they seemed numb,
torpid, quite incurious.   (10-12)

> These lines remind me that manatees are mammals,
> and so they don't breathe underwater. They have to
> come "up for air"—which explains, I guess, the
> idea that they're between "breathing and drown-
> ing": if they don't come up, they'll drown; so
> they live most of their time in a state between
> breathing and drowning. I still don't know why
> they're said to be "jacketed." Perhaps Clampitt is
> inviting us to see their skin, which looks sort of
> loose and baggy, as a kind of jacket.

                        No
imagining these sirenians
dangerously singing. Or
gazing up yearningly: so much
for the Little Mermaid. True,
the long-lashed little ones
could have been trademarked
"Cute" by the likes of Walt Disney.   (12-19)

A number of things at this point are puzzling:
for instance, why are the manatees called "sirenians"? What is a sirenian, in other words, and why
might one imagine them "dangerously singing"? And
what's the connection to the Little Mermaid?

Whenever something is puzzling, I usually try
doing some research. In this case, a quick look in
The Columbia Encyclopedia is revealing: the entry
for "manatee" refers us to "sirenian," which is
the name of a biological order, "Sirenia." (The
only other living sirenian, or sea cow, is called
a dugong.) Right above "sirenian," we find
"Siren," the name for sea nymphs in Greek mythology who sang so beautifully that sailors would
crash into the rocks around their island. So, the
manatees, although they're sirenians, aren't like
the Sirens. So that's one puzzle solved.

The entry also reports the speculation that manatees, "which nurse on the water's surface, are
the source of the mermaid legends." Clampitt's
speaker finds the manatees so "numb, torpid, quite
incurious," that it's impossible to imagine them
as Sirens or mermaids. Contrasting them to the
Little Mermaid is of course particularly comical
given the huge bulk of these floating blobs. They
are, according to the entry, "sluggish, largely
nocturnal bottom feeders," weighing perhaps five
hundred pounds and eating as much as a hundred
pounds of vegetation a day. Even so, we must note

that the "long-lashed little ones" are "Cute"
enough for Disney. So another puzzle is solved.

The entry also may help clear up another question: manatees, we read, have gray skin that is
"completely hairless" (except for bristles around
the mouth). The skin has folds and wrinkles in it:
so maybe that is why it appears to be a jacket to
the speaker.

His world's over that way,
suitably for a peninsula where
the cozy mythologies we've
swindled ourselves with, on
taking things easy, might even
come true: sun-kissed nakedness
on the beach, year-round, guilt-free
hibiscus and oranges, fountains
welling up through the limestone,
the rumor of Ponce de León, having
found the one he was looking for,

living at ease in, some say
Boca Raton, other Cádiz. A last
bedtime placebo?   (20-33)

This section makes clear that the speaker is
indeed in Florida at the Kennedy Space Center,
where the shuttle launches, near Orlando and
Disneyworld "over that way." We dream, the speaker
says, of "taking things easy" in Florida, living
in paradise forever like a successful Ponce de
León. Such dreaming doesn't do anything, but it
may make us feel better anyway, like a "placebo."

Still, we keep
looking up.   (33-34)

What does it mean to say "Still, we keep looking
up"? Perhaps it means that our dreams of content-

ment ("sun-kissed nakedness on the beach") aren't
entirely satisfying: we still keep looking up,
waiting for some discovery-or, in this case, for
Discovery. We all want to see something.

That clear morning,
just warm enough for a liftoff,
the fabulous itself could be seen
unwieldily, jacket by jacket,
in the act of shedding, as
a snake does its husk, or
a celebrant his vestments:

the fiery, the arrowy tip of it,
of the actual going invisible,   (34-42)

>   These lines strike me as a wonderful way of
> describing a launch: the shuttle disappearing as
> it rises is "the actual going invisible." The
> shuttle's voyage becomes "the fabulous itself" in
> the act of "shedding"-being reborn or transformed
> like the snake or the celebrant. If you've seen a
> launch, even on television, you know that the
> shuttle does seem to move "unwieldily," rotating
> slowly as it goes up, lumbering so it seems, at
> least at first, toward the heavens.

trailing its vaporous, ribboning
frond as from a kelp bed,
the umbilical roar of it
stumbling behind, while up in
the belly of it, out of their
element, jacketed, lolling
and treading, the discoverers
soar, clumsy in space suits.   (43–50)

>   The comparison of the booster rocket's vapor
> trail to a "ribboning frond as from a kelp bed" is
> very strange, isn't it. What's the point of such
> an odd description? It takes us, obviously, to the

manatees, who eat such fronds in kelp beds. It
begins to link, it seems to me, the astronauts to
the manatees. The connection becomes stronger as
Clampitt uses "jacketed" and "lolling" to describe
the human "discoverers," the same words used to
describe the manatees.

   In what ways are the astronauts like the manatees? Clampitt suggests that the astronauts are
also in a sense "out of their element." They are
"treading," not in water, but as if they were. And
they appear, like the manatees, to be "clumsy in
space suits."

What are we anyhow, we warmth-
hungry, breast-seeking animals?
At Blue Spring, a day or so later,
one of the manatees, edging
toward discovery, nudged a canoe,
and from across the wet, warm,
dimly imaginable tightrope,
let itself be touched.   (51–58)

   If we had any doubts about what the oppositions
are in this poem, and how they're brought together, this final section makes these matters very
clear, doesn't it? When Clampitt asks "What are we
anyhow, we warmth- / hungry, breast-seeking animals?", who is the "we" here? At the beginning of
the poem, it is the manatees who "come upriver" to
where "it's / always warm," and it seems clear
that the "warmth-hungry" we includes both human
"discoverers" as well as manatees (who breast-feed
their young on the surface, we recall).

   With the final scene of the manatee "edging
toward discovery," Clampitt most strikingly unites
manatees and humans. The manatees are also "looking up," reaching out. They may seem clumsy, numb,

quite incurious, but the astronauts, as they float
around "out of their element," also seem clumsy,
lolling. Clampitt uses "jacketed" to describe both
human and manatee (although I still find this word
a bit confusing). In letting itself be touched,
the manatee is aligned with humanity, becoming
really a courageous discoverer, like the crew of
Discovery.

  But what is the "wet, warm, / dimly imaginable
tightrope" that the manatee reaches "across"? It
must be, I suppose, the water, or the surface of
the water, and Clampitt's point would seem to be
that the manatee, while appearing to be clumsy, is
actually pulling off quite a feat. Inhabiting the
water, living between breathing and drowning, is
like walking a tightrope. Likewise, the astronauts
on Discovery may seem clumsy "jacketed" in their
suits, but they are in reality "the fabulous
itself."

At this point I think I understand the poem fairly well.
That is, I understand how the poem's two topics are related.
Manatees lolling about in the warm water; human beings
shooting themselves into space: what could be more different? And yet Amy Clampitt brings the two together.

Or does she?

Shaping

Is it possible to turn this reading of the poem around, to
tease out another, conflicting meaning? To begin to deconstruct this poem, let's think a bit about the oppositions that
seem to be brought together. The worlds of manatees and
humans appear to be far apart—as different as "that country"
and Byzantium in Yeats' "Sailing to Byzantium." The manatees seem dramatically unlike discoverers: "numb, / torpid,
quite incurious." Manatees are even unlike the partly human,
the mermaids and sirens. In Yeats' poem, as we just saw,

Cleanth Brooks's New Critical reading finds that the golden bird unifies the poem, combining the worlds of nature and art. Likewise, in Clampitt's poem a number of images seem to unify the opposing worlds, as the human discoverers come to seem like the manatees, "lolling," "treading," "jacketed." The closing image of one manatee "edging / toward discovery" most directly shows us how the manatee shares the human urge to "keep / looking up" and to reach out and explore. We are both, manatee and human, "warmth- / hungry, breast-seeking animals." Whereas Yeats' poem unifies art and nature, Clampitt's poem brings together the realms of animal and human. So it seems.

But if the poem appears most obviously to say that manatees and astronauts are similar or linked (out of their elements, awkward, seeking discovery), is it possible to suggest that the poem also undermines this unifying theme? What is being overlooked or suppressed in Clampitt's unifying move? Here are some notes toward a deconstructive reading.

> < > Apparent unity: the manatee is said to be "edging toward discovery," like the Discovery astronauts it seems.

> > < Reversal: But who really is the discoverer in this situation? The manatee passively "let itself be touched" after it "nudged" the canoe. Although we may think at first that the manatee is "edging toward [its own] discovery," the more reasonable inference is that the manatee is "edging toward discovery" by the canoe-goers. Does the manatee discover anything? Not that we know. There's really no evidence that the manatee has moved beyond being "numb, / torpid, quite incurious."

> < > Apparent unity: "we" are "warmth- / hungry, breast-seeking animals."

> > < Reversal: This assertion connects the manatees to us only in a superficial way. More carefully considered, this description actually distances the mana-

tees from "the discoverers" in their "space suits":
the astronauts surely aren't seeking warmth or breasts
in space. There is something else that drives humanity
to explore, to "keep looking up," and that intellectual curiosity is not shared, so far as we can tell, by
the manatees.

   < > Apparent unity: "jacketed" is used to describe
both manatees and astronauts.

   > < Reversal: The meaning of "jacketed" as it
applies to manatees is never made clear. I can think
of two senses in which the astronauts are "jacketed."
They're actually wearing jackets; and they're
enclosed, in the sense of this definition of "jacket":
"a metal casing, as the steel covering around the barrel of a gun or the core of a bullet." I don't see how
the manatees are "jacketed" in either of these senses.
Applied to both manatees and astronauts, the term
really emphasizes the gap between the two when we
examine it closely.

   < > Apparent unity: The poem says "the fabulous
itself could be seen / unwieldily, jacket by jacket,
/ in the act of shedding, as / a snake does its husk,
or / a celebrant his vestments": the reference to a
snake and a celebrant again seems to link animal and
human activities, subtly implying that the "jacketed"
manatees and humans are discovering "the fabulous
itself."

   > < Reversal: But aren't these two images actually
pulling in different directions? A snake shedding its
skin is not performing a voluntary, self-conscious
act. The celebrant, however, makes the fabulous visible by shedding "his vestments"—a voluntary, self-
conscious act. In removing his religious, ceremonial
garments, the celebrant reveals somehow, Clampitt
says, the mystery and the wonder he has participated

in: the fabulous itself. At least, that's how I read
these difficult lines.

   I would have thought that the fabulous would be
glimpsed in the celebrant putting on his vestments,
and that the act of removing them would reveal the
mundane and ordinary world. But Clampitt has imagined
the lift-off as an act of shedding, and so images of
"shedding" become images of discovery. The gap in
meaning results from the difference between a reptile
engaging in an automatic, biological function, and a
conscious human disengaging from a spiritual event.

   < > Apparent unity: The notion that the astronauts
are "out of their / element" may seem to reflect the
manatees' situation, living in water but breathing
air.

   > < Reversal: But the implicit comparison doesn't
hold up because the astronauts really are out of their
element, totally unsuited to live in space without the
creation of an artificial environment. Manatees, on
the other hand, live on the border between air and
water: that is their element. Birds fly in the air,
and build nests in trees and other places. We wouldn't
say they're "out of their element" in either situation. Again, we see how the poem's effort to unify
animal and human comes apart. Manatees are different:
they can't live out of their element; we can, at least
for certain periods.

At this point, I'm looking at the phrase "cozy mythologies
we've / swindled ourselves with," mythologies that "might
even / come true" in Florida, Clampitt says, in the land of
Walt Disney. And I'm thinking that the poem itself offers a
"cozy mythology" about manatees and humans, suppressing
the essential differences. From living in Florida for three
years, I remember that a great deal of attention is paid to the

manatees—they're endangered, and they're uniquely huge and strange. The state offers a manatee tag for automobiles, and the funds raised go to a "Save the Manatee" campaign. The main threat to manatees in Florida today seems to be from motorboats: as the manatees float up to the surface, boaters fail to see them and run over them, inflicting severe injuries with the propellers. A manatee hospital has even been set up to treat injured manatees, and boat speeds have been restricted in some areas. We are trying to live *with* the manatees; many tourists every year get in the water and swim with them. One could argue that we are forgetting our differences, assuming that manatees are in some crucial way like ourselves, when really perhaps we should leave them alone, banning boats and recreation in the waters they inhabit. At any rate, this reading of Clampitt's poem opens up uncertainties in our understanding of them.

Drafting

At this point I think I have enough ideas to draft an essay. Where should I start? First, I need to set up the task, letting the reader know what I'm trying to do: namely, I'm trying to show how the poem appears to link human and manatee, but really doesn't. I want to start fast, diving right in; and since the ending most dramatically unifies manatee and human, with the two actually touching with the final word, I'm going to try starting with the ending of the poem. The word "discovery" occurs in the final lines, and since it's the title, I need to pay attention to it. The final image occurs in response to a question, it seems, and so it makes sense to move next to the question itself. Then I'll present the other evidence I've generated: "jacketed," "out of their element," and the snake/celebrant problem. That's my tentative plan as I start writing, very much aware that I may change my mind.

Here's the essay that resulted after a draft and a little polishing.

HUMANITY AND MANATEE: AMY CLAMPITT'S
"DISCOVERY"

This paragraph intro-
duces the issue: why is
the poem partly about
manatees and partly
about humans? The
conclusion is crucial,
asserting indirectly
their unity.

The conclusion of Amy Clampitt's
"Discovery" follows a profoundly
challenging question: "What are we
anyhow, we warmth- / hungry, breast-
seeking animals?" Right before this
question, the poem refers to astronauts, "discoverers" who are "clumsy
in space suits," so it seems reasonable to assume that "we" refers to
human beings. But rather than trying
to say explicitly what "we" are anyhow, answering a question about
human nature that has occupied
philosophies and religions for cen-
turies, the poem offers instead a
little story about a manatee:

At Blue Spring, a day or so
    later,
one of the manatees, edging
toward discovery, nudged a canoe,
and from across the wet, warm,
dimly imaginable tightrope,
let itself be touched.

While this story might seem at
first an evasion of the question,
the poem repeatedly links manatees
and humans, giving them the same
qualities, using the same words to
describe them both. Thus, this story
implicitly answers the question
about human nature by pointing once
more to manatees: we are more like
them, and they are more like us,
than we might have thought. Like
the manatee, we are "edging toward

discovery," reaching out to other beings.

But a careful examination of the implied links between manatees and humans reveals that the similarities are actually questionable. Ultimately, as this paper will show, it is unclear whether the poem's comparison helps us understand the nature of either humans or manatees—or just compounds the mystery.

This paragraph directly presents the thesis: the linking is problematic.

Let us begin with the strongest unifying agent of manatee and human, the phrase "edging toward discovery." The word "discovery" links the manatee's action to the poem's title and to the space shuttle Discovery. The poem does not say that Discovery in particular is being launched at the time the manatees "come upriver," but "the latest rocket" clearly is one of the shuttles. And the description of the astronauts, "jacketed, lolling and treading," "clumsy in space suits," seems designed to remind us of the manatees, who are described in the first section in the same terms—"lolling, jacketed," and "numb, torpid" (which certainly suggests clumsiness).

The strongest evidence for unity, "edging toward discovery," is introduced here.

But in what sense is the manatee "edging toward discovery"? Although the same words are used to describe astronaut and manatee, the similarity of their roles in the act of discovery seems uncertain. Whereas the astronauts self-consciously and

The manatee is not a discoverer but an object of discovery.

actively venture out into space, the
manatee passively "let itself be
touched." Such a surrender may seem
essentially different from the
behavior of the human "discoverers,"
either in the shuttle or the canoe.
One could argue, of course, that the
manatee is discovering how it feels
to be touched by human beings. But
the astronauts do not rocket into
space to deliver themselves to the
touch or observation of other
beings; and the people in the canoe
are not said to be allowing the manatee to see what their hands feel
like. There's no solid evidence that
the manatee discovers anything or
moves beyond being "numb, / torpid,
quite incurious." So, "edging toward
discovery" only seems initially to
unite manatee and human; upon
reflection, it may exhibit their
differences, or at the least call
their likeness into doubt.

The question itself
applies better to the
manatee.

The question itself—"What are we
anyhow, we warmth- / hungry, breast-
seeking animals?"—may seem to refer
to both manatees and humans. The
poem begins by noting how the manatees have "come upriver" to Blue
Spring seeking warmth; and as mam-
mals, the manatees do breastfeed
their young. But this deep question
also puts a gap between manatee and
human, because the astronauts surely
aren't seeking warmth or breasts in
space. There is something else that
drives humanity to explore, to "keep

looking up," and that intellectual, self-conscious curiosity is not shared, so far as we can tell, by the manatees. Although "we" may be "warmth-hungry" and "breast-seeking," the suggestion that these are essential qualities limits and narrows what it means to be human.

"Jacket" applies better to humans.

Likewise, "jacket" or "jacketed" appears four times in the poem, and would seem to be an important term connecting manatee and human, unifying the poem's two subjects. The term is applied to both manatees, who are "lolling, jacketed, elephantine," and to the astronauts, who are "jacketed, lolling and treading." But again the link is problematic. The astronauts are "jacketed," it would seem, because they have on jackets, and because they are encased in metal—"jacketed" in the sense of "a metal casing, as the steel covering around the barrel of a gun or the core of a bullet," as *Webster's* puts it. Are the manatees "jacketed" in either of these senses? The other two occurrences refer to "the fabulous itself" being revealed "jacket by jacket," which seems simply to mean "layer by layer," or "casing by casing." Thus, although the repeated use of the term may seem to bridge the poem and its subjects, it really does not in any clear or direct way. The connection is superficial, and it gives way to a gap: manatees do not really

come in jackets in any literal
sense; humans do.

More evidence: other
gaps.

In a number of other ways the
poem's two subjects break apart upon
analysis. The notion, for instance,
that the astronauts are "out of
their / element" may seem to reflect
also the manatees' situation, living
in water but breathing air. But the
astronauts really are out of their
element, totally unsuited to live in
space without the creation of an
artificial environment. Manatees, on
the other hand, need to live on the
border between air and water: that
is their element. Humans do not need
to live on the border of space and
earth. Or, again, the reference to a
snake and a celebrant again seems to
link animal and human activities.
But aren't these two images actually
pulling in different directions? A
snake shedding its skin is not performing a voluntary, self-conscious
act. The celebrant, however, makes
the fabulous visible by shedding
"his vestments"—a voluntary, self-
conscious act. In removing his religious, ceremonial garments, the celebrant reveals somehow, Clampitt
says, the mystery and the wonder he
has participated in: the fabulous
itself. For the snake, the fabulous
itself would seem to be the instinctual act of shedding. The gap in
meaning results from the difference
between a reptile engaging in an
automatic, biological function, and

a conscious human disengaging from a
spiritual event.

Conclusion: the unity
may be a myth, or is at
least uncertain.

The poem refers to the "cozy
mythologies" of paradise and eternal
youth that "might even come true" in
Florida. Another myth may be the
illusion that manatees and humans
are alike in some essential way. The
poem asserts that unity, but at the
same time it points out the difference, the otherness, of the manatees. We may drive our boats and
canoes where they live; we may touch
them; but it may be misleading to
think we understand them—or even
ourselves. The "discovery" may well
be the question of "What are we anyhow"?

PRACTICING DECONSTRUCTIVE CRITICISM

I offer here two texts for deconstructive efforts, along
with some questions I hope you find helpful.

Questions

1. What is the most obvious statement the following
   advertisement attempts to make? What sort of attitudes, feelings, assumptions, does the advertisement
   attribute to part of its audience? What effect does it
   strive to create?
2. How might the advertisement tend also to create the
   attitudes, feelings, assumptions it strives to reduce or
   remove? That is, does the advertisement do contradictory things? How does this conflict influence its effec-
   tiveness?

Cut through the anxiety, the unknown, the hassle...

At USC we offer free Back-To-School workshops that answer all your questions about going back "to hit the books."

If you're 25 years or older, our workshops are designed just for *you*. You'll discover opportunities for adults at USC that make your dreams possible, whether they are finishing that degree you started years ago or going to college for the first time. We'll help you understand admission, advisement and registration procedures. And you'll be surprised by the wide range of subjects and flexible times and locations of our courses.

Join our workshop during USC Showcase '93 on Saturday, April 3, 9:30 - 11:00 a.m. at 900 Assembly Street, room 17.

Call today to reserve your space!

USC...ADULTS *are a part!* **•777-9446**
University of South Carolina Division of Continuing Education

3. Look closely at the details of the advertisement and how they reveal (as deconstruction insists all texts

must) what is being excluded or suppressed. For example, what does the imperative to "Cut through the anxiety, the unknown, the hassle" acknowledge? If the slogan next to the phone number were to be spoken, what would it say? How does the pun in this slogan divide and complicate it?

London (1794)
William Blake

I wander thro' each charter'd street
Near where the charter'd Thames does flow,
And mark in every face I meet
Marks of weakness, marks of woe.

In every cry of every Man,   5
In every Infant's cry of fear,
In every voice, in every ban,
The mind-forg'd manacles I hear.

How the Chimney-sweeper's cry
Every blackening Church appalls;   10
And the hapless Soldier's sigh
Runs in blood down Palace walls.

But most thro' midnight streets I hear
How the youthful Harlot's curse
Blasts the new-born Infant's tear   15
And blights with plagues the Marriage hearse.

Questions

1. What is a charter? What would it mean for a street to be "charter'd"? How about a river (the Thames in this poem)?

2. "Charter'd" is repeated in the first two lines. What other words are repeated in the poem? What might be the purpose of such repetition?

3. In *The Pursuit of Signs* Jonathan Culler reviews some of
the many interpretations this famous poem has generated, and he notes that one of two different structures
has been perceived to organize the entire poem. The
first way of thinking about the poem's structure sees it,
as Culler says, as a "synecdochic series, where a list of
particulars are interpreted as instances of a general
class to which they all belong" (69). What in your opinion might be the "general class" to which the particulars in the poem belong? That is, the chimney sweep-
er's cry, the hapless soldier's sigh, and the harlot's curse
are instances of what? What do they have in common?

4. The second way of thinking about the poem's structure
sees it (again following Culler) as an *"aletheic reversal:*
first a false or inadequate vision, then its true or adequate counterpart" (69). Where, in your opinion, might
the shift from a false vision to a true one occur? How
would you describe these two visions? (Hint: where
does the poem shift from universal statements—
"every," "every"—to more specific ones?)

5. How does the idea of "mind-forg'd manacles" contribute to the structure of the poem? (Your answer to
this question may overlap with previous answers.) Is it
a particular or a general, a member of a class, or a
class?

6. How many examples are offered in the last two verses?
What are they examples of? How are they parallel?
(You might think in terms of victim—action—institution.) Is there any problem with their parallelism?
    No critic, Culler says, takes the statement that the
chimney sweep's cry appalls the church at face value
(*Signs* 70). How does the structure of the other two
examples affect the way we think about the chimney
sweep? Again, think in parallel terms. Why would
critics find it necessary to explain the example of the
chimney sweep?

7. What sense can you make of the last verse? What are
the difficulties in understanding it?

8. The speaker of the poem marks (or hears) the sweep cry, the soldier sigh, and the harlot curse. This structural parallelism encourages us to assume a parallelism of meaning. What are the problems with determining such a unity? That is, can you argue that in fact the poem does not make sense—at least not any one sense, but rather that it goes in conflicting directions?

9. Are the "mind-forg'd manacles" the product of the Church, the Palace, and Marriage? (Most readers seem to assume so.) Can you turn this inference around and argue otherwise? Could the sweep, the soldier, and the harlot create their own manacles?

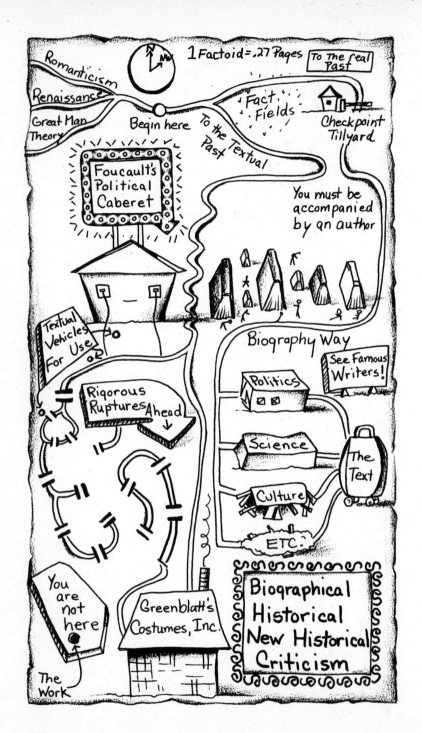

CHAPTER 5

CONNECTING THE TEXT
Biographical, Historical, and New Historical Criticism

*We know somewhat, and
we imagine the rest.*

—Samuel Johnson

THE PURPOSES OF BIOGRAPHICAL, HISTORICAL, AND NEW HISTORICAL CRITICISM

Even the most rigorously formal New Critic or the most introspectively responding reader may make some use of biographical or historical information. It just makes common sense to wonder who wrote a particular work, and when, and how, and in what circumstances. With the advent of deconstruction, altering all our notions of language and knowledge, we also have new conceptions of authorship and historical circumstances. Thus, this chapter considers what happens when biographical, historical, and new historical concerns move to the critical foreground.

Biographical Criticism

If we think of a literary work primarily as a personal achievement, the accomplishment of a great mind, then biographical criticism offers to help us understand both the work and its creator, as we relate one to the other. Take, for instance, the following poem.

When I Consider How My Light Is Spent (1655?)
John Milton

When I consider how my light is spent,
    Ere half my days in this dark world and wide,
    And that one talent which is death to hide
Lodged with me useless, though my soul more bent
To serve therewith my Maker, and present   5
    My true account, lest He returning chide;
    "Doth God exact day-labor, light denied?"
I fondly ask. But Patience, to prevent
That murmur, soon replies, "God doth not need
    Either man's work or His own gifts. Who best   10
    Bear his mild yoke, they serve Him best. His state
Is kingly: thousands at his bidding speed,
    And post o'er land and ocean without rest;
    They also serve who only stand and wait."

Biographical criticism would insist on the importance of knowing something about the author—perhaps most importantly, in this case, that Milton had lost his eyesight by 1651. Without this fact, it could be argued, the reader might wonder what sense to make of the phrase "how my light is spent," since "going blind" would be only one of many possible meanings (how my day is spent, how my insight is used up, how my lover is tired out, and more). Knowing about Milton's life may also help us to appreciate the poem's significance: the speaker of the poem is not, it may seem, merely a fiction, an assumed character, contemplating some hypothesis; rather, the speaker has some connection to a real man, a writer, contemplating the horror of his own blindness.

Of course, as one guide to writing about literature puts it, you should "avoid equating the work's contents with the author's life" (Griffith 115); obviously a piece of writing isn't the same thing as a person's life. Still, although the writing and the life "are never the same," are we obliged to conclude that writers do not sometimes try to express themselves truthfully? If we must conclude that "When I Consider" is "fictional" in the same sense that *Star Wars* is fictional, then we may lose some of the poem's power. For most readers this poem is considerably more moving if we imagine that Milton is writing about himself.

Just as Milton's life may illuminate the poem, the poem may also help us to understand Milton's life. It has been thought by more than one critic that Milton was a misogynist, a "domestic tyrant" as the *Oxford Companion* puts it (654), cruelly ordering his daughters about, sternly dictating to his successive wives (three in all). This poem may suggest perhaps that Milton tended to think of the universe in terms of servants and masters, and that he viewed himself as a servant to God. God's "yoke" is light, even though it employs thousands speeding "o'er land and ocean without rest," and the servant's job is simply to serve in whatever capacity. The servant is in fact so inconsequential that "God doth not need / Either man's work or His own gifts." As Milton insists to himself that he must strive to serve even if that serving means simply standing, the submissiveness in the poem reflects the sort of subservience Milton apparently expected (and thought he had earned) from those who served him. He may have treated those around him like his servants, but he also saw himself in the same way, as the servant to another master.

Historical Criticism

Biographical criticism is the natural ally of historical criticism. We can hardly understand one person's life without some sense of the time and place in which he or she lived, and we can hardly understand human history without trying to think about the individual humans who made it. Historical criticism considers how military, social, cultural, economic, scientific, intellectual, literary, and (potentially) every other kind of history might help us to understand the author and the work.

In the case of Milton's poem, the most obvious historical context might well be the political situation of England: in 1655, about the time the poem is supposed to have been written, England was struggling to recover from a civil war that had ended with the beheading of Charles I in 1649. After this regicide, of which he approved, Milton was deeply involved in politics, serving as Latin secretary to the newly formed Council of State, and writing on numerous political and religious controversies. Against the backdrop of this political turmoil, the references in the poem to the "one talent" and the urgency of using it might suggest additional meanings. (He is alluding of course to Jesus's parable of the poor servants who simply buried their talents and the good servant who used his single talent for profit.)

Perhaps Milton felt called to straighten out his country by employing his gift for language; the government and the church must have seemed at times to be falling apart before his eyes. With his one talent, his gift for writing, perhaps Milton felt he should be saving the nation. But he puts this self-imposed burden in a new light in the poem when he reminds himself that God does not need his help—that others do God's bidding, and that his own job description may have changed dramatically with his impairment. He is telling himself that all he must do now is "stand and wait," ready to serve when he can. (What Milton most spectacularly would wait for, as it turns out, was his masterwork, *Paradise Lost*, the story of Adam and Eve and their loss of Eden.)

The history of literature itself has also been considered especially important for the understanding of particular works. Milton's reader needs to recognize that "When I Consider" is a sonnet, but it would also be nice to know what sonnets Milton had read, how this sonnet relates to others, and what other poems or other kinds of works Milton knew.

Such literary background is almost always helpful and often seems essential.

In the study of renaissance literature, for example, students have for decades read E. M. W. Tillyard's *The Elizabethan World Picture* in order to understand the background of Shakespeare, Ben Jonson, Christopher Marlowe, and other Elizabethan writers. Tillyard aimed, as he said, to explain the Elizabethans' "most ordinary beliefs about the constitution of the world" (viii), and he showed clearly and repeatedly how this basic knowledge is essential to our understanding. For example, Tillyard says English citizens who lived during the reign of Elizabeth (1533–1603) believed in "a doctrine of plentitude." They imagined an order in the universe whereby every entity filled a particular position in a "chain of being," stretching from the lowest possible inert element to the highest, from the lowest plant to the highest, and from the lowest creature to the highest (25–33). In *Paradise Lost*, Milton's Raphael, an angel, explains this "chain of being" to Adam, showing him how everything is ranked, and every level of possible being is filled. And Adam explains to Eve one consequence of this hierarchical "plentitude":

> Millions of spiritual Creatures walk the Earth
> Unseen, both when we wake, and when we sleep:
> All these with ceaseless praise his works behold
> Both day and night. (32)

Imagining that Milton inherited the Elizabethan idea of the chain of being may help to understand the ending of "When I Consider." Specifically, we get a better sense of the reference to the "thousands" who speed at God's bidding, without rest. They are part of the "millions" of possible creatures existing in the scale between Milton and God; and, if God has a place (but not a need) for those who actively serve him, he also must allow in the scheme of things for some who serve in every other possible way—including standing and waiting. Thus, Milton's passive role is required of him; it is right; it is his place in the universal chain of being.

New Historicism

The kind of historical background provided by Tillyard depends, as Jean Howard says, on three assumptions:

(1) "that history is knowable";

(2) "that literature mirrors or at least by indirection reflects historical reality"; and

(3) "that historians and critics can see the facts of history objectively." (18)

In the past two decades these assumptions, which seem reasonable enough at first glance, have been convincingly called into question by an outpouring of theory and practice, including deconstruction and reader-response criticism. The starting point for this work is a simple observation: "history" is textual. We read about it; we experience it in words, which are used to explain the physical evidence. We don't have access directly to the past; we have a "story" about it. The Battle of Antietam, for instance, is a textual phenomenon. It does not exist. Our tendency to separate history and literature—seeing one as fact, the other fiction; one as the background to the other—is collapsed by this insight. So we cannot directly observe history, nor be scientific or objective about its facts or remains, because history must be interpreted; our reading of it is as subjective as our reading of any other texts.

To see how subjective history is, you probably need only read two accounts of the same event (preferably from newspapers with different political stances). There simply isn't any objective historical "reality" out there, since the past is always absent, gone by, removed. As Hayden White puts it, history becomes "a story of a particular kind" (60). History is shaped by its necessary textuality. The pastness of the past means, again, that it exists now only as an absence, an empty space that is written upon ultimately by language. Its content and its meaning are open to interpretation.

If history and literature are both texts, then literature is potentially as much a context for history as history is for literature. Elizabethan plays may be seen to "reflect" political events, but Elizabethan politics may also be seen as the consequence of theatrical productions. We may think of certain political events, the coronation of Elizabeth or state trials for treason, for instance, as being "staged" like plays. We will want to think about how "When I Consider" might have influenced history.

Even the reality of Milton's blindness as a "background" for the poem is produced textually for us, and it must be interpreted. It cannot be taken simply as a freestanding fact. What did blindness mean? Would it have been seen as a punishment? As a special gift or calling? Would Milton see himself as a Homeric figure, in the tradition of Ancient Greece's great blind poet? Was Milton's blindness a kind of protection, affording him some exemption from prosecution when the new government failed and Charles II returned to the throne? Why does Milton see himself as essentially helpless, unable to work, to do "day-labor," even though he can still compose? Was writing not considered work?

Although such speculative questions might also be pursued by traditional biographical and historical criticism, new historicism provides a new way of addressing them. A new historicist critic might elect to examine the whole issue of vision in Milton's day, of "light" versus "darkness," of insight versus sight, of writing versus working, and much more, as a textual matter. Since Milton's blindness is for us a textual phenomenon, the new historicist would feel free to study medical texts, economic texts, optics texts, rhetoric texts, and any other texts that might help explain how "blindness" functions in Elizabethan texts: how is "blindness" constructed? Whether Milton would actually make such connections could be considered, but it would not necessarily be essential to the significance of the investigation. The new historicist critic would be more likely than the traditional historical critic to consider the possibility that Milton's blindness was psychosomatic, or feigned, or any other hypothesis that might be productive, because the new historicist assumes that history is a story, a construct, necessarily written and re-written.

The most catalytic figure in this rethinking of history has been Michel Foucault, who has persistently attempted, in Eve Bannet's words, "to break down the familiar units, categories, continuities and totalities through which history, society and the symbolic order are traditionally interpreted" (96). We should note that Tillyard did not himself claim that every Elizabethan endorsed every aspect of "the Elizabethan world picture"; in fact, he repeatedly qualified his position by citing contrary opinions. Still, Tillyard does call his work *The Elizabethan World Picture*, and the exceptions are designed to support his generalizations. New historicists, following Foucault, endeavor to expose the complexities, exceptions, divergences, gaps, and anachronisms in our characterizations of any period. While Tillyard sees the chain of being as a reassuring and pervasive principle of order for Elizabethan thinkers, Stephen Greenblatt considers how such myths serve the ideological interests of Elizabethan culture, discouraging dissent and subversion, and he shows how *King Lear*, for example, both affirms and undermines such cultural directives. Greenblatt's argument thus becomes an intervention into the traditional way of looking at Elizabethan England.

In addition to opposing or questioning traditional schemes of history, new historicism also tends to focus on the production of "knowledge" at a particular time and place. Foucault for example shows how the modern conception of "the mentally ill" came into being, taking the same cultural position that those with leprosy had held. Most startling, Foucault argues that "madness" has not been a stable historical event, but is rather an invention, a construct, creating an excluded "other" category. Reversing the usual idea of asylums as benevolent and rehabilitative, Foucault describes their character as judicial and punitive—judging without appeal and incarcerating without trial. Similarly, Foucault reverses the widespread view that sexuality has been repressed in modern Western culture, arguing instead that sexual behavior has been increasingly discussed, classified, prohibited, authorized, and exposed. Drawing on texts from widely diverse fields, Foucault describes how the categories of the perverse and abnormal have been constructed.

Since new historicists are interested in how historical "knowledge" is produced, they are naturally interested in the effects of power and ideology, whether these appear in "literature" in the usual sense or in any other texts. How we see the "facts"—indeed, whether we see a set of facts—depends upon the controlling system of assumptions and operations (or ideology). This unavoidable interest in power has made new historicism especially appealing to those critics interested in economy and class—usually designated as Marxist criticism. Marxist critics see the individual person as a product of society's system of value, and therefore exposing how the individual is constructed by class and economy is vitally important.

In Milton's poem, we may note the anguish that is piled upon his loss of sight because he also finds himself unable to carry out "day-labor." Milton has identified his "self" with his work, and must therefore insist upon his willingness to work—in fact, he must insist that he *is* working by only standing and waiting.

In other words, against the assumptions of the traditional history, of the sort practiced by Tillyard, we may place the assumptions of the new historicism:

(1) History is knowable only in the sense that all texts are knowable—that is by interpretation, argument, speculation.

(2) Literature is not simply a mirror of historical reality; history in fact isn't a mirror of historical reality. Literature is shaped by history, and even shapes history; it is also distorted by history, and is even discontinuous with history.

(3) Historians and critics must view "the facts" of history subjectively; in fact, the "facts" must be viewed as their creation.

HOW TO DO BIOGRAPHICAL, HISTORICAL, AND NEW HISTORICAL CRITICISM

To do biographical criticism, you need to know as much as you can about the life of the author, and then apply that knowledge. To do historical criticism, you need to know history and apply it. New historicism complicates things a bit, because you ought to know the author's biography—even though the author's personality is a cultural construct, a textual effect; and you ought to know history (or histories)—even though the "facts" are always subject to questioning, supplementation, opposition. There is no telling what else you ought to know, since any and every discipline may shed some productive light on the way power is represented in various texts. Since you can't know everything, follow your instincts and your interests: useful connections or disconnections may be identified anywhere.

Or, to put these strategies into a sequence:

1. Determine the historical setting of the work. Investigate the author's biography.

2. Consider how the historical or biographical background helps us to understand the work. Or, consider how the work contradicts or stands apart from the usual historical or biographical background.

3. Consider what other texts of the same time might be related to the text. Identify the ideology that is shaping this system of texts.

Although these approaches require some research and patience, they are interesting and often very rewarding.

THE WRITING PROCESS: SAMPLE ESSAYS

The work I want to focus on in this section is a compelling short story, first published in the October 27, 1962, issue of *The New Yorker*.

Reunion (1962)
John Cheever

1   The last time I saw my father was in Grand Central Station. I was going from my grandmother's in the Adirondacks to a cottage on the

Biographical Research

- For convenient access to essential facts about the life of a major figure—*Encyclopaedia Britannica* or another major encyclopedia. As a rule, however, you don't want to cite general encyclopedias in your essay; just use them to get started.

- For more details—the *Dictionary of National Biography* (British), the *Dictionary of American Biography,* or the *Dictionary of Literary Biography.*

- For information on contemporary authors— *Contemporary Authors.*

- Also useful—*Biography Index, Oxford Companion to English Literature, Oxford Companion to American Literature,* and the other *Oxford Companions.* An especially appealing resource is *The Atlantic Brief Lives,* which offers brief and often brilliant biographies of writers and other artists by authoritative scholars.

- For book-length biographies—check the catalogue in your library. Check the publication date of the biography; new facts and resources are coming to light all the time, although a newer biography is not necessarily a better one. Also, book reviews can help you evaluate a particular biography: *Book Review Index* covers the most sources; *Book Review Digest* includes excerpts from the reviews.

Historical Research

- For detailed surveys of literary history—the *Oxford History of English Literature* (13 volumes); F. E. Halliday, *A Concise History of England; from Stonehenge to the Atomic Age,* or Robert Adams, *The Land and Literature of England.* A delightful mini-view of American literature appears in the first chapter of *An Incomplete Education.* The standard heavy-duty history of American literature is *The Literary History of the United States,* edited by Robert E. Spiller (2 volumes).

New Historical Research

Some suggestions for places to look for materials:

- Popular or noncanonical literature: children's stories, adolescent fiction, romances, adventure stories, and so forth.

- Primary materials for other disciplines: music theory, psychology, criminology, architecture, and so forth.

- Newspapers and magazines. These can offer you descriptions of events and leads to other texts.

- Artifacts from the period. Think like an archeologist trying to make sense of the physical remains of a particular time. For instance, a delicate and ornate snuffbox from the eighteenth century may illuminate the sort of cultural environment in which, say, Mozart's delicate and ornate music could be written.

Cape that my mother had rented, and I wrote my father that I would be in New York between trains for an hour and a half, and asked if we could have lunch together. His secretary wrote to say that he would meet me at the information booth at noon, and twelve o'clock sharp I saw him coming through the crowd. He was a stranger to me—my mother divorced him three years ago and I hadn't been with him since—but as soon as I saw him I felt that he was my father, my flesh and blood, my future and my doom. I knew that when I was grown I would be something like him; I would have to plan my campaigns within his limitations. He was a big, good-looking man, and I was terribly happy to see him again. He struck me on the back and shook my hand. "Hi, Charlie," he said. "Hi, boy. I'd like to take you up to my club, but it's in the Sixties, and if you have to catch an early train I guess we'd better get something to eat around here." He put his arm around me, and I smelled my father the way my mother sniffs a rose. It was a rich compound of whiskey, after-shave lotion, shoe polish, woollens, and the rankness of a mature male. I hoped that someone would see us together. I wished that we could be photographed. I wanted some record of our having been together.

2   We went out of the station and up a side street to a restaurant. It was still early and the place was empty. The bartender was quarreling with a delivery boy, and there was one very old waiter in a red coat down by the kitchen door. We sat down, and my father hailed the waiter in a loud voice. *"Kellner!"* he shouted. *"Garçon! Cameriere! You!"* His boisterousness in the empty restaurant seemed out of place. "Could we have a little service here!" he shouted. "Chop-chop." Then he clapped his hands. This caught the waiter's attention, and he shuffled over to our table.

3   "Were you clapping your hands at me?" he asked.

4   "Calm down, calm down, *sommelier,*" my father said. "If it isn't too much to ask of you—if it wouldn't be too much above and beyond the call of duty, we would like a couple of Beefeater Gibsons."

5   "I don't like to be clapped at," the waiter said.

6   "I should have brought my whistle," my father said. "I have a whistle that is audible only to the ears of old waiters. Now, take out your little pad and your little pencil and see if you can get this straight: two Beefeater Gibsons. Repeat after me: two Beefeater Gibsons."

7   "I think you'd better go someplace else," the waiter said quietly.

8   "That," said my father, "is one of the most brilliant suggestions I have ever heard. Come on, Charlie, let's get the hell out of here."

9   I followed my father out of that restaurant into another. He was not so boisterous this time. Our drinks came, and he cross-questioned me about the baseball season. He then struck the edge of his empty glass with his knife and began shouting again. *"Garçon! Kellner! Cameriere! You!* Could we trouble you to bring us two more of the same."

10   "How old is the boy?" the waiter asked.

11   "That," my father said, "is none of your God-damned business."

12   "I'm sorry, sir," the waiter said, "but I won't serve the boy another drink."

13   "Well, I have some news for you," my father said. "I have some
      very interesting news for you. This doesn't happen to be the only
      restaurant in New York. They've opened another on the corner.
      Come on, Charlie."

14   He paid the bill, and I followed him out of that restaurant into
      another. Here the waiters wore pink jackets like hunting coats, and
      there was a lot of horse tack on the walls. We sat down, and my
      father began to shout again. "Master of the hounds! Tallyho and all
      that sort of thing. We'd like a little something in the way of a stirrup
      cup. Namely, two Bibson Geefeaters."

15   "Two Bibson Geefeaters?" the waiter asked, smiling.

16   "You know damned well what I want," my father said angrily. "I
      want two Beefeater Gibsons, and make it snappy. Things have
      changed in jolly old England. So my friend the duke tells me. Let's
      see what England can produce in the way of a cocktail."

17   "This isn't England," the waiter said.

18   "Don't argue with me," my father said. "Just do as you're told."

19   "I just thought you might like to know where you are," the waiter
      said.

20   "If there is one thing I cannot tolerate," my father said, "it is an
      impudent domestic. Come on, Charlie."

21   The fourth place we went to was Italian. *"Buon giorno,"* my father
      said. *"Per favore, possiamo avere due cocktail americani, forti, forti.
      Molto gin, poco vermut."*

22   "I don't understand Italian," the waiter said.

23   "Oh, come off it," my father said. "You understand Italian, and
      you know damned well you do. *Vogliamo due cocktail americani.
      Subito."*

24   The waiter left us and spoke with the captain, who came over to
      our table and said, "I'm sorry, sir, but this table is reserved."

25   "All right," my father said. "Get us another table."

26   'All the tables are reserved," the captain said.

27   "I get it," my father said. "You don't desire our patronage. Is that it? Well, the hell with you. *Vada all'inferno.* Let's go, Charlie."

28   'I have to get my train," I said.

29   "I'm sorry, sonny," my father said. "I'm terribly sorry." He put his arm around me and pressed me against him. "I'll walk you back to the station. If there had only been time to go up to my club."

30   "That's all right, Daddy," I said.

31   "I'll get you a paper," he said. "I'll get you a paper to read on the train."

32   Then he went up to a newsstand and said, "Kind sir, will you be good enough to favor me with one of your God-damned, no-good, ten-cent afternoon papers?" The clerk turned away from him and stared at a magazine cover. "Is it asking too much, kind sir," my father said, "is it asking too much for you to sell me one of your disgusting specimens of yellow journalism?"

33   "I have to go, Daddy," I said. "It's late."

34   "Now, just wait a second, sonny," he said. "Just wait a second. I want to get a rise out of this chap."

35   "Goodbye, Daddy," I said, and I went down the stairs and got my train, and that was the last time I saw my father.

In what follows we turn from the primary text to other texts, seeking connections. These connections might be used to argue for the story's unity or disjunction, or to explain the psychology of the characters, or in any number of other ways. But here I am interested primarily in how the story might reflect Cheever's personal history and feelings, in the first example, and the how the story is shaped by a system of ideas regarding prestige, identity, suicide, and alcohol in the second example.

A BIOGRAPHICAL ESSAY

Preparing to Write

A search of the electronic card catalogue at my school's library revealed thirteen books with John Cheever as their subject. I retrieved the seven that weren't checked out and requested the others to be held for me. Then I started skimming and reading, looking especially for materials relating to "Reunion," but also learning as much about Cheever as I could. Here's a sampling of the notes I took:

FROM *JOHN CHEEVER* by Lynne Waldeland (Boston: Twayne, 1979):

- "Reunion" is from *The Brigadier and the Golf Widow,* Cheever's "best volume of short stories," according to William Peden (91).

- The stories share a theme of transformation.

FROM *THE LETTERS OF JOHN CHEEVER,* edited by Cheever's son, Benjamin (New York: Simon and Schuster, 1988):

- Regarding the original publication of "The Brigadier and the Golf Widow," the title story of the volume in which "Reunion" would later appear: Cheever writes to a friend that he went into *The New Yorker* offices to correct the galleys (the trial printing) of the story and found that Bill Maxwell had cut the story "in half." Cheever went along, he says, with the cut in the office, but then later called from a bar and cursed Maxwell, who was at home entertaining "Elizabeth Bowen and Eudora Welty" (two famous writers), telling Maxwell that if he cut the story "I'll never write another story for your [sic] or anybody else" (232). Cheever's letter concludes this way: "Anyhow the magazine had gone to press and they had to remake

```
the whole back of the book and stay up all night
but they ran it without the cut" (232-33).
```

Maxwell's recollection, reported by Benjamin, is very different: Maxwell says he thought the story had two endings, and so he was going to see how Cheever liked it with only one. He had no plan to cut the story at all without Cheever's approval; the story wasn't about to go to press (Cheever had found it on Maxwell's desk), and there was no all-night reworking; Bowen and Welty had visited his house, but never at the same time (233).

How can Cheever have the story so wrong? Does he have no allegiance to the truth, preferring to spin a good tale? Or does his letter describe the truth, at least as he remembers it? The letter seems to have been written immediately afterward: how could his memory be so immediately faulty? Intrigued by this problem, I turned to the introduction to the volume of letters, written by Cheever's son, Benjamin. Benjamin Cheever makes clear that "my father's interest in telling a good story was greater than his interest in what we might consider the facts" (20). Cheever's letters thus become a kind of rehearsal for his fiction, as he practices shaping reality into better narrative material. Benjamin notes that he has "included excerpts from his journals and his fiction, so that one can see the life—sometimes the same incident—reflected differently through the prism of his prose" (20).

For anyone undertaking biographical criticism, the implications here are clear: we should be particularly cautious regarding the "facts," especially as reported by Cheever; at the same time, we should be aware that Cheever does work his life into his stories, apparently sometimes in rather direct ways.

The following passages also caught my attention:

• Benjamin writes:

```
The most difficult part for me, as a son, was the
extent of my father's homosexuality. It's impos-
sible for me to be objective about this, or to
```

> separate his fears from my own, but he was cer-
> tainly troubled by the issue. (16)

- Benjamin writes:

> He used to say that I must wish I had a father
> who didn't drink so much, and I'd always say no.
> I suppose this makes me what Alcoholics Anonymous
> would call an enabler, somebody who makes it all
> right for the alcoholic to destroy himself. Maybe
> so, but I thought then and think now that you
> have to take the people you love pretty much the
> way you find them. Their worst qualities are
> often linked with their very best ones. (17-18)

- Also, reminding me of the father's smells in
  "Reunion," Benjamin writes:

> it remains that while I am not a heavy drinker
> myself, or a smoker, I still find the smell of
> gin and tobacco a delicious combination. (18)

Finally, the following passages are especially interesting
in the context of biographical criticism. Benjamin Cheever
says:

> The connection between his life and his work was inti-
> mate, but it was also mysterious. My father was fond
> of saying that fiction was "crypto-autobiography." One
> obvious reason for this statement is that it protected
> him from the attacks of friends and family who felt
> that they'd been libeled in his prose. (21)

FROM THE FIRST CHAPTER OF *JOHN CHEEVER* by Samuel
Coale, "Cheever's Life" (New York: Frederick Ungar,
1977):

- Cheever's father was a shoe salesman who was out of
  work late in life, and his mother opened a shop for
  the family to survive, selling first their own
  belongings. Cheever's father resented, apparently,
  her independence and competence and his own help-
  lessness.

FROM *HOME BEFORE DARK,* a life of Cheever by his daughter, Susan (Boston: Houghton, 1984):

- e. e. Cummings was Cheever's "first model" (59). Susan Cheever remembers attending with her father a poetry reading by Cummings. When Cummings saw Cheever, "The force and openness of their affection for one another seemed to shake that airless, heavily draped room" (60). Susan remembers particularly, she says, sitting with her father as Cummings read "my father moved through dooms of love" (60), the elegy to Cummings' father.

- Cummings died in 1962, the same year "Reunion" was published.

- A passage that's interesting in the context of the father's use of foreign languages to attract waiters in "Reunion":

  Although he spoke minimal French, he always called the French classics by their original names: *Les Faux-Monnayeurs, La Chartreuse de Parme, Le Rouge et le Noir.* In his last years—a time when he was so well respected that a lot of people assumed he spoke two or three languages—he began dropping French words into his conversation. When he was sent his own books in French translations, he kept them on the desk or his bedside table. With Italian, he was even worse. He spoke a stilted, conversational Italian, but he used it at every opportunity, and he even insisted on re-Italianizing all Americanized Italian words or names. (He always insisted on calling my editor Nan Talese "Nan Talayzee," for instance.)

  "Che cosa di buona oggi?" he would ask any dark-haired waiter, whether he was at the Four Seasons or the Highland Diner on Route 9 in Ossining. They were always very polite. (113-14)

- Susan Cheever also offers this passage, which reminds me of Charlie's awareness of the smell of his father and suggests that Cheever longed for the sort of father that his character, Charlie, did not have:

  "There is the presence of a father—stern, unintelligent and with a gamey odor—but a force of counsel and support that would have carried one into manhood," my father wrote in his journal. "One does not invest the image with brilliance or wealth; it is simply a man in a salt and pepper tweed, sometimes loving, sometimes irascible and sometimes drunk but always responsible to his son."

  My father didn't have this ideal, tweedy parent he dreamed of in his journal who would have "equipped him for manhood." He spent much of his life looking for counsel and support from surrogate fathers and ultimately, painfully, rejecting them. (128)

- Late in Cheever's life, according to Susan, when he had achieved some fame:

  He dropped names shamelessly. It was no longer safe to tease him about favorable reviews. In restaurants, he let headwaiters know that he was someone important. Since this kind of behavior was new to him, he wasn't particularly graceful about it. Walking down Park Avenue with him once, after a lunch at the Four Seasons ("Che cosa di buona oggi?"), I noticed that he was smiling his public smile at everyone who passed—just in case they recognized him, I suppose. (210-11)

FROM SCOTT DONALDSON'S BIOGRAPHY, *JOHN CHEEVER* (New York: Random, 1988):

- Cheever's mother told him he was a mistake: "If I hadn't drunk two Manhattans one afternoon, you

never would have been conceived" (19). And his
father wanted him aborted, even inviting the abortionist to dinner, an event that appears in both
The Wapshot Chronicle and *Falconer.*

- In the story "National Pastime," the father won't
teach the son to play baseball, which causes the
son real embarrassment and trauma (20).

FROM *THE JOURNALS OF JOHN CHEEVER,* edited by Robert
Gottlieb (New York: Knopf, 1991):

- Cheever writes:

  Having drunk less than usual, having, as my
  father would say, gone light on the hooch, I find
  myself, for the first time in a long time, free
  of the *cafarde.* Quarter to nine. Eastern day-
  light-saving time. It would be pleasant to consider this a simple matter of self-discipline.
  Thunder and rain in the middle of the afternoon;
  the first of the month. Our primordial anxiety
  about drought and its effect on the crops, the
  crops in this case being three acres of lawn and
  forty-two rosebushes. (135-36)

  I dislike writing here about boozefighting, but
  I must do something about it. A friend comes to
  call. In my anxiety to communicate, to feel the
  most in warmth and intimacy, I drink too much,
  which can be two drinks these days. In the morning I am deeply depressed, my insides barely
  function, my kidney is painful, my hands shake,
  and walking down Madison Avenue I am in fear of
  death. But evening comes or even noon and some
  combination of nervous tensions obscures my memo-
  ries of what whiskey costs me in the way of physical and intellectual well-being. I could very
  easily destroy myself. It is ten o'clock now and
  I am thinking of the noontime snort. (103)

> Year after year I read in here that I am drinking
> too much, and there can be no doubt of the fact
> that this is progressive. I waste more days, I
> suffer deeper pangs of guilt, I wake up at three
> in the morning with the feelings of a temperance
> worker. Drink, its implements, environments, and
> effects all seem disgusting. And yet each noon I
> reach for the whiskey bottle. I don't seem able
> to drink temperately and yet I don't seem able to
> stop. (103)

> Never having known the love of a father has
> forced me into love so engulfing and passionate
> that there is no margin of choice. (177)

At this point I had invested about twelve hours in doing
research—skimming, reading, taking notes. I decided to move
on to the next phase: organizing this material and relating it
to "Reunion."

Shaping

Simply by selecting some observations rather than others,
I was already in a sense organizing my materials. But I wasn't
quite sure why I was attracted to these biographical materials, and so I spent some time reading over my notes and looking for links and patterns. For each note, I tried to think of
some words or phrases that would characterize the material.
The following topics seemed the most obvious:

1. Fiction as "crypto-autobiography."
2. The need for the father's love.
3. Alcoholism.
4. The father's smells.
5. The father's coldness.
6. The father's love.
7. The father's failure.
8. Foreign languages (and name-dropping).

Next, I went through the materials again and numbered them according to the list above, thus allowing me to group together all of the materials that dealt, for instance, with the relationship of Cheever's fiction to his life.

At this point, before I could tell how to arrange my organized materials, I needed a main idea: I couldn't tell how to order my materials if I didn't know what I was trying accomplish. Employing a biographical stance, I knew that I was trying to determine how our understanding of Cheever's life enlarges or affects our understanding of his story. In Cheever's case, such an approach seems especially promising, given Cheever's own acknowledgement of the intimate relationship between his life and art.

But how would I characterize that relationship? At this point, before I launch into that speculation, you may want to take a few moments and see how you'd apply the biographical information to the story. What would your main idea be?

One striking finding is that Cheever and the father in "Reunion" resemble each other: each is an alcoholic father afraid that he is neglecting or hurting his children. Cheever struggles not to drink before noon, and then, losing that battle, struggles not to get out of control. The father in the story also seems to be fixated on his drinking, forgetting apparently about feeding Charlie lunch. After only one drink with Charlie, he orders "Bibson Beefeater," suggesting perhaps that he has already been drinking beforehand. The father in the story also seems to be like Cheever in his desire to show off his knowledge of foreign languages, and the father also does a bit of name-dropping. Although Cheever and his wife never divorced, they seem to have lived most of their lives on the edge of that gulf. Seeing Cheever in the father, seeing Cheever's awareness of his own shortcomings reflected in the father, I tend to have more sympathy for the father.

But there are also significant ways in which the young boy, Charlie, is like Cheever. Cheever felt distanced from his father, even as he longed for his love. He felt his father to be mysteriously cold—"the greatest and most bitter mystery in my life." Even Cheever's sensitivity to the way his father smelled, recorded in his journal, is a trait we see in Charlie.

Cheever did not have a secretary, but his father did, at least until he lost his job. We know that Cheever felt his father neglected him, just as Charlie's father, who has not seen him in three years, is "a stranger." In fact, Cheever believed his father wanted him aborted.

But so what if Charlie's father is like Cheever's father, and like Cheever? And Charlie is also like Cheever and perhaps like Cheever's son? What do these parallels explain? Well, what *needs* to be explained? What do you find most remarkable or puzzling about the story? For me, two things are strange:

1. Charlie says his father will be "my future and my doom." Why will his father be his doom? How does he know "that when I was grown I would be something like him"?

2. Charlie provides a portrait of his father that is at first perhaps a bit amusing but is ultimately grotesque. In the end Charlie's father seems to be a kind of monster, obsessed with getting "a rise" out of the newsstand clerk while the son he hasn't seen in three years is leaving. Why does Charlie, after telling us how "terribly happy" he was to see his father, reveal nothing of his feelings? We can guess how Charlie felt, but we do not know. Why the absence of feeling—at least in the telling (which may not be truthful)?

Does Cheever's relationship to the two characters offer any sort of explanation to both questions? I think so, and that idea becomes my tentative thesis:

> Cheever resented his father's alcoholism and inattention and at the same time longed for his love; he desired to turn away from his father, putting the pain of his neglect behind him, and at the same time he wanted to turn toward his father, to bridge their distance. This love/hate conflict is intensified by Cheever's awareness that he is in certain crucial ways like his father. In "Reunion" Charlie does not directly express his disgust and rage at his father

because his position is essentially the same as Cheever's: in hating his father, Charlie (like Cheever) is closing off the possibilty of resolution; in hating his father, Charlie (like Cheever) is hating himself.

This thesis, as is usually the case, suggests an organization for the essay:

1. Cheever's fiction meaningfully echoes his life: thesis.
2. Charlie's father and Cheever's father.
3. Charlie and Cheever.
4. Charlie's father and Cheever himself.
5. Conclusion.

Drafting

You might want to sketch out your own draft of an essay based on the plan above before you read the one that follows.

JOHN CHEEVER'S "REUNION" AS "CRYPTO-AUTOBIOGRAPHY"

The intro sets up the problem: why is Charlie's father unsympathetically portrayed?

In John Cheever's "Reunion," the portrait of Charlie's father seems in the final analysis harsh and unforgiving. Not having seen his son in three years, the father proceeds at their meeting to drink himself into an abusive, obsessive state. He is never overtly mean to Charlie to be sure, but he is also far from attentive. Before the meeting, he did not respond personally to his son's letter asking about the lunch, letting his secretary arrange it instead; and throughout the visit he seems intent only on getting drinks and exerting his authority over waiters, showing little or no interest in the well-being of his son. As Charlie leaves, his father is unable even to say goodbye appropriately because he is so intent on getting "a rise" out of the newspaper clerk.

Yet Charlie's opinion is not explicitly presented.

And yet, despite his father's distressing behavior, Charlie does not directly express his feelings about the day's events. In the first paragraph he tells us that he was "terribly happy" to see his father, that he even wished they could be photographed together, but at the same time he says he immediately knew, the moment he saw his father, that he was "my future and my doom." Even with this emotional load, Charlie appears simply to report what happened without betraying his own reaction. But much is left out, leaving the reader to guess what Charlie is feeling, how this event has affected him, why this was the "last time I saw my father." Was he so outraged, hurt, saddened, confused, embarrassed, or something else that he determined never to see him again? Or did his father die soon afterward? The story is so brief that it is difficult to speculate with any confidence on Charlie's motivations, or even on his accuracy, yet it is so vividly told that it is difficult not to speculate.

Thesis is introduced here.

Perhaps this distancing is precisely what Cheever wanted: to tell a story about a father and a son, presenting deeply moving events without really exposing what they mean. To understand Cheever's purpose, and thereby understand his story better, we need to look at Cheever's own experience of father-son relationships. The justification for relating life to fiction is particularly strong in Cheever's case since the same incident oftentimes is recounted in his letters and journals and then employed in his fiction. Even when Cheever was supposedly reporting a real event, his "interest in telling a good story was greater than his interest in what we might consider the facts," as his son Benjamin put it (20). As Benjamin wrote, "The connection between his life and his work was intimate," and Cheever was even "fond of saying that fiction was `crypto-autobiography.'" In fact there are obvious autobiographical elements in "Reunion," and decoding them does shed some light on the story.

Cheever's life connects to the story.

First, we should note that Cheever was profoundly troubled by his relationship to his father: late in life he called his father "the greatest and the most bitter mystery in my life," and he revealed that the problem of learning to love a father "appears in all the books and stories" (Susan Cheever, 209-10). We do not need to know much about Cheever's childhood to imagine why

Cheever's father and Charlie's father.

he kept trying to sort it out. Not
only did Cheever's mother tell him
he was a mistake ("If I hadn't drunk
two Manhattans one afternoon, you
never would have been conceived"),
but also, as Cheever's daughter
says, "his father wanted him aborted, even inviting the abortionist to
dinner, an event that appears in
both *The Wapshot Chronicle* and
Falconer" (19). Charlie's father is
in some crucial aspects like
Cheever's father: alcoholic, insecure, sarcastic, self-centered.
Unlike Charlie's father, Cheever's
father was not divorced, but there
were tremendous hostilities between
his parents, leading to drunken
infidelities, threatened suicides,
and violent arguments—which formed
much of the substance of Cheever's
fiction.

Charlie and Cheever.   If Charlie's father is like
Cheever's father, Charlie is also
a reflection of Cheever. Charlie,
like Cheever, wants to love his
father, but he finds a man who is
apparently uninterested in him and
careening out of control. In his
hunger for love, Charlie tries to
connect with his father on some more
primitive level, smelling his father
"the way my mother sniffs a rose,"
and finding "a rich compound of
whiskey, after-shave lotion, shoe
polish, woollens, and the rankness
of a mature male." Cheever was also

extraordinarily moved by smells, telling his publisher at one point that he was "a very olfactory fellow," and not to try to remove any of the smells in his book.

Cheever and his father.

But Cheever does not seem to express his rage and disappointment very directly through Charlie. Surely part of the obstruction is Cheever's realization that he is in many ways like his father, Frederick Cheever, a shoe salesman who became unemployed and bitter in the mid-1920s. John Cheever was not technically out of work, but he did not have a regular job, and he struggled for much of his life to make ends meet. Most obviously, like his father—like Charlie's father—Cheever could not control his drinking. In an entry from the early journals (late forties and fifties), Cheever writes, "Year after year I read in here [in his journal] that I am drinking too much, and there can be no doubt of the fact that this is progressive" (103). Although Cheever finds everything about his drinking "disgusting," still "each noon I reach for the whiskey bottle." Cheever was evidently aware of the effect of such behavior on a son, as Cheever's own son, Benjamin, writes, "He used to say that I must wish I had a father who didn't drink so much, and I'd always say no" (18).

Cheever and Charlie's
father.

In fact, Charlie's father's habit
of baiting waiters in foreign
tongues may have been modeled on
Cheever's own behavior, as a passage from Susan Cheever's biography
of her father reveals. After com-
menting on how Cheever, even though
"he spoke minimal French," began
"dropping French words into his
conversation," she goes on to say,
"With Italian, he was even worse,"
using it "at every opportunity,"
especially in restaurants (62).

Summary

Thus Charlie's statement that his
father was "my future and my doom"
resonates on several levels.
Cheever, the model for Charlie, had
become "something like" his father.
And Cheever's father was "something
like" Charlie's father, just as
Charlie would become "something
like" Cheever himself. For Charlie
to hate his father would involve
him in hating himself, his own
future self; yet he could hardly
approve affectionately of his
father. But more than that: for
Charlie to express his hatred
toward his father, Cheever would
have to acknowledge his own hatred
for his father, which would likewise involve him in a self-destruc-
tive disgust. Cheever could not
find a way to love his father, but
he could not find a way to hate him
either. And so he was driven to
write about him endlessly, search-
ing for a way to describe the relationship and resolve it.

WORKS CITED

Cheever, John. *The Brigadier and the Golf Widow.*
New York: Harper, 1964.

——. *The Journals of John Cheever.* Ed. Robert
Gottlieb. New York: Knopf, 1991.

——. *The Letters of John Cheever.* Ed. Benjamin
Cheever. New York: Simon & Schuster, 1988.

Cheever, Susan. *Home Before Dark.* Boston: Houghton,
1984.

Donaldson, Scott. *John Cheever.* New York: Random,
1988.

A NEW HISTORICAL ESSAY

Preparing to Write

Where could I look for some clues to the ideology shaping Cheever's story? I decided that one place to look, thinking of "Reunion" as part of a cultural system, would be *The New Yorker* magazine in which the story was first published. Knowing the story came out in 1962, I found it in the October 27th issue: the whole story appears on page 45.

I studied the magazine, trying to absorb the culture of 1962, the book and movie reviews, the current events, the articles, the advertisements, time-traveling back a little over thirty years. I did not imagine one issue of one magazine could contain an entire culture, but I did assume that a close inspection of one issue might suggest a great deal about the world *The New Yorker* presented to its readers. I tried to imagine myself as an anthropologist studying a foreign and unknown culture—in this case, the culture of *The New Yorker*'s writers, advertisers, and readers. In reading through the magazine, I was struck very quickly by two messages, which seemed to appear relentlessly in various ways. Both messages arguably still permeate our culture, but they seemed especially prominent in this "foreign" setting. Perhaps

I was simply paying close attention to what I ordinarily try to ignore.

Put bluntly, I found the magazine telling its readers again and again to consume—to purchase, to view, to possess, to ingest—and to display the quality of their discerning consumption. Most insistently, it seemed that readers were being told to consume superior alcoholic beverages; directly in some thirty-six ads, and indirectly in ads for other products. An ad for Japan Airlines pictured a happy couple in the act of taking drinks from an attentive hostess; another for Caron perfumes depicted a beautiful woman clinking a brandy glass with her lover.

I was also struck by the exhortations to wear superior clothing, urging readers to display their wealth and excellent taste. Such exhibition was motivated, sometimes blatantly, sometimes subtly, by the promise of acceptance and affection. These messages—consume and display—appeared most obviously in the advertisements, but they could also be discerned in the articles and even the cartoons. They often appeared together.

Shaping

If we recognize that Cheever's story appears in a context saturated with recurrent encouragements to drink (for status and success) and to display one's status and success, what difference does it make? How does this context affect our reading of the story? How does the story affect our reading of the context, for that matter?

One effect might be to reconsider our assessment of Charlie's father's drinking. In New Historicist fashion, stressing ideology over individuals, I would argue that Charlie's father is not an autonomous agent, fully responsible for his failures. Rather, Charlie's father is to some degree a product of a value system he has learned too well. He has simply learned to seek affection and status in alcohol. His efforts to display his sophistication in languages and to demonstrate his dominance over the various waiters are also the effect of a powerful (but pitiful) desire for status.

This view of the father's fundamental insecurity and lone-
liness, which he attempts to erase by drinking and asserting
himself, reminds me of some passages in Cheever's journal.

- Writing about his inability to control his drinking,
  Cheever writes: "I could very easily destroy myself"
  (103). Charlie's father, like Cheever, is destroying himself slowly. Cheever and his character are being driven
  by emotional pain and insecurity to seek relief in the
  way that their culture has prescribed—asserting their
  status, consuming alcohol.

We do not know in "Reunion" why Charlie's father and
mother were divorced, and we may assume that Charlie has
not seen his father for three years because his father is
uncaring. Cheever's journal may help us to consider other
possibilites consistent with the facts of the story—namely
that Charlie's mother may have prevented his father from
seeing him. Perhaps she considered his father so worthless
that she did not want Charlie to see him again. Perhaps
Charlie's father feels so guilty that he considers himself
unworthy of his son's attention.

Finally, I should mention one more journal entry in
which Cheever records the visit of a friend: "in my anxiety to
communicate, to feel the most in warmth and intimacy, I
drink too much, which can be two drinks these days" (103).
The advertisements and cartoons link intimacy and affection
to alcohol, and Cheever does the same thing here. Again,
Charlie's father's behavior needs to be reconsidered.

At this point, it seems clear that I have way too much
material for a brief essay—which means that I'm in good
shape. But don't I need to dig further, examining all *The New
Yorker* issues of 1962, and *Good Housekeeping* and *Reader's
Digest* also, and everything else that can be recovered? Not
really, although it's always nice to know as much as you can.
My claim is simply that a certain community (the readers of
The New Yorker) at a certain slice of time (1962) were being
exposed to a certain set of messages. Rather than having to
dig up a whole city, the new historicist can construct a tentative system of meaning from the close analysis of selected

artifacts. The point is not that one document influenced another, but rather that at this moment within this community all documents participated in certain common assumptions.

So, looking over my notes, freewriting and brainstorming, I come back to my focus on Charlie's father as a reflection of a system of meaning. I try organizing my material in the following way:

The emotional view: Charlie's father as a deviant jerk.
Thesis: The analytical view: Charlie's father as a product of his time.
Advertisements and cartoons suggest alcohol confers status and affection: manliness.
Cheever and Charlie's father: drowning self and pain in drink.

Drafting

You might wish to draft an essay yourself at this point, then compare your application of the materials to mine.

HOW TO MAKE AN ALCOHOLIC DRINK: CHEEVER'S "REUNION" IN ITS CONTEXT

The opening orients the reader to the story and the issue: the father's lack of affection.

In John Cheever's "Reunion," Charlie's father appears to be the worst sort of parent. After three years of separation (following a divorce), the father doesn't respond to his son's letter, but rather has his secretary arrange their meeting. He greets his son in a strange way, with no apparent affection:

"Hi Charlie," he said. "Hi, boy. I'd like to take you up to my club, but it's in the Sixties, and if you have to catch an early train I guess we'd better get something to eat around here."

Although he puts his arm around Charlie, his subsequent behavior seems to confirm his callous self-absorption, as he apparently forgets about lunch and thinks only of drinking and insulting waiters. The visit ends with Charlie saying goodbye, for the last time, to a father who seems interested only in harrassing a newsstand clerk.

This paragraph introduces a possible explanation: the father's values are shaped by his culture.

But before we entirely dismiss Charlie's father, we might consider his motivation. What does he think he is doing? Where has he learned such behavior? Certainly Charlie is a victim of his father's indulgent inattention; but is Charlie's father also a victim in any way? In *The New Yorker* magazine in which "Reunion" first appeared, we find a set of directives that help to explain the behavior of Charlie's father, which may well be motivated not by any sort of disregard or animosity toward Charlie, but rather by the desire for status and affection. This desire is fueled by a system of values reflected in and even shaped by *The New Yorker.*

Evidence: Ads for alcoholic beverages focus on status.

Again and again advertisements in the October 26th issue of 1962 convey to the readers the paramount importance of status, rank, superiority. One of the most blatant of these ads asks the question "Are you a status seeker?" If you like "Italian restaurants," the ad continues, "foreign cars," "antique

furniture," and finally "Lord
Calvert" whiskey, then you apparently are a status seeker (as you
should be, the ad implies). The
association of alcoholic beverages
with nobility, and therefore "status," is a recurrent theme. Grand
Marnier is "The Emperor of
Liqueurs," and another scotch is
named "House of Lords." Old Hickory
is drunk by "all the nicest people,"
and several couples in formal
evening attire are depicted. The
drink identifies you as a superior
being, among "the nicest people,"
which does not in this context seem
to mean the most polite or philan-
thropic.

Other ads and status.

Other ads for non-alcoholic products also reinforce this desire for
status. One ad pictures an aristo-
cratic man, sneering slightly, in an
overcoat, standing behind a large,
exotic-looking dog, with the caption
"Which has the pedigree?" Of course,
it isn't the dog, or the man; it's
the coat. Buying this coat, the ad
implies, gives you a pedigree you
can wear. This anxiety about the

Clothing and status.

status of one's clothing, or how
one's clothing expresses one's status, is also employed by advertisements for alcoholic drinks. One ad
depicts a man from the neck down,
dressed in a tuxedo, carrying a fur
coat with a large label clearly
exposed. The caption says, "When a
label counts, it's Imported O.F.C.,"

and we can easily see that the label
in the fur coat is the same as the
label on the bottle of whiskey to
the right of the text.

Here the focus on
labels is applied to
clothing and whiskey.

When does a label count? When one
is concerned about the display of
status and superiority, a concern
that this and many other ads serve
to amplify and exploit. A tuxedo and
a fur coat represent the pinnacle of
fashion, and we can imagine that the
physically fit man, draping the fur
coat over his arm, is waiting for
his companion to come claim the
coat. The man's head is not pictured
because with the right label, his
appearance doesn't really matter—and
the reader can imagine his own head
on that body. Tellingly, the ad says
almost nothing about how the whisky
tastes ("Rich. Light."), but stress-
es rather that it is "In immaculate
good taste." This designer whiskey
confers status, prestige, and even
companionship; who cares what it
tastes like?

The claim: Charlie's
father is motivated by
anxiety, created in
part by these cultural
values.

This anxiety about one's status
and the implication that drinking
alcoholic beverages will elevate it,
which pervade the advertisements and
even the cartoons in *The New Yorker*,
arguably shape the character of
Charlie's father, and Cheever as
well. Charlie's father has his secretary make the arrangements for
meeting his son in order to establish that he has a secretary. He
wants his son to realize that he has

status—because he has absorbed the
cultural lesson that his self-worth
depends on it. He mentions "my club"
for the same reason, I would argue:
to convey that he has a club, even
though it is conveniently too dis-
tant to be used. Likewise, his display of foreign languages and his
manic rudeness toward the various
waiters are pitiful efforts to
impress his son with his sophistication and power. At the end, as he
struggles to "get a rise" out of the
newsstand clerk, he is trying des-
perately to show his son how clever
and superior he is. That is why he
says "just wait a second, sonny": he
is putting on this performance for
his son, not for his own amusement.
His interest in his son and his
excitement are subtly suggested by
his arrival "at twelve o'clock
sharp." He's eager to see his son;
he simply does not know how to
impress his son, and his response is
an effort to establish his status.

Even his alcoholism is
related.

Even Charlie's father's desperate
pursuit of alcohol reflects his anxiety about his status. Not only can
we speculate that his nervousness
drives him to medicate himself with
liquid depressants; we can also see
how his pursuit of drinks reflects
his awareness of the association,
created in advertisements and other
cultural messages, between alcoholic
consumption and affection. Charlie's
father is seeking to create a bond

with Charlie in a way that advertisements even today continue to
promote. Charlie's father wants to
create an "it-doesn't-get-any-bet-
ter-than-this" moment; when the second waiter refuses to serve Charlie,
his father immediately leaves
because he wants more than a drink
for himself; he hopes the drinks
will lead to affection and bonding.

Conclusion: these val-
ues are destructive.

But they are really self-destruc-
tive, as Cheever makes clear.
Charlie's father does not establish
his status, and his quest for drinks
does not create a bond. Instead, the
day's events extinguish the contact
between father and son, just as the
father's drinking represents a slow
self-extinction. Cheever has exposed
the lie in the advertisements sur-
rounding his story.

PRACTICING BIOGRAPHICAL, HISTORICAL, AND NEW HISTORICAL CRITICISM

Here are some possibilities to get you started.

1. If you were going to begin today to write a screenplay, a short story, a novel, a poem, or a play, what would it be about? Sketch out a rough draft or outline, or write the work if possible. Then consider how biographical, historical, or new historical criticism might relate to your work.

2. Choose another magazine from 1962 (*Good Housekeeping, Life, Reader's Digest, The Atlantic,* for instance) and compare its system of values to *The New Yorker*'s, as I've described it. How does this expanded

vision of 1962 affect your view of "Reunion"? What if "Reunion" had appeared in *Good Housekeeping,* for instance?

3. Here are two cartoons from the same *New Yorker* issue containing "Reunion." Discuss the system of values they imply. How might they be related to "Reunion"?

"*He's got this gimmick, see. He's completely honest.*"

Drawing by Stan Hunt; © 1962, 1990 The New Yorker Magazine, Inc.

"You're going to get a great summation! He's smashed!"

Drawing by Rowland B. Wilson; © 1962, 1990 The New Yorker
Magazine, Inc.

164

6

MINDING THE WORK
Psychological Criticism

When a member of my family complains that he or she has bitten his tongue, bruised her finger, and so on, instead of the expected sympathy I put the question, 'Why did you do that?'

—Sigmund Freud

THE PURPOSE OF PSYCHOLOGICAL CRITICISM

Psychology began in a sense when the first person, rather than just reacting to another person's behavior, wondered instead, "Why did you do that?" Modern psychology begins with Freud, not simply because he wonders so intensely, but because he offers a compelling answer: we do things, Freud asserted, really weird and silly things sometimes, for reasons that are to some degree hidden, inaccessible, beyond our direct control or awareness. These hidden motivations come from what Freud called *das Unbewusste*, which means literally "the unknown" but is usually translated into English as "the unconscious," that part or activity of one's mind that is unknown even to its possessor. Although both the term "unconscious" and the general concept predated Freud, his theories revolutionized the study of the mind.

There is in fact only one major form of psychotherapy that is not based in some important respect on Freudian concepts—behavior therapy. For a psychological theory, behaviorism seems strangely unconcerned with the mind. Basing their approaches on B. F. Skinner's work, who in turn drew largely on Ivan Pavlov, behaviorists view psychological problems as bad habits: the patient has learned unproductive or destructive behaviors and must unlearn them and take up others. Every other therapy, despite some vast differences, depends in crucial ways on Freud. To understand modern psychology and to practice psychological criticism, you need to start with Freud and particularly with his conception of the unconscious mind.

Obviously, you needn't stop there. Maslow's hierarchy of needs, or Erikson's theory of adult development, or any other psychological theories (including your own) may prove very illuminating. I focus here on Freud because his work is historically the starting point, because his ideas are so familiar to educated people, because his works continue to generate challenge and controversy, and because Freud's work nicely illustrates the application of psychology to literature. His theories were based in significant ways on literary works. There's just no way to survey here the whole field of psychology. So I encourage you to study psychology, expanding your understanding of Freud, and exploring also the theories of others.

The therapeutic procedure Freud developed was designed to help those patients whose conscious lives were being troubled or even overtaken by unconscious fears or desires. It involved having the patient lie on a couch and talk freely about whatever came to mind, roaming back through childhood, dreams, fantasies, whatever, thereby allowing the patient and the analyst to gather enough data to speculate about what was going on in the hidden country of the unconscious. By slowly exposing the effects of the unconscious, peeling back layer after layer of disguised and suppressed fears and desires, Freud's "talking cure" was designed to enlarge the mental "territory" of the conscious mind. When the patient, with the analyst's help, could expose these unconscious materials, Freud believed that their power over the patient would be lessened and even dissipated.

When Freud failed to comfort his injured family members, he was not simply creating work for future therapists (unconsciously?), but he was rather assuming that an apparently irrational action like biting one's own tongue might actually have some important underlying explanation. Freud did not expect his family to express their unconscious motivations ("I bit my tongue because I want to tell you to drop dead, but I know I shouldn't," for instance); rather, he hoped to unearth some evidence of how an unconscious desire was being first covered up or denied and then expressed in a disguised way. He was, in his own way, trying to be a good father.

Freud's theory of the unconscious also revolutionized the study of the mind and launched modern psychology by assuming that the unconscious is inherently sexual. Even children are sexual beings, Freud pointed out, thus scandalizing many of his Victorian contemporaries. Not a few people continue to be scandalized. How this unsettling insight affected Freud's work can be seen in the story of "Little Hans," one of his most famous and remarkable cases. When Hans was brought to Freud at age five, he refused to go outside because he was hysterically terrified that a horse would bite him. Through Hans's father, Freud was able to learn that at age three-and-a-half Hans's mother had tried to discourage him from touching his own genitals by saying that if he didn't stop, the doctor would come to "cut off your widdler and then what will you widdle with?" Freud deduced that Little Hans had noticed that horses had large genitalia and that his mother did not appear to have any, apparently proving that she knew what she was talking about. In the uncanny logic of Little Hans's unconscious mind, castration and horses became all jumbled up with his love for his mother, and the competition with his father for that love. Freud helped the father reassure Little Hans that his own penis was in no danger, curing his irrational fear.

It is, however, incorrect to think of Freud simply as that guy who thought of everything in terms of sex. For one thing,

Freud's idea of sexuality includes much more than simply the act of sex. Rather, Freud focused on the entire drive toward physical pleasure, which he saw as being constantly in conflict with opposing forces. This conflict is necessary for rather obvious reasons: without it, we would be unable to function in a civilized society. But our desires, when they cannot be expressed and released, must go somewhere. Hence, the need for an unconscious, a kind of storage vault for psychic energy. In this mental hydraulic system, as Freud sees it, some of the repressed energy does leak out in various disguised ways—in dreams, slips of the tongue, jokes, creative writing.

This mechanism for submerging unacceptable desires is well-known today as "repression," and it is for Freud an essential activity. Mental illness, then, in which the unconscious is unable to contain satisfactorily the repressed material, becomes different only in degree, not kind, from "normal" mental health.

There's already plenty in the little bit I've discussed to make anyone uneasy: we don't know what's going on in our minds even though that activity is influencing our thinking and behavior. The mechanism whereby our fears and desires are being repressed is the same mechanism that leads to mental illness—meaning that "normal" is a relative term, since we're all unavoidably a little out of touch; the drive toward pleasure is relentlessly struggling to overpower our grip on the realities of our culture. I haven't even gotten to the Oedipus complex, which, despite its "utter centrality to Freud's work," as Terry Eagleton says (156), is nonetheless outrageous—so disturbingly bizarre that, from a Freudian perspective, there must be something to it.

Freud concisely describes this fundamental sexual phenomenon of early childhood in "The Ego and the Id" (1923). In this accessible paper Freud explains how the young boy invests his desire and affection in his mother, developing an "object-cathexis" for her. The baby's desire for physical contact with his mother obviously begins with the mother's breasts, but the boy will ultimately want to possess his mother entirely. As his "sexual wishes in regard to his mother become more intense," Freud says, his father is increasingly "perceived as an obstacle to them." At this point, desiring his mother, blocked by his father, the young boy has acquired what Freud calls "the simple positive Oedipus complex" (640). Freud is alluding to the ancient myth in which Oedipus, in the course of saving a city, happens unknowingly to kill his father and marry his mother.

Obviously, the desire to do away with the father and join with the mother cannot be acted out without disastrous consequences, and it must therefore be repressed, put out of sight. This "primal repression," as Freud calls it, is in fact what creates the unconscious, making a place for repressed desires. But if nothing more than this repression happens, then the Oedipus complex will persist in the unconscious, exerting its relentless pressure and eventually creating psychological trouble—a "pathogenic effect." This ill effect is avoided, Freud says, when the Oedipus complex is destroyed, a process that is brought about by the boy's perception that his father is superior.

And here is where most readers of Freud tend to drop their jaws or even toss the book across the room, because the threat of the father is focused, Freud believes, in the threat of castration. Fearing that the father may negate his affection for the mother by castrating him, the boy (understandably enough) begins a process of transferring his desires elsewhere. (What little Hans was experiencing was thus a more intense variation of a "normal" process.) The part of the mind that "retains the character of the father," who comes to stand for the restraints of "authority, religious teaching, schooling, and reading," Freud calls the "superego." In struggling to control the ego, the superego is opposed by the id, the repository of basic instincts and desires. The relationship between the id and ego, as Freud puts it in his *New Introductory Lectures on Psychoanalysis*, is like that "between a rider and his horse" (108). The rider is supposed to direct the horse's energy, but sometimes the rider has "to guide his horse in the direction in which it itself wants to go."

Think of the id as Jack Nicholson or Roseanne Arnold, irreverent, indulgent, spontaneous, raucous. Think of the ego as Robert Duvall or Meryl Streep—smooth, adaptable, responsible, an actor. And the superego is like Christopher Reeve or Miss Manners—principled, moral, wholesome, occupied with doing the right thing.[1]

Thus, Freud offers two maps of the mind. First, conscious versus unconscious; then later, this division is refined into the id, ego, superego model. The id is largely the territory of the unconscious, and the ego and superego are mostly conscious.

Freud has not been alone in revising his ideas. His earliest followers rather quickly offered major additions, divergences, and rejections of various Freudian features. Melanie Klein, for instance, emphasized the turbulence of the pre-Oedipal period when the child wants to possess and destroy the mother. Harry Stack Sullivan turned from Freud's emphasis on internal conflicts to concentrate on the individual's relationships with important people in his life. The "good" mother, Sullivan says, conveys security and contentment to the child, whereas the "bad" mother communicates her anxiety and distress to the child, who must adjust his or her own behavior to modify the mother's stress. Carl Jung downplayed Freud's emphasis on sex and supplemented the individual unconscious with the idea of a "collective unconscious" that contains themes and images inherited by all humans. Jungian approaches to psychological criticism look for such recurrent themes and images across time and across cultures, seeing them as clues to the structuring of the collective unconscious mind.

Today little of Freud's work is accepted without substantial modification or challenge. Fortunately, in order to do psychological criticism you don't need to wait until the truth of all Freud's particular theories has been settled; and you don't need to understand all the various refinements and refutations and wholescale rethinkings of Freud that continue to appear. The more you know about psychology, to be sure, the more options you're likely to have as a critic. But all you really need to understand in order to do psychological criticism is Freud's fundamental concept of the unconscious—a concept that has remained the unchallenged starting point for most subsequent psychological theories. The purpose of psychology depends on bringing to consciousness the hidden fears and desires that disturb and control our lives. And the purpose of psychological criticism likewise is to direct Freud's question—"Why did you do that?"—to authors, or characters, or readers. Looking at the author, psychological criticism tries to go beyond the biographical facts to expose the underlying motivations—motivations and meanings that the author herself or himself may not have glimpsed. Looking at a character, psychological criticism treats the author's creation as a person whose behavior can be explained psychologically. Looking at the reader, psychological criticism considers how the reader's motivations shape the meaning of the work.

The next section discusses how to carry out such tasks.

HOW TO DO PSYCHOLOGICAL CRITICISM

Psychology and literary criticism have been intertwined from their very beginnings. Plato noted that poets indulge in a kind of madness when they write, stirring up the audience's passions and emotions. A well-ordered republic, Plato thought, would be better off without poets. Aristotle countered Plato's argument with the position that literature has a healthy psychological effect; in the case of tragedy, it purges excessive fear and pity. Longinus felt that literature could cultivate the audience's sense of the sublime, elevating and refining their sensibilities.

Freud's practice of using literary works to illustrate his theories, or test them, or even suggest them, has been continued by psychological thinkers of every variety. Alfred Adler, for instance, one of the earliest theorists to break away from Freud, believed his own psychological insights were drawn largely from literary works; he even asserted that "the artist is the leader of mankind on the road to absolute truth" (329). In "Creative Writers and Day-Dreaming" (1908) Freud lays the foundation for applying psychology to literature. The author's creative production is, for Freud, like the material of a dream: it is a "day-dream," shaped and therefore disguised substantially by the unconscious mind. A work of literature then is like the material the analyst receives from his or her patients. Acts of literary criticism and psychological analysis begin to look very much alike, if they are not in fact the same. In both cases, the interpreter examines a text and reconstructs an underlying meaning and significance.

Since these underlying meanings of the patient's or the author's stories belong by definition to the realm of the hidden and directly unknowable, a certain amount of creativity and imagination on the part of the interpreter are not only authorized but also called for. In addition to creativity, some basic concepts and terms will be useful. These originate with Freud, but they've become part of the psychological vocabulary, and to varying degrees they've even filtered into the common language.

I've already mentioned *repression*, the mind's essential strategy for hiding desires and fears. But out of sight does not mean out of mind in this case. Consider for a moment the following poem, which despite its simplicity has received much critical attention:

A Slumber Did My Spirit Seal (1800)
  William Wordsworth

A slumber did my spirit seal;
I had no human fears:
She seemed a thing that could not feel
The touch of earthly years.

No motion has she now, no force;   5
She neither hears nor sees;
Rolled round in earth's diurnal course,
With rocks, and stones, and trees.

This poem appears in a series of poems about "Lucy," a girl who died young. No historical "Lucy" has been found by researchers, and she appears to have been a fiction. If we ask Freud's question of Wordsworth, "Why did you do that?", we will have to make up our own answer: even if he were alive, Wordsworth's own answer could not be trusted because the real reason for the poem might well be hidden in his uncon-scious. So let us ask ourselves, what wish or fear or desire might Wordsworth be expressing here in a disguised form?

When Wordsworth wrote this poem, he was living with his sister in deep poverty in Germany, enduring an extremely cold winter. His sister, Dorothy, was his lifelong companion, living with him throughout his marriage. Several of Wordsworth's poems are dedicated to her; several of his poems in fact borrow from her quite brilliant journals. Wordsworth and his sister were very close.

When Wordsworth sent this poem to Samuel Coleridge, Coleridge wrote to another friend that "in some gloomier moment" Wordsworth had "fancied the moment in which his sister might die." If the poem is in some way about the death of Wordsworth's sister, then it certainly does represent a pro-found fear for Wordsworth. And yet, the poem is oddly unemotional. The speaker "had" no fears; "she" feels nothing; the speaker's "spirit" is sleeping and sealed off.

To a psychologist (or a psychological critic), the experi-ence of an event without any of the expected response is called *isolation*. In Cheever's "Reunion," I would argue, Charlie employs isolation to deal with the last time he saw his father. He doesn't overtly deny his emotions, or try to explain them away, or express them; he appears simply to ignore them, disconnecting from them, selectively telling us what happened. One could also argue, I think, that Hemingway's soldier exhibits isolation in "A Very Short Story."

But why would Wordsworth refuse to acknowledge the profound grief one would expect to arise at the idea of his sis-ter's death? A psychological view, looking at the intimacy of Wordsworth's relationship with his sister, would have to won-der if perhaps he isn't protecting himself against desires he cannot acknowledge. If Wordsworth did have an incestuous desire for his sister, whom he certainly loved deeply, acknowl-edging that desire would certainly cause him great psycholog-ical pain. In fantasy, in his poetry, he could deal with that desire indirectly by imagining his sister, or her surrogate Lucy, as being dead. Channeling an unacceptable urge into some artistic creation is called *sublimation*. We see it in

Lucille Clifton's "forgiving my father," which transforms her hatred for her father into a work that moves her toward forgiveness. Sublimation is no doubt at work in Mary Astell's *Proposal* (see Chapter 7), in which her inevitable rage against an oppressive patriarchy becomes the driving force behind her proposal for women to secede.

If Wordsworth is substituting Lucy for Dorothy, he is also engaging in *displacement,* which inserts a safe object of emotion for a dangerous one. We might argue for example that Milton's focus on his blindness, in "When I Consider How My Light Is Spent," is a substitute for a more frightening loss of light, his death.

But perhaps we're on entirely the wrong track here, or perhaps there are simply other tracks available. My initial reading of Wordsworth's poem was that "she" is his own spirit. Otherwise, what sense does the initial line make, "A slumber did my spirit seal"? He imagines his own death, and depicts his soul as being feminine. "I had no human fears" becomes an instance then of *denial,* in which one simply falsifies reality, flatly and directly refusing to accept it. While repression buries the emotion and other strategies hide or disguise it, denial looks right at it and says it isn't there. Denial can be a more ominous symptom as it signals a break with reality. When Hemingway's soldier says he doesn't want to see any of his friends, it seems likely he's engaging in denial.

One could also argue, pursuing a different angle, that the critic who claims Wordsworth's poem deals with his incestuous desires is practicing *projection:* "Oh yeah, I see Wordsworth's repressed incestuous desires," the critic says, when it is actually his or her own incestuous desires, projected onto Wordsworth, that are being seen and avoided.

Or, one could argue the whole enterprise of criticism is motivated by *intellectualization,* a strategy for avoiding uncomfortable emotions by rationalizing them, analyzing them, talking and talking and talking about them. Intellectualization is isolation for intellectuals.

If we imagine that Wordsworth was terrified of ghosts and spirits, that he feared they were wandering all over the place, and that he was especially convinced that he would become a restless ghoul himself, then we could see the poem as a *reaction formation,* in which one is convinced that the opposite of a terrible situation is actually the case. Although Wordsworth, in this scenario, is convinced that spirits roam the earth, he keeps telling himself insistently that "slumber" actually seals one's spirit, leaving it as dead as a rock. In "My Father's Martial Art," Stephen Shu-ning Liu says his father and his Master are sitting on O Mei mountain. To the extent that he believes this statement he is arguably employing a reaction formation, for the poem makes rather clear that his father is dead. He cannot come down and hush the traffic. He—at least his body—isn't sitting anywhere.

As you're thinking about how to apply psychological theories to literature in specific ways, you might also consider the more general effects of a psychological perspective. I'd like to bring two consequences to your attention.

Students often ask English teachers, "Do you really think the author intended to mean all that?" Which means of course, "Aren't you being too clever, reading too much into this, making a big deal out of something that isn't there?" After Freud, the question becomes irrelevant. The author himself or herself can't really know what was intended because of the inevitable involvement of the unconscious mind. We may think we intend one thing, but our unconscious intentions may be very different and much more complex. Our intention may even be contradictory because the unconscious mind isn't worried about logical consistency. By analyzing the work closely, we may gain some insight into what the author really intended—but we're always just guessing. At the least, we can be confident that the meaning of any statement is richer than it seems.

This point brings me to the second consequence of an awareness of psychological criticism, which is closely related to the first one. After Freud, what idea could possibly be too far out to consider? Psychological theories ought to encourage you to be creative in speculating about the motivations of characters, authors, or readers. When students write uninteresting papers, it's often because they're too vague on the one hand, or too cautious on the other. I would like to think that an acquaintance with psychological criticism will tend to loosen your imagination.

THE WRITING PROCESS: A SAMPLE ESSAY

Hamlet, as you might imagine, has been the subject of considerable psychological analysis, beginning most notably with Ernst Jones's *Hamlet and Oedipus,* which made much of Hamlet's bedroom scene with his mother. In some versions of the play, Sir Laurence Olivier's for instance, Hamlet's physical attraction to his mother is shockingly obvious, as Hamlet pushes his mother onto her bed, holding her down, ranting and raving about her affection for Claudius, his uncle, the murderer of his father, now his step-father. I'm going to look at a passage that seems to me much less promising. If there are psychological analyses of this passage, I'm not aware of them. In fact, I thought at first, after picking the passage at random, that a psychological reading wouldn't work. So, you're going to see the evolution of a psychological reading of this passage.

But first, you'll see the passage. In this scene, from act four, scene four, Hamlet has just observed the army of Fortinbras moving to attack a part of Poland. The land the two armies are fighting over is insignificant; Fortinbras' captain says he wouldn't pay "five ducats" to farm it. And yet thousands of men and thousands of ducats will be wasted to fight over it. Hearing this, Hamlet speaks the soliloquy below. Read it carefully and consider what you might say about it from a psychological perspective.

Hamlet 4.4.32–66 (1600)
William Shakespeare

How all occasions do inform against me,	*inform against:*
And spur my dull revenge! What is a man,	*accuse*
If his chief good and market of his time	*market: product*
35 Be but to sleep and feed? a beast, no more.	

Sure He that made us with such large
  discourse,   *discourse: reasoning
                                                        power , language*
Looking before and after, gave us not
That capability and godlike reason
To fust in us unus'd. Now whether it be   *fust: develop mold*
40 Bestial oblivion, or some craven scruple   *craven: cowardly*
Of thinking too precisely on th' event—   *event: the result*
A thought which quarter'd hath but
  one part wisdom
And ever three parts coward—I do not know
Why yet I live to say, "This thing's to do,"
45 Sith I have cause, and will, and strength,   *Sith: since*
  and means
To do't. Examples gross as earth exhort me: *gross: huge, obvious*
Witness this army of such mass and charge,
Led by a delicate and tender prince,
Whose spirit with divine ambition puff'd
50 Makes mouths at the invisible event,   *makes mouths:
Exposing what is mortal and unsure   taunts, scorns*
To all that fortune, death, and danger dare,
Even for an egg-shell. Rightly to be great
Is not to stir without great argument,
55 But greatly to find quarrel in a straw
When honor's at the stake. How stand I then,
That have a father kill'd, a mother stain'd,
Excitements of my reason and my blood,
And let all sleep, while to my shame I see
60 The imminent death of twenty thousand men,
That for a fantasy and trick of fame
Go to their graves like beds, fight for a plot
Whereon the numbers cannot try the cause,
Which is not tomb enough and continent
65 To hide the slain? O, from this time forth,
My thoughts be bloody, or be nothing worth!

Preparing to Write

One first strategy to generate ideas is simply to list some
basic psychological concepts and look for them in the passage. For instance:

Isolation: What is Hamlet not feeling that he should
be feeling? This question seems easy to answer.
Hamlet himself tells us that he should be feeling
bloodthirsty rage, yet his revenge is "dull." So he
tries to exhort himself to feel what he should,
rather than existing in a "bestial oblivion," feeling nothing.

Intellectualization: Hamlet offers two possible explanations for his delay in lines 39–41. "Bestial
oblivion" (or isolation) is one; "thinking too precisely on th' event" (or intellectualization) is
the other. Both these strategies are used to avoid
feeling emotions—which is precisely what Hamlet
sees himself doing.

Repression: What is Hamlet ignoring? What obvious
feeling does he totally pass over? Certainly he
recognizes that he should be vengeful but isn't;
but Hamlet seems to look right past what would seem
most important: he doesn't want to die. If Hamlet
kills Claudius, he may lose his own life. He may
have, as he says, "cause, and will, and strength,
and means / To do't," but he has no guarantee that
he can do it safely. This avoidance is, I think, a
major repression, and it is bound to express itself
somewhere. In fact, this whole passage can be seen
as an effort to ignore what he is most pressed to
say: that he fears throwing away his life.

Projection: Does Hamlet use projection to disguise his
feeling that taking his revenge will mean throwing
away his life? There is his reference to the "delicate and tender prince" who is willing to expose
"what is mortal and unsure" for the sake of "an
egg-shell." Of course Hamlet does not know how the
other prince feels, or really whether he is "delicate and tender." The other prince may well believe
that the upcoming battle is a small but glorious
part of an epic campaign—not that he is fighting

for an eggshell, but that the battle is strategi-
cally, symbolically, historically, personally of
major proportions. It is in fact Hamlet who, deep
inside, feels that he, a delicate and tender
prince, a student and theatre-goer, is being asked
to act like a warrior and throw away his life for
an eggshell. He says, "That guy is throwing his
life away for an eggshell." His unconscious meaning: "I'm throwing my life away for an eggshell."

A problem here: can we really say that Hamlet
views his cause as an eggshell? He has "a father
kill'd, a mother stain'd." These would seem to be
more than an eggshell. But his revenge will not
alter his father's death. He'll be just as dead
after Hamlet acts. Nor will Hamlet's revenge undo
the stain on his mother. Although men will "find
quarrel in a straw / When honor's at the stake,"
her honor has already been tarnished by Claudius,
hasn't it? Early in the play Hamlet has referred to
his world as "an unweeded garden / That grows to
seed, things rank and gross in nature / Possess it
merely" (I.ii.135-37). So the world and his cause
are no more than an eggshell for Hamlet.

Displacement: Instead of venting his anger at
Claudius, who is dangerous, Hamlet is attacking
himself.

Denial: Hamlet says he does not know why he hasn't
acted, but the reason is right in front of him: he
doesn't want to be like the twenty thousand men
already marching to their meaningless deaths. He is
denying that he knows.

Reversal: Hamlet says that the twenty thousand men are
marching to their "imminent" deaths "to my shame."
Isn't he turning that around, however? Isn't it
really to their own shame? Hamlet acknowledges that
their deaths will not mean anything significant;
shouldn't they be ashamed of such senseless slaugh-

ter? The ground won't even be able to hold them,
Hamlet says; but that has already been true of the
bodies Hamlet has encountered: his father won't
stay put; Polonius's body eludes the court;
Ophelia's body floats away and surfaces again in
her grave. One must wonder if the ground can ever
contain the bodies put into it.

Reaction formation: Does Hamlet convince himself that
the exact opposite of something bad, something that
he doesn't want to confront, is going on, and that
it is good? Hamlet knows that he must eventually
carry out his revenge, giving in to a need for
revenge that does not make conscious sense to him.
His ego is being pressed by the superego, who is
literally his father figure, calling for justice.
His ego is also being pressed by his id, which
hungers for violence, indulgence. He wants to give
in to something bad: the violent energy of his id.
But he tells himself he doesn't want to.
    Let's try that again. Hamlet knows unconsciously
that he must behave violently, like an animal, a
savage, in order to carry out his revenge. He must
become a beast. Yet he tells himself the opposite.
He is a beast, he says, if he doesn't carry out his
revenge. His unconscious conflict can be seen in
the word "spur"—see below.

The conflict in Hamlet's mind over whether he should be a
beast or not, whether he should exercise "godlike reason" or
not, seems designed for relating to the id, ego, and superego.
So I used those terms as prompts in my invention phase.

Id— Hamlet says all occasions "spur" his revenge—as
if it were a horse. Freud in fact compares the id
to a horse. It is Hamlet's id that will have to
motivate his revenge: logically, he can't do it.
But, Hamlet doesn't want to be "a beast," in "bestial oblivion." If he lets the id's horse run, however, that's exactly what he'll be.

Ego— So his ego is caught in the middle. Driven to commit suicide without any consciously satisfying reason.

Superego— Justice, the moral code, the stand-in for the father: in this case, the ghost of the father isn't just in his head, he's walking about. Like the id, Hamlet's superego calls for revenge, which the ego recognizes as requiring its own extinction. No wonder Hamlet is caught in the middle, unable to act. He says at the end his thoughts will be bloody—but not his actions.

Is this enough material for an essay? How would you organize it?

Shaping

Is there a thesis floating around in the brainstorming above? It seems clear that I'm returning again and again to the question of why Hamlet is not taking his revenge. Why is he standing there talking rather than doing something? He thinks he should be killing people, or at least one particular person, yet he hasn't yet done it. And the conclusion of his speech, which seems to announce his action, on closer analysis just says his thoughts will be bloody. The next scene in the play isn't Hamlet bursting in on Claudius and cutting his throat.

So, my thesis might be that this passage helps us understand Hamlet's hesitation—his mental conflict. How? Why? First, I list what I think I know:

1. Hamlet's father and his superego (one stands in for the other) call for justice. Morality has been violated and it must be set right. "Honor's at the stake," as Hamlet says.

2. For some reason, this call to violence is insufficient. Hamlet avoids coming to terms with it for much of the play. How?

3. I said when I was developing ideas that Hamlet's
   unconscious wants to be bloody. But that really
   doesn't make sense, does it?

Let us imagine that Freud's comparison of the id to a horse is very appropriate. Let us further imagine that when Hamlet says the occasions should "spur" his revenge, he is speaking about the kinds of urges and passions that Freud assigns to the unconscious. So why is Hamlet's unconscious unwilling to kill Claudius? For the reader who assumes Hamlet's behavior is motivated—that "Hamlet" can be discussed as if he were a personality, and not a set of lines in a play, a fiction—this unwillingness is the nub of the problem.

Acting as a psychological critic, I want to persuade my audience to accept my explanation of Hamlet's behavior. To do that, I need to look some more at the text, and ask a few more questions.

Why would anyone be unwilling to kill someone who deserved it? I've already discussed pretty thoroughly above that Hamlet doesn't want to throw away his life. He's not convinced, even though his superego or his father tell him he should be, that killing Claudius is worth it. But this stuff is logical: this is the "thinking too precisely" that Hamlet mentions. The other reason, the "bestial oblivion," is more primitive.

I haven't yet drawn on Freud's crucial Oedipal complex, and it finally occurs to me that here's where it comes into play: Hamlet doesn't want to kill Claudius because at some level he can't blame Claudius. When Hamlet says he stands with "a father kill'd, a mother stain'd," he is in exactly the Oedipal position that Freud says the unconscious desires to be in. Hamlet calls these events "Excitements of my reason and my blood," and they are exciting, but not in a way that he consciously recognizes. He finds at some deeper level himself excited and unable to be enraged at Claudius for carrying out his own deep-seated wish.

At this point, I think I have the plan of an essay:

The problem: how can this passage be used to help
readers understand Hamlet's hesitation?

The answer: we see him using some classic strategies to avoid two realities: (1) killing Claudius will probably involve getting himself killed, and he just can't justify that; (2) killing Claudius will involve killing himself in a symbolic sense because Claudius has done what he wanted to do, unconsciously: kill his father and sleep with his mother.

THE PSYCHOLOGY OF HAMLET'S
HESITATION: A READING OF 4.4.32–66

Introduces the problem: why does Hamlet hesitate?

Shakespeare's *Hamlet* would be a simple case of king-killing and revenge except for one thing: Hamlet hesitates. Like Mona Lisa's smile, Hamlet's delay in carrying out his revenge is puzzling because we do not know his motivation. Some possible reasons are obvious. Perhaps he is not sure that the ghost is telling the truth. Perhaps he is waiting for the perfect revenge, when Claudius is doing something evil rather than praying, thus increasing the near-certainty that he will go to hell. Perhaps he wants to survive his revenge-taking. Perhaps he just wants to be sure he can succeed.

Possible explanations.

But Hamlet himself doesn't agree with these.

Any or all of these reasons might well be sufficient to explain Hamlet's delay, but Hamlet does not himself accept these reasons. In act 4, scene 4, after repeated efforts at self-analysis, Hamlet can still say:

> I do not know
> Why yet I live to say, `This
> thing's to do,'

Sith I have cause, and will, and
    strength, and means
To do't. (43-46)

If Hamlet does not know by this
time why he is waiting, then perhaps
the cause of his delay is not conscious or rational.

Oedipus complex
extended to hesitation.

Hamlet's psychology has often
been examined. The idea that
Hamlet's attitude toward his mother
is motivated by an Oedipus complex
is well known. But Hamlet's hesitation to revenge his father's death
can also be profitably connected to
his unconscious psychology as an
examination of his soliloquy in act
4, scene 4 will show. Hamlet is
unable to admit to himself that
"honor" is not a sufficient reason
for self-sacrifice; nor is he able
to understand that he identifies
with Claudius, despite his detesta-
tion of him.

After observing Fortinbras and
his army advancing to fight and die
for a small piece of worthless
ground, Hamlet exclaims: "How all
occasions do inform against me, /
And spur my dull revenge!" (32-33).
When Hamlet says that all occasions
"spur" his revenge, he compares his
mind to a horse being spurred. But
the next few lines clash with this
metaphor: "What is a man, / If his
chief good and market of his time /
Be but to sleep and feed? a beast,

A problem: revenge
equals the bestial.

no more" (33-35). Hamlet wants his
revenge to be bestial, yet he cen-

sures those who act like beasts.
He's caught in a dilemma: how to be
"spurred" without becoming less than
human?

Hamlet's denial of the realm of
Freud's id, the realm of bestial
desires, is expanded upon in the
next few lines:

> Sure He that made us with such
>   large discourse,
> Looking before and after, gave
>   us not
> That capability and godlike
>   reason
> To fust in us unus'd. (36–39)

In saying that we are made "with
such large discourse," Hamlet is
pointing out the vastness of man's
reasoning ability, which makes him,
Hamlet believes, "godlike." Unlike
the id, man's ego is able to look to
the future and the past, "Looking
before and after." We should use
that reason. But using our reason
does not promote violent action, as
Hamlet's next few lines indicate:

> Now whether it be
> Bestial oblivion, or some craven
>   scruple
> Of thinking too precisely on
>   th' event—
> A thought which quarter'd hath
>   but one part wisdom
> And ever three parts coward—I do
>   not know
> Why yet I live to say, "This
>   thing's to do,"

                        Sith I have cause, and will, and
                            strength, and means
                        To do't. (39-46)

                        Neither bestial oblivion nor the
                    rational mind seem conducive to
                    revenge. After asserting that he
                    should use his reason, rather than
                    letting it get moldy, Hamlet says
                    that reasoning blocks decisive
Humankind ought not   action. To kill Claudius, Hamlet
be bestial.   must assume a "godlike" role, hand-
                    ing out justice; yet his godlike
                    faculty does not support such dan-
                    gerous action, any more than his
                    bestial instincts support it.

                        Consciously unaware of this con-
                    flict, Hamlet continues to berate
                    himself, saying "Examples gross as
Reasoning works   earth exhort me." That is precisely
against revenge.   the problem: his reason obstructs
                    his action, and the examples exhort-
                    ing him are "gross as earth." The
                    kind of primitive, bestial violence
                    required of Hamlet is foreign to
                    him. He has suppressed his bestial
                    self even as he recognizes on one
                    level that it needs spurring. Hamlet
                    seems to think he is exhorting him-
                    self to action when he points to the
                    massive army, which is "Exposing
                    what is mortal and unsure / To all
                    that fortune, death, and danger
                    dare, / Even for an egg-shell"
Furthur support.   (51-53). But the logical absurdity
                    of the example actually works
                    against Hamlet's desire: anyone who
                    thinks about it at all will realize
                    that it is stupid for men to die for
                    an eggshell.

Hamlet's cause is not an
eggshell, and the next few lines
indicate further just how deluded
Hamlet is in his comparisons:

> Rightly to be great
> Is not to stir without great
> argument,
> But greatly to find quarrel in a
> straw
> When honor's at the stake.
> (53-56)

His case is not a straw, and the
idea that one should not stir "without great argument" actually justi-
fies his delay, even though Hamlet
consciously believes he is talking
himself into taking action. What is
perhaps most intriguing here, however, is the question of how Hamlet's
"honor" is involved. The play would
seem to be about murder, regicide,
and justice. Compared to these,
honor would seem to be a minor concern.

But the relevance of honor
emerges in the next lines:

Honor and revenge.

> How stand I then,
> That have a father kill'd, a
>   mother stain'd,
> Excitements of my reason and
>   my blood,
> And let all sleep, while to my
>   shame I see
> The imminent death of twenty
>   thousand men,
> That for a fantasy and trick of
> fame

> Go to their graves like beds,
>   fight for a plot
> Whereon the numbers cannot try
>   the cause,
> Which is not tomb enough and
>   continent
> To hide the slain? (56-65)

Hamlet feels that his mother is "stain'd," even though it is unclear that she knows anything about Claudius's murder. But Hamlet has already shown himself to be obsessed with his mother's sexuality, especially in the bedroom scene. And the lines following the mention of his mother's stain demonstrate Hamlet's subconscious expression of his own desire. He refers to the "Excitements of . . . my blood," and to "sleep," to "fantasy" and a "trick," and to "beds." While Hamlet is consciously focused on burying the dead in an insufficient tomb, his bestial self is concerned with his mother's womb and dying in a sexual sense.

Thus we can see that Hamlet fails to take action because his rational ego and his bestial id block his revenge, and because his own Oedipal desire to do what Claudius has done—kill his father and possess his stained mother—tends to defuse his resolve. We may notice that the conclusion of his soliloquy does not call for bloody actions. Instead, he says, "O, from this time forth, /

Honor and the Oedipal urge.

Conclusion: Hamlet's psychological conflicts account for his hesitation.

```
My thoughts be bloody, or nothing
worth!" (65-66) Hamlet's psychologi-
cal conflicts block his action. He
cannot actively seek revenge;
revenge must come to him, and when
it does, his hesitation will be jus-
tified by his own doom.
```

PRACTICING PSYCHOLOGICAL CRITICISM

Freud's theories, as numerous critics have observed, take the male sex as the norm. How does the Oedipus complex apply to little girls? Their first physical pleasure is also contact with the mother; do little girls wish to sleep with their mothers and kill their fathers? Freud was himself mystified by the problem of applying his theories to women, the "dark continent" as he once called them, but he did try to explain how girls passed through the Oedipus complex. Instead of "castration anxiety," which causes the little boy to submit to reality and his father, turning his desires elsewhere, the little girl perceives that she is already "castrated." Is there then no reason that the little girl should turn her affections from her mother? Freud's solution was the notorious concept of "penis envy"—an idea that continues even today to drive people up the wall. The little girl turns to her father, Freud said, because she realizes that her mother also has been "castrated." This envy is hardly as powerful as the fear of castration, it would seem, and Freud did believe that the superego of women was not as powerfully formed as that of men, and that women consequently had weaker ideas of justice and authority. The complementary idea of womb envy apparently did not occur to Freud, but it seems equally if not more plausible.

If this all seems too bizarre, let me briefly suggest once more why I'm bringing this up here. Freud's thinking is the foundation of psychological criticism, and the Oedipus complex is central to Freud. Freud's struggles to make this complex work for little girls resulted in his concept of penis envy. And this concept can be interestingly tested with the following poem.

A Narrow Fellow in the Grass (1866)
Emily Dickinson

A narrow Fellow in the Grass
Occasionally rides—
You may have met Him—did you not
His notice sudden is—

The Grass divides as with a Comb—   5
A spotted shaft is seen—
And then it closes at your feet
And opens further on—

He likes a Boggy Acre
A Floor too cool for Corn—   10
Yet when a Boy, and Barefoot—
I more than once at Noon

Have passed, I thought, a Whip lash
Unbraiding in the Sun
When stooping to secure it   15
It wrinkled, and was gone—

Several of Nature's People
I know, and they know me—
I feel for them a transport
Of cordiality—   20

But never met this Fellow
Attended or alone
Without a tighter breathing
And Zero at the Bone—

Questions

1. This poem was one of the few poems published while Dickinson was alive. It appeared under the title "The

Snake," which was not Dickinson's title, but the addition of an editor. Does that title detract from the poem?

2. Which words in the poem seem odd in the context of a snake?

3. From a Freudian perspective, paraphrase the poem: that is, narrate what happens.

4. Why does Dickinson make the speaker of this poem "a Boy"?

5. What might "Zero at the Bone" mean? What fear or desire might be expressed by this phrase?

O to Be a Dragon (1951)
Marianne Moore

If I, like Solomon, . . .
could have my wish—
my wish . . . O to be a dragon,

a symbol of the power of Heaven—of silkworm
size or immense; at times invisible.   5
Felicitous phenomenon.

Questions

1. Can this poem be related to Dickinson's "narrow Fellow" poem?

2. In what way does a psychological perspective alter your reaction to this poem?

Note

[1] In *An Incomplete Education* Judy Jones and William Wilson compare the id, ego, and superego to Nicholson, Duvall, and Reeve (402).

CHAPTER
7

GENDERING THE TEXT
Feminist Criticism

*I am already performing a
feminine critical act, namely
refusing to speak from a
position of supposed neutral-
ity and pseudoscientific
objectivity.*

—Naomi Schor

THE PURPOSE OF FEMINIST CRITICISM

All criticism has political implications, but feminist criticism is openly political. Like feminism itself, feminist criticism aims to identify and oppose the various ways women are
excluded, suppressed, and exploited. For Jonathan Culler and
others, the task of feminist criticism is even larger. As Culler
puts it, "feminist criticism" is "the name that should be
applied to all criticism alert to the critical ramifications of
sexual oppression, just as in politics 'women's issues' is the
name now applied to many fundamental questions of personal freedom and social justice" (56).

It is possible to resist the premises of feminist criticism.
One can argue, for instance, that Western society has actually
been structured to protect women from the brutalities of war
and commerce, allowing them to be nurturers, mothers, and

homemakers. Rather than exploiting or suppressing women, this line of thinking goes, Western society has celebrated and cherished them. While I have no doubt this idea may be sincerely held, and even to some degree supported, it will not stand up to analysis.

It overlooks the way that insulation and honor are themselves a kind of suppression and exclusion. (If a woman is put on a pedestal, she can't *do* much of anything up there.) And it assumes that women are the weaker sex (emotional, unstable, passive, irrational), needing protection, unable to compete with men. But all women are not weaker than all men in any way. Many women are taller, stronger, smarter, and more aggressive than many men. These qualities are the yardsticks of a man-oriented or patriarchal culture; but even by those values, which may be questioned, generalizations about "men" and "women" are troublesome.

In fact, even dividing humankind into men and women can be problematic since there is no simple genetic or physiological test that will clearly divide all humans into "male" and "female." Determining clear *psychological* differences between the sexes appears to be even more complex and elusive. Although we can articulate certain stereotypical ideas of "masculine" or "feminine" thinking, we could not use these features to sort males and females perfectly—any more than we could use height, or weight, or muscle mass.

Such difficulties have led to the idea that it would be more useful to think of sexuality in terms of a continuum rather than two totally distinct opposites. This idea requires us to distinguish "sex" (the biological status of male and female) from "gender" (our conceptions of "man" and "woman"). As Simone de Beauvoir put it, "One is not born a woman, one becomes one" (301). An individual, in other words, may be born female, but that status does not entail the attributes of "woman" as our culture has defined them. Our conceptions of femininity, Beauvoir is saying, are social constructions that are imposed on individuals. Or, as Thomas Laqueur puts it, in his recent detailed history of the ways we have invented our ideas of gender, sex "is situational; it is explicable only within the context of battles over gender and power" (11); and "two sexes are not the necessary, natural consequence of corporeal difference" (243).

It is always possible that you just don't agree that women have been oppressed and that generalizations based on sexual orientation or gender are dumb. What would be the purpose of feminist criticism for such a person? Can such a non-feminist even do feminist criticism? For that matter, can a man do feminist criticism? At the risk of irritating or even outraging some of my readers, I think the answer is that *anyone* can do feminist criticism—and do it "honestly." One of the wonderful things about words is that we can use them to try out ideas, to speculate, to put on roles and explore. We construct arguments and conduct analyses not only to persuade others but also to investigate things for ourselves—if we have an open, critical mind, that is. Writing is a process of learning.

If you already inhabit a feminist outlook, then applying it to literature may help you understand it better. And if this way of thinking isn't where you find yourself today, it won't hurt you to visit and try to think like a native for a while. You'll enlarge your outlook; you may even decide to stay. At the least you'll have a better understanding of feminist thinking. Your performance as a feminist critic (or any other sort of critic) may be an act, a role you've taken on, but it need not (and ought not) be an *insincere* performance. One can *pretend* to play Macbeth or Willie Loman, or one can sincerely *play* these characters. Your job is to immerse yourself in feminist criticism, genuinely attempting to appreciate its insights, even if you don't finally accept them.

And when is feminist criticism appropriate? It's always a possibility, an available option. The way to see if a feminist approach is appropriate is to try it out. Even if the text isn't obviously dealing with feminist concerns, a feminist approach may be revealing. In fact, the absence of women or their concerns may be quite significant. For some texts, admittedly, a feminist reading may require considerable care and imagination. But, again, the pervasiveness of sexual bias in our society ensures, I would argue, that most texts will readily provide ample materials for a feminist response. Just as we expose the presence of a virus by assuming its existence and then running tests to establish its effects, we ought likewise to assume the existence of bias and prejudice and make efforts to expose its effects. When feminist criticism can find nothing to talk about, when all its tests come out negative, then its work will be done. Then we can assume that traditional literary studies will sufficiently include issues of sex and gender; then we can neglect to consider the implications of our actions in the context of such issues. Then we will live in a very different world.

HOW TO DO FEMINIST CRITICISM

According to Cheryl Torsney, feminist criticism is not a single method, but rather a patchwork or "a quilt" of different methods stitched together with a common conviction: "that one can read, write, and interpret as a woman" (180). This plurality of approaches is one reason that Robert Con Davis says it may well be "that the future of literary studies is being decided in current feminist theory and criticism" (161), as various ways of reading are stitched together, blended, contrasted, and questioned. My survey of critical approaches ends with feminist criticism because it can draw on each of the theories described here, as well as on others. Any act of criticism, to be sure, is likely to draw on various strategies, blending together complementary and sometimes even contradictory assumptions and practices. But feminist criticism is perhaps uniquely positioned to benefit, and benefit from, other approaches.

I'll focus here then on two pervasive concerns of feminist criticism: how women have written, and how women have been written. The first of these concerns deals significantly with the status of women writers, and its most influential formulation is probably Virginia Woolf's *A Room of One's Own*, published in 1929. Woolf's impetus can be seen in her revealing thought experiment: what if, Woolf asks, Shakespeare had

had a sister, equally as brilliant and talented as Shakespeare himself? What would have become of her? She would not have had the same educational opportunities, the same financial independence, the same social freedom or professional access. Obviously, her career would have been strikingly different from Shakespeare's. In fact, Woolf doubts that she would have had a career at all. In "Professions for Women," Woolf explains how her own career has been obstructed by narrow conceptions of womanhood, which offered virtually no role for serious women writers. In calling for "a room of one's own," Woolf is asking for the freedom and the space for all Shakespeare's sisters to speak honestly out of their own experiences, without assuming male pseudonyms or adopting masculine voices.

Some extraordinary women, as Woolf makes clear, somehow did manage to write, and this tradition of women's writing is extremely important because "We think back through our mothers if we are women" (79). Without some sense of these "mothers," the woman writer will be unable to make a creative room of her own, being forced instead to suppress her unique voice and attempt to fit into the mansions of the male tradition. Literary history—a *new* literary history that includes women—thus becomes a vital action, making it possible for women to write as *women*, whatever that means. (For Woolf it appears to have included the freedom to transcend gender.)

The effects of the effort to recover women's writing have been dramatic: most obviously, the canon of honored, "serious" literature has been enlarged to include more works by women (an alternative canon of women's writing has also arisen), and certain genres long considered minor or secondary have received serious attention. Women did write in the major genres (fiction, drama, poetry), but their creative energies also found outlets in letters, journals, diaries, and other long-neglected forms. In recovering this work of their "mothers," feminist critics have often invoked Woolf, attempting to describe the "precious speciality" (in Woolf's words) of this nearly lost tradition of women's writing. For Elaine

Showalter, this engagement with women's writing calls for a "distinctly female vision." In *A Literature of Their Own* (1977), obviously building on Woolf's project, she uses the term "gynocriticism" to refer to this study of women by women.

The second concern has to do with the way women have been written—that is, with the image of women in literature. The most influential work here, without question, is Simone de Beauvoir's *The Second Sex*, published in French in 1949. Beauvoir's point is simple but powerful: females have been depicted in literature and culture as either Mary or Eve, the angelic mother or the evil seductress. Such a representation of women, especially in works by men, serves to make women unreal, other, the absence of maleness, rather than anything positively female or mutually human: it is especially pernicious when it is unnoticed and is perceived to be "natural" or "realistic." The work of the reader, then, is to expose this opposition—misogyny (woman seen as monster) or idealization (woman seen as saint)—thereby undermining its power by exposing its artifice. Notable followers of Beauvoir's tradition include Mary Ellman, whose *Thinking about Women* (1968) argues that gender stereotypes in literature are applied not only to characters but to *everything;* and Sandra Gilbert and Susan Gubar, whose *Madwoman in the Attic* (1979) argues that women writers both accept and reject the angel vs. seductress stereotypes, thereby creating their own distinctive vision.

These two concerns—woman as writer, woman as written—can be illustrated by looking briefly at Mary Astell's *A Serious Proposal to the Ladies,* published in 1692. We should note first that merely reading Astell's work verges on a feminist act. Her *Proposal* certainly has not held a secure place in the traditional canon. In Tillotson, Fussell, and Waingrow's popular *Eighteenth-Century Literature,* published in 1969, Astell's work does not appear (the volume covers 1660–1800). Representative works of some ninety men do appear, spread over 1538 pages. Women writers are virtually ignored: three are represented, occupying less than two pages. Let's recap that score: men—1538; women—1 and a fraction. In John

Mahoney's anthology for the same period, *The Enlightenment and English Literature*, published about eleven years later (1980), we might expect to see more women writers, especially given the surge of interest in feminist criticism in the 1970s. But there are in fact no women at all in Mahoney's anthology.

Such neglect points to the need for alternative collections, such as Sandra Gilbert and Susan Gubar's *Norton Anthology of Literature by Women*, which covers the middle ages (fourteenth century) to the present, and presents fifteen women writers (including Astell) in its eighteenth-century section; or Roger Lonsdale's *Eighteenth-Century Women Poets*, which offers the work of over one hundred women; or Robert Uphaus and Gretchen Foster's *The 'Other' Eigthteenth Century: English Women of Letters*, which presents in some depth the work of twenty-two women, including Astell. But merely offering alternatives to the traditional surveys seems to many people entirely inadequate, leaving the writing of women in a secondary, supplementary position. It is no longer plausible, after the advent of feminist criticism, to argue that women writers are justifiably omitted from the standard anthologies ("the canon") because their writing is inferior to the writing of men. For one thing, women's writing has gone largely unread, even in graduate survey courses, so that even "experts" in eighteenth-century literature may know little about Astell or any other female writer; one cannot say that the writing of men is better without having read the writing of women. For another thing, the standards used to construct "the canon" are the invention of mostly male critics and scholars, who are themselves the product of the exclusion of women: women aren't included now because they haven't been included in the past, and the cycle perpetuates itself. Feminist criticism therefore may show how some works by women meet the traditional standards of excellence, but it may also challenge the arbitrariness of those same patriarchal notions of excellence.

Consider the following two passages from Mary Astell's *Serious Proposal*. In the first Astell announces precisely what her proposal is; in the second she summarizes her plan. As you read these two passages, labeled A and B respectively, pay attention to how women are presented. What images of "woman" do the passages convey? (I have numbered the sentences for easy reference.)

(A)

(1) Now as to the proposal, it is to erect a monastery, or if you will (to avoid giving offence to the scrupulous and injudicious, by names which though innocent in themselves, have been abused by superstitious practices), we will call it a religious retirement, and such as shall have a double aspect, being not only a retreat from the world for those who desire that advantage, but likewise, an institution and previous discipline to fit us to do the greatest good in it; such an institution as this (if I do not mightily deceive my self) would be the most probable method to amend the present, and improve the future age.

(2) You are therefore ladies, invited into a place, where you shall suffer no other confinement, but to be kept out of the road of sin: You shall not be deprived of your grandeur, but only exchange the vain pomps and pageantry of the world, empty titles and forms of state, for the true and solid greatness of being able to despise *them*. . . .
(3) Happy retreat! which will be the introducing you into such a paradise as your mother Eve forfeited, where you shall feast on pleasures, that do not, like those of the world, disappoint your expectations, pall your appetites, and by the disgust they give you put you on the fruitless search after new delights, which when obtained are as empty as the former; but such as will make you truly happy now, and prepare you to be perfectly so hereafter. (4) Here are no serpents to deceive you, whilst you entertain yourselves in these delicious gardens. (5) No provocations will be given in this amicable society, but to love and good works, which will afford such an entertaining employment, that you'll have as little inclination as leisure to pursue those follies, which in the time of your ignorance passed with you under the name of love, although there is not in nature two more different things, than true love and that brutish passion, which pretends to ape it. (6) Here will be no rivalling but for the love of the God, no ambition but to procure his favour, to which nothing will more effectually recommend you, than a great and dear affection to each other.

(B)

(7) The ladies, I'm sure, have no reason to dislike this proposal, but I know not how the men will resent it to have their enclosure broke down, and women invited to taste of that tree of knowledge they have so long unjustly monopolized. (8) But they must excuse me, if I be as partial to my own sex as they are to theirs, and think women as capable of learning as men are, and that it becomes them as well. (9) For I cannot imagine wherein the hurt lies, if instead of doing mischief to one another, by an uncharitable and vain conversation, women be enabled to inform and instruct those of their own sex at least; the holy ghost having left it on record, that Priscilla as well as her husband, catechized the eloquent Apollos and the great Apostle found no fault with her. (10) It will therefore be very proper for our ladies to spend part of their time in this retirement, in adorning their minds with useful knowledge.

Since Astell's "Proposal" is considered a feminist classic, it is interesting to note how she appears to reinforce the idea of women as weak sensualists, daughters of Eve, tending toward sin. Astell tells "the ladies" that their "confinement" will allow them to "be kept out of the road of sin," as if women can resist temptation only if they are removed from it (2). Further, she explicitly links all women to Eve, asserting that this "Happy retreat" will introduce them "into such a paradise as your mother Eve forfeited" (3). Astell's ladies will be able to re-enter or re-create paradise not because they are any stronger or smarter than Eve, the epitome of feminine susceptibility, but because there will be "no serpents to deceive you" in Astell's "Happy retreat" (4).

In addition, the inducements Astell offers "the ladies" are themselves sensual, as if she can tempt them into a second paradise only by promising pleasure—in fact, the same pleasure for which women originally were ejected: in the garden of Eden, it was of course the forbidden fruit from the tree of knowledge that Eve could not resist; in Astell's retreat, women will get to enjoy such fruit once more, being able to *"feast* on pleasures" more durable than those of the world, avoiding "the *fruitless* search after new delights," entertaining themselves in these *"delicious* gardens" of learning (3). Astell seems here to be reinforcing the stereotype that women are controlled by their appetites: to entice them to learn, she discusses knowledge as if it were food—a "delicious" and fruitful "feast." Astell further seems to accept the conventional sexism of depicting women as aesthetic objects, concluding that it is proper for women to be "adorning their minds with useful knowledge" (10)—as if knowledge were valuable as an adornment, an intellectual sort of ribbon or bow to make women more attractive. In consecutive sentences, Astell promises ladies that the retreat will "entertain" (4), providing "entertaining employment" (5), as if women only seek diversion, avoiding diligence.

This reading of Astell's "Proposal" deals admittedly with only a portion of her text, but it could be extended easily, and it illustrates sufficiently, I think, one activity of feminist criticism: exposing stereotypes of women. Although this exposure is often at the expense of male authors, we should not be surprised to find such sexism in Astell's text, despite her place as an early feminist: how could she entirely evade the assumptions of her time? As Janet Todd puts it:

> If 'feminism,' in a 1970s sense, claims absolute equality of the sexes and complex identification of roles, then no women in eighteenth-century England advocated it; if it implies equal opportunity, then probably only Mary Wollstonecraft, who hinted at female politicians while extolling motherhood, might qualify. But if a feminist is one who is aware of female problems and is angry or irritated at the female predicament, then almost every woman writer and many men could claim the title. (qtd. Ruthven 17)

We are all products of our culture, our language, our myths, and our history; therefore attempting to identify the negative or stereotypical images in Astell's work does not constitute an attack on her. The vision of educated women in "A Proposal to the Ladies" *is* extraordinary.

In addition to this negative strategy of unmasking prejudices, feminist criticism also undertakes the positive business of reading women's writings with a particular attentiveness to their difference either from male texts or from the dominant discourse, supposed to be controlled by men, and therefore "patriarchal." Such a recuperative reading of these passages from Astell's "Proposal," rather than targeting the depiction of women, might look more closely at what Astell was attempting to do with these images. How does Astell's own gender affect her discourse and its aim? As a woman, writing in the late seventeenth century, proposing a kind of "monastery" to educate women, Astell addresses her text "A Serious Proposal *to the Ladies*," but any reflection at all must acknowledge that her audience had to include men. It would have been impossible, after all, in her day, to create the sort of institution Astell proposes without the approval and even the active support of men. Astell depicts herself as speaking to "the ladies," but she intends to be overheard by those holding the power. How does this dual audience affect her writing?

The most obvious critical strategy would be to look for contradictions, or for assertions that can be taken two ways, or for two different phrasings of the same assertion, as Astell speaks different things to different audiences with the same text. In fact, it seems reasonable to assume that Astell's position is hardly unique, that other women writers confronted a divided audience. Indeed, for Gilbert and Gubar, a strategy of both conforming to and undermining patriarchal cultural conventions has distinguished women's writing since Jane Austen. Although Astell's work appeared over a century before Austen's, much the same (if not worse) conditions applied.

What examples of a double-voiced discourse do you find in Astell's passages? For a start, we might notice that Astell first says her proposal is to "erect a monastery" for single women, but she quickly alters "monastery" to "religious retirement" (sentence 1). Astell says she makes this change to avoid the prejudice against the term "monastery," which would have linked her project to Catholic monks, who had a reputation in Astell's day, among some anti-Papists anyway, for dabbling in the supernatural ("superstitious practices," as Astell says). But Astell might have used "nunnery" or "priory" instead of "monastery"; so why did she first offer the term associated with monks, then withdraw it? Because, I would argue, "monastery" makes clear to one part of her audience that she is offering them a chance to move into a domain heretofore jealously controlled by men. By saying she wants "to *erect* a monastery," Astell subtly underscores the masculine privilege she wants to usurp. Lest some male readers be threatened by women assuming such erections, Astell immediately portrays her project as a "retreat," a "confinement," a withdrawal into a feminine space, not a masculine intrusion. But the empowering potential of the retreat's "delicious gardens" has already been indicated to Astell's discerning reader.

Having glimpsed this potential power, the ladies, Astell says in the second passage, will "have no reason to dislike this proposal." But, she continues, "I know not how the men will resent it to have their enclosure broke down, and women invited to taste of that tree of knowledge they have so long unjustly monopolized" (7). Earlier, Astell has taken pains to make sure her proposal is not seen as an invasion, but rather a retirement. And in the body of her proposal, Astell has repeatedly limited the ambition of her idea, making it less threatening to men: she does not believe a woman needs to study "languages" as diligently as men, but only as "are necessary to acquaint her with useful authors"; she does not desire "that women should teach in the church, or usurp authority where it is not allowed them," but only that they be allowed "to understand our duty, and not be forced to take it upon trust for others" (page 116). But this subsequent image reverses the earlier one of "retreat": instead of the women confining themselves, they will be *breaking down* the "enclosure" of the men. If this proposal describes a retreat, it is a retreat into the intellectual space already occupied by men.

Likewise, although Astell has repeatedly alluded to Eve's weakness, confirming the patriarchal myth of mankind's fall, and thus reassuring part of her readers that she understands the dangerous and sinful nature of women, her concluding reference to the Genesis story also reverses the implications of the earlier allusions. Somehow Eve's disastrous deed, tasting the fruit from the forbidden tree of knowledge, has become precisely the activity that men have "so long unjustly monopolized" (7). Although Astell has appeared to reinforce the male-oriented view of the fall of "man," this version of the story now becomes problematic: men have been zealously indulging in the same activity for which Eve has been unceasingly castigated. How can "tasting" of the tree of knowledge be considered evil? Isn't knowledge good? Why have men monopolized it?

Astell thus shrewdly intimates that men—with God-like presumption—have built their own paradise or "enclosure," eating from the tree of knowledge themselves, while forbidding women to partake. Despite her earlier concessions to the limited ambition of women's learning, Astell's position in the later passage is much bolder, asserting that women are "as capable of learning as men are, and that it becomes them as well" (8). This radical position is balanced, but not obscured, by Astell's more modest stances earlier. But even these earlier references to the weakness of women can be played two ways.

For instance, when Astell points out to the ladies that her "Happy retreat" will be "introducing you into such a paradise as your mother Eve forfeited" (3), she appears to be acknowledging woman's sinful nature and offering a chance to undo the Fall. But there is a dramatic difference between these first and second paradises: no Adam will inhabit Astell's, for it will include single women only. This lack of men does not appear in the least to be a deterrent to the ladies' happiness; on the contrary, Astell's retreat will allow women to avoid "that brutish passion, which pretends to ape" true love. Instead of the love of men, which Astell suggests is animalistic, simian even, she holds out the promise of the ladies' "great and dear affection to each other" (6). The positive significance of this male absence is rather subtly conveyed by what must be seen as the most appealing aspect of this second paradise: "Here are no serpents to deceive you, whilst you entertain your selves in these delicious gardens." A single serpent ruined the first paradise for Eve (and the rest of us); but in pointing to this crucial difference, Astell uses the plural "serpents." Given the phallic symbolism of serpents, we can easily conclude that Astell is talking about bipedal serpents—the same ones who have now enclosed the tree of knowledge (which women had the courage to eat from!), keeping women out.

In this case, as I have read these passages, the negative view of women that emerges in one sort of feminist criticism (woman as written), becomes part of a positive strategy in the other kind (woman as writer).

THE WRITING PROCESS: A SAMPLE ESSAY

Let's see what opportunities a feminist approach affords a reader of the following poem, written by Samuel Johnson in 1746, about fifty years after Astell's proposal. Although he was struggling to make his reputation in 1746, Johnson would go on to become arguably the eighteenth century's greatest and most versatile writer, the second-most quoted author in our language (behind only Shakespeare).

Before you read the poem, it may be be helpful to know (if you don't already) that "Stella" was often used in eighteenth-century poetry as a kind of generic name for a beautiful, youthful, charming woman. Likewise, "nymph" in this period also usually refers to such a woman, although the word literally means, in Greek and Roman mythology, a female spirit that inhabits and somehow embodies a feature of nature. (For instance, there might be a nymph of the Ohio River, who would be the spirit of the river, standing for it and living somehow "in" it.) So a nymph or a Stella would be a beautiful woman that one could imagine being part of a lovely rural setting. "Stella" and "nymph" in this poem refer, it seems clear, to the "Miss _____" of the title. And this person seems, at some point anyway, to have been a real person: when the poem first appeared, its title was "To the Honble [short for "Honorable"] Miss Carpenter," who was Alicia Maria Carpenter, daughter of Lord Carpenter. A manuscript has the same title. But Anna Williams reprinted the poem in her *Miscellanies* with the current title; and since Johnson presumably assisted Williams with her collection of poems (Williams was a blind poet, given lodging and support by Johnson), it is likely he made or approved of the change.

Now read the poem several times, noting your reactions and questions on paper.

To Miss _____ On Her Playing upon the Harpsichord In a Room Hung with Some Flower-pieces of Her Own Painting (1746)
Samuel Johnson

When Stella strikes the tuneful string
In scenes of imitated spring,
Where beauty lavishes her pow'rs
On beds of never-fading flow'rs,
And pleasure propagates around   5
Each charm of modulated sound,
Ah! think not, in the dang'rous hour,
The nymph fictitious, as the flow'r,
But shun, rash youth, the gay alcove,
Nor tempt the snares of wily love.   10
    When charms thus press on ev'ry sense,
What thought of flight, or of defence?
Deceitful Hope, and vain Desire,
For ever flutter o'er her lyre,
Delighting, as the youth draws nigh,   15
To point the glances of her eye,
And forming, with unerring art,
New chains to hold the captive heart.
    But on these regions of delight,
Might Truth intrude with daring flight,   20
Could Stella, sprightly, fair and young,
One moment hear the moral song,
Instruction with her flow'rs might spring,
And wisdom warble from her string.
    Mark, when from the thousand mingled dyes   25
Thou see'st one pleasing form arise,
How active light, and thoughtful shade,
In greater scenes each other aid;
Mark, when the diff'rent notes agree
In friendly contrariety,   30
How passion's well-accorded strife
Gives all the harmony of life.
Thy pictures shall thy conduct frame,
Consistent still, though not the same;
Thy musick teach the nobler art   35
To tune the regulated heart.

Preparing to Respond

After you've invested some effort in the poem, becoming familiar with it, compare the results of your reading to my own, printed below. The numbers in my notes refer to the line numbers of the poem.

> READING NOTES ON "TO MISS _____"
>
> Line 1: "strikes the tuneful string"? I suppose this means her playing upon the harpsichord.
>
> Line 2: "In scenes of imitated spring"? What does this mean? It must refer to her paintings of "some flower-pieces," which would be an "imitated" spring.
>
> Line 4: "never-fading flow'rs"—because they're painted, not real.
>
> Lines 7–8: The warning here seems odd: "think not ... / The nymph fictitious, as the flow'r," as if someone couldn't tell the difference between a girl playing the harpsichord and a painting! There must be something else going on here.
>
> And why is this hour dangerous? Because of "the snares of wily love" (line 10). The speaker is afraid he will fall for the nymph if he doesn't watch out. Or, rather, he's afraid the "rash youth" (line 9) will fall. Is he the rash youth?
>
> Lines 11–18: This section makes clear that the speaker fears the effect of Stella upon the youth. Her artistry will capture him if he is not careful, creating "New chains to hold the captive heart."
>
> Lines 19–24: In this section the speaker points out that the tremendous power Stella has to take prisoners might also be used for good: "Instruction" might come from her painting (line 23); "wisdom" might come from her music (line 24). To get these benefits, "Truth" will have to "intrude with daring

flight" into "these regions of delight." What does
this mean? That her art and music will have to do
more than just give pleasure, or seduce the affections of rash youths. Stella herself will have to
"hear the moral song" if her charms are to have
some useful purpose.

Lines 25–34: We're told to "mark," or take note of,
the way painting works, and then the way music
works. Specifically, we're told to notice how all
the different "mingled" colors come together to
make "one pleasing form," and how all the
"diff'rent notes" come together in "friendly contrariety."

Lines 35–36: I think these lines make clear why we are
instructed to "mark" how conflicting dyes and notes
come together in harmony. The speaker is most concerned earlier in the poem by the charms of
Stella's music and painting, which could make a
"captive" of the "rash youth." These charms could
be the forces for good, however, as the third section asserts. This fourth section then explains how
harmony comes from contrariety. So what is the
"contrariety" here? The speaker wants Stella's
pleasure to be opposed or complemented or completed
by instruction. The sensual indulgence of her art
will serve some higher purpose if her painting
could "thy conduct frame," and her music could
"tune the regulated heart."

Who is "thy" is these closing lines? Stella? The
youth? The speaker? The reader? My guess would be
all of the above. Stella is being addressed—the
poem is "To" her after all, which might mean "in
honor of" or "to be sent to." But other readers
clearly are meant to overhear, or "oversee" the
advice, especially the rash youth, perhaps Johnson
himself.

Now we want to evolve a feminist reading of the poem.

Johnson is not, I think it's safe to say, a neglected woman writer, and so the feminist approach that seems most promising here would focus on the following questions:

- What role does sex or gender play in this work?
- What image of women is conveyed by the poem?
- How is the relationship between men and women depicted?

Some material toward answering these questions is already beginning to appear, I think, in my notes above: the speaker of the poem clearly sees Stella, or her charms, or the charms of her music and painting, as "dang'rous"; and Stella is encouraged to add Truth and Instruction to the pleasures of her charming arts. The next step will be to identify materials that will allow me to address the questions above, and then to think about the audience I'm trying to reach, and what I'm trying to accomplish. Feminist criticism characteristically tries to intervene in the ongoing traditional discussion. How can a feminist perspective on this poem affect our thinking?

Before you look at my annotations starting on the following page, I encourage you to look at the poem again yourself, then compare my notes to your own.

Shaping

My first impression had been that the poem celebrated Stella's (or Alicia Carpenter's) artistic and musical talents, and encouraged her to add instruction and virtue to those charms. Focusing on a feminist stance altered my own view, and what emerged here for me was the speaker's unrelenting vision of Stella as a threat. As I continued to re-read the poem, I was surprised by the intensity of the speaker's fear: what is so threatening about a young lady playing a harpsichord in a room with some her paintings? The declared danger is her effect on the youth—love, or infatuation, or lust, which becomes some sort of loss of independence and autonomy. Everything I saw as I annotated seemed aimed at one

To Miss _____ On Her Playing upon the Harpsichord *→ Art, charm, seduction*

In a Room Hung with Some Flower-pieces of Her Own Painting

When Stella strikes the tuneful string

In scenes of imitated spring, *— Not real*

Where beauty lavishes her pow'rs *Excessive, unnatural*

On beds of never-fading flow'rs,

pleasure is O.K., but it shd. be so promiscuous? And pleasure propagates around

Each charm of modulated sound, *Charm*

Ah! think not, in the dang'rous hour, *The danger? Falling in love or lust.*

The nymph fictitious, as the flow'r

But shun, rash youth, the gay alcove, *stay in the open.*

Nor tempt the snares of wily love. *As if she is going to trap him like an animal.*

When charms thus press on ev'ry sense,

What thought of flight, or of defence?

Deceitful Hope, and vain Desire, *overwhelming*

Eve For ever flutter o'er her lyre,

Delighting, as the youth draws nigh,

To point the glances of her eye,

And forming, with unerring art,

Art vs. Nature (Art — bad)

New chains to hold the captive heart.   *Love = Prison*

Like a decadent red-light district?

But on these regions of delight,

Might Truth intrude with daring flight,   *Truth = Nature = Moral*

Could Stella, sprightly, fair and young,

One moment hear the moral song,   *Her lust song vs. moral song.*

Instruction with her flow'rs might spring,

And wisdom warble from her string.

Mark, when from the thousand mingled dyes   *Not real*

Thou see'st one pleasing form arise,

How active light, and thoughtful shade,

In greater scenes each other aid;

Mark, when the diff'rent notes agree   *Mix art with nature. Dangerous, unstable balance?*

In friendly contrariety,

How passion's well-accorded strife

Gives all the harmony of life.

Thy pictures shall thy conduct frame,

Consistent still, though not the same;

Thy musick teach the nobler art   *Impose order on her unfettered, dangerous art*

Tune = art. Art to tame art?

To tune the regulated heart.

thing: neutralizing, controlling, managing somehow the tremendous feminine power that Stella's charms represent—the power to enchain the heart of any rash youth, which certainly must include the speaker, who (I can't help suspecting) may be Johnson himself.

My goal at this point is beginning to emerge, as I realize that I want my audience to see that Johnson's overt morality may be something more oppressive: the poem aims to control "Stella," or get her to control herself; and the reason for this effort is precisely that the speaker fears he cannot control himself. It is not imperative to bring Adam and Eve into the discussion, but the poem does seem to re-play that enduring story: woman as temptation, who causes man to fall. In other words, the poem seems to demonstrate once more Simone de Beauvior's thesis that women tend to be presented as Eve or Mary, evil temptress or virginal saint. I imagined an audience that might think I'm making too much out of this—seeing something sinister when it's just a poem about self-control; so I planned to try to anticipate this reaction and provide careful, balanced support.

I jotted down my supporting ideas and played around with them until some logical progression began to emerge. Here is the order I came up with (the items may make more sense when you see them in my draft essay):

1. Erasing Miss _____ 's name: the title

2. Thesis: Johnson aims to blank out women's sensuality and danger

3. Johnson's audience: Miss _____ ostensibly, but really a warning to the youth; to the reader; ultimately to Johnson himself

4. Surface message to "Stella": include instruction/wisdom

5. Restrictive actions become clearer in the end: to tune and to frame

6. Stella as danger: sensual enslavement ("Chains")

7. Sensual disorientation—what is real?

8. Promiscuity (woman as potentially uncontrol-
   lable desire):
     painting "lavishes" on "beds"
     music "propagates"

9. Stella is not real—a fiction: the speaker as
   confused as the youth

10. "Truth" called in: regulate Stella's art

11. Add instruction to pleasure

12. Morality for the youth's benefit, not hers

13. Identity: Limit hers to save his

Drafting

The next step was to transform my individual ideas and
annotated poem into a rough draft, which I could then revise
and polish. This step, as always, takes some time and
patience; but if you're sufficiently prepared and you have
adequate time, it has its substantial satisfactions. You may
want to sketch out your own essay before you look at mine.

BEWARE OF WOMEN WITH HARPSICHORDS
AND PAINTINGS: ON SAMUEL JOHNSON'S
MISOGYNY

Introduces the poem
and the problem: the
erasure of "Miss
Carpenter."

The title to one of Samuel
Johnson's occasional poems is perhaps most revealing in what it
leaves out: "To Miss _____ On
Her Playing upon the Harpsichord, In
a Room Hung with Some Flower-pieces
of Her Own Painting." Why has the
woman's name become a blank, especially since "Stella" appears in the
first line, and since the poem was
originally addressed "To the Honble
Miss Carpenter" (the "honourable"
Alicia Maria Carpenter, daughter of
the second Lord Carpenter)? Why has
Johnson erased Miss Carpenter and

ignored "Stella," presumably his
pseudonym for her? (The poem
appeared first in Dodsley's *Museum*
in November of 1746; it was reprinted with the altered title in a collection "edited" by Johnson's
friend, Anna Williams, who was
blind, and who relied heavily on
Johnson's assistance. I am assuming
Johnson is responsible for the title
change.)

Thesis: the poem
is about the threat
of women (women
as Eve).

This paper argues that Johnson
has removed Miss Carpenter's name
because the poem really is about the
threat that women pose and the need
to blank them out, erase them, neu-
tralize them, render them less dangerous. Although the poem is
addressed "To Miss _____," its
more urgent message is directed at
another audience, the unnamed "rash
youth" in the poem, who stands for
anyone like the speaker, like
Johnson, who is foolish enough to go
near a woman with a harpsichord and
some paintings—or any other props
for that matter.

The surface reading:
set-up for what fol-
lows.

The poem, to be sure, may appear
on a superficial reading to be nothing more than advice to a young
artist and musician, encouraging her
to include instruction in her per-
formances, adding morality, virtue,
"Truth," to the pleasures of her
forms and harmonies. The poem's conclusion summarizes this surface message:

Thy pictures shall thy conduct
    frame,
Consistent still, though not the
    same;
Thy musick teach the nobler art
To tune the regulated heart.
(33-36)

The frame as
containment

But why, we must ask, does
Johnson (or the speaker) believe
that Stella's "conduct" needs a
"frame"? Why does her heart need to
be tuned and "regulated"? Although
framing and tuning are laudable when
applied to music or art, Stella is
not a painting or a song, and
Johnson's conclusion makes her an
object and expresses a criticism:
Stella needs to be closed in, limited, set apart (framed); she needs to
be standardized, fixed, corrected
(tuned). And the reason for this
discipline and confinement is, quite
simply, she is "dang'rous" (7).

Sexuality is
dangerous.

The danger, specifically, is that
Stella threatens to enslave any
"rash youth" with her art, both
aural and visual, forming "New
chains to hold the captive heart"
(18). Her "unerring" art, Johnson
says, is so powerful that the poor
youth is totally disoriented in the
poem's first section, unable to tell
what is real and what isn't: the
flowers, Johnson feels compelled to
tell the youth, are not real; the
woman is. The point seems absurd
(imagine telling someone this),

until we realize exactly what the threat of "the dang'rous hour" is: it is sexuality, sensuousness, passion, "wily love"; and these entities are so powerful that they make truth and fiction run together.

But the distinction between the woman and her art is crucial. Her art is promiscuous and enduring: her painting "lavishes her pow'rs / On beds of never-fading flow'rs"; "pleasure propagates around" with her music, indiscriminately pleasing all. But the youth should not confuse the painted beds or melodious propagation with real beds, real propagation: the woman is not a fiction or a fantasy, receptive to his "Hope" or "Desire" (13)—his "Deceitful Hope, and vain Desire." But the speaker, like the rash youth, is having trouble seeing what is real: "Stella," after all, is not the woman's name. She is the speaker's creation. The reality is that her "charms," which "press on ev'ry sense" at the moment, cannot be totally framed or regulated because the speaker and the youth participate in their perception. And because Stella, the "real" Stella, cannot be possessed, the overwhelming hope and desire that she stirs up become dangerous, threatening to engulf the identity of the youth, who will become simply the one who hopes and desires, the victim of his own imagination.

Imagination is
dangerous.

Conclusion: Miss
Carpenter must be
contained and blanked
out by the poem;
women are dangerous.

Rather than give in to the illu-
sory "regions of delight," Johnson
calls in the pleasure police—
"Truth," who will supposedly rein in
"Stella, sprightly, fair, and young"
by exposing the artificiality of her
charms. Sensual indulgence, Johnson
asserts, should be neutralized by
"friendly contrariety," as reason
cancels out passion. The act of
removing "Miss Carpenter" from the
poem, then, leaving an empty space,
is simply the logical extension of
Johnson's effort to frame, regulate,
abstract, and oppose the passion of
women. Since the youth cannot control his imagination and desire,
losing his ability to tell truth
from art, then Stella must restrain
her art. To save his identity, the
poem takes away hers.

Revision: Gay and Lesbian Criticism

Earlier I referred to Jonathan Culler's assertion that
"feminist criticism" is "the name that should be applied to all
criticism alert to the critical ramifications of sexual oppression" (56). Certainly the forms of "sexual oppression" in our
society are more varied than this chapter has acknowledged
so far, and we might expand our consideration here to
include gay and lesbian studies, which have made impressive
contributions to the study of the literature in the past two
decades.

If we consider my own draft above, it seems clear that I
have made a revealing and unwarranted assumption: the
"rash youth," I have taken for granted, is a male. Specifically,
I have assumed that the youth is a heterosexual male enam-
ored of the presumably heterosexual Stella. But the sex of the
youth, as you may have noticed, is actually nowhere indi-

cated in the poem. If it is sexist to use "he" to refer to men and women (and it clearly is), then it's similarly heterosexist to assume that undesignated romantic or sexual relationships always refer to heterosexual couples, isn't it? Johnson doesn't make the sex of the rash youth clear, and he therefore opens up various other readings. Consider for a moment how the possibility that the youth is female might alter or further expand our reading of the poem.

For instance: the poem's caution against "pleasure" might immediately take on a different hue, for the "dang'rous hour" might be the one in which the youth is tempted to fall in love with another woman. And the odd injunction, "think not . . . / The nymph fictitious, as the flow'r" makes considerable sense, as the speaker warns the youth not to imagine that the nymph would be receptive to a lesbian encounter; or (alternatively) the speaker warns the youth not to imagine that the nymph is actually a man. The nymph is not "fictitious"; she is only what she appears to be, and falling in love with her would be disastrous for the female "youth," lesbian or not. Even though "charms thus press on ev'ry sense," the youth is being advised to resist these "New chains."

More specific is the warning to "shun, rash youth, the gay alcove, / Nor tempt the snares of wily love." An alcove is "a small, recessed section of a room, a nook" (*Webster's*)—or in other words, a closet. If "gay" had meant "homosexual" in Johnson's day (it apparently did not), then avoid "the gay alcove" would mean shun "the gay closet"—avoid being a hidden homosexual. For modern readers, "gay alcove" does suggest such a meaning, which it is difficult (for some readers anyway) to erase from the poem. Further, it would be difficult to say with certainty that "gay alcove" could not possibly have suggested to Johnson, extremely sensitive to connotations, the great lexicographer, something of its future meaning. (For a similarly anachronistic reading of "gay" in Alexander Pope's poetry, see Atkins, 124.)

Even "wily love" covertly suggests the danger of the "snares" of lesbianism, since "wily" has the same root word, *wigle* (Old English), as "witch." At least, we can now see better the point of the poem's conclusion, advocating "diff'rent notes," "friendly contrariety," and "well-accorded strife": Johnson's heterosexism urges us to endorse "difference" in love, attacking (in rather cloaked terms) same-sex love, which belongs in a closet we shouldn't enter.

The reading I have sketched here is obviously only one possibility—a rather daring one in fact. I can also see an entirely different reading in which the youth is a gay man, and "shun the gay alcove" means "stay out of the closet; accept your sexuality."

Feminist, gay, and lesbian approaches have much in common and often appear in alliance. Their shared aim is to expose stereotypes and fight prejudice, dismantling oppressive ideas of two natural sexes or genders, uniformly opposed and attracted. The question whether homosexuality represents a choice or a destiny, a matter of preference or biology, is finally irrelevant to the more fundamental question of freedom and tolerance.

PRACTICING FEMINIST CRITICISM

I hope at this point you have some idea of the way feminist criticism can make writing about literature more interesting and revealing. More importantly, I hope you can see how doing feminist criticism involves you in an important exploration of our culture and your own principles. After feminist criticism, it is especially difficult to say that the study of literature has no real relation to our lives. Literature is a particularly revealing and influential part of the myriad culture that surrounds and shapes (with or without our compliance or resistance) you and me. Feminist criticism can help us see that, and perhaps do something about it.

As I've suggested above, feminist criticism can be applied (at least in theory) to any work—including not just "great" novels or poems or plays, but also television shows, movies, detective stories, science fiction, advertisements, greeting card verse, bumper stickers, whatever. To get you started (if you're not already) as a practicing feminist critic, I've provided below two well-known poems. Each responds richly, I think, to a feminist persective, and I offer some questions after each poem that I hope will stimulate your thinking in that direction.

Shall I Compare Thee to a Summer's Day? (1609)
William Shakespeare

Shall I compare thee to a summer's day?
Thou art more lovely and more temperate.
Rough winds do shake the darling buds of May,
And summer's lease hath all too short a date.
Sometimes too hot the eye of heaven shines,   5
And often is his gold complexion dimmed;
And every fair from fair sometimes declines,
By chance, or nature's changing course, untrimmed.
But thy eternal summer shall not fade,
Nor lose possession of that fair thou ow'st;   10
Nor shall death brag thou wand'rest in his shade,
When in eternal lines to time thou grow'st.
    So long as men can breathe or eyes can see,
    So long lives this, and this gives life to thee.

Questions

1. The poem aims to be flattering, it seems clear, but what is the basis of its flattery? That is, what does the speaker value?

2. It is usually assumed that this poem is addressed to a woman. Is there any support for this supposition in the poem itself? What is the sex of the speaker of the poem? Do these questions alter your perception of the poem, or open up alternative readings?

3. If the loved one is a woman, how does this poem reinforce conventional ideas about aging and beauty? How is a person not like a summer's day?

4. How comforting would the final couplet be to the person addressed? What is the source of the loved one's immortality? Who has the power? How does the poem reinforce this power?

My Life had stood—a Loaded Gun (1863?)
  Emily Dickinson

My Life had stood—a Loaded Gun—
In Corners—till a Day
The Owner passed—identified—
And carried Me away—

And now We roam in Sovereign Woods—   5
And now We hunt the Doe—
And every time I speak for Him—
The Mountains straight reply—

And do I smile, such cordial light
Upon the Valley glow—   10
It is as a Vesuvian face
Had let its pleasure through—

And when at Night—Our good Day done—
I guard My Master's Head—
`Tis better than the Eider-Duck's   15
Deep Pillow—to have shared—

To foe of His—I'm deadly foe—
None stir the second time—
On whom I lay a Yellow Eye—
Or an emphatic Thumb—   20

Though I than He—may longer live
He longer must—than I—
For I have had the power to kill,
Without—the power to die—

Questions

1. What is "Vesuvian"? (You'll find a dictionary helpful.)
   What is an "Eider-duck"? What is the "Yellow Eye"?
   What do you think the "emphatic Thumb" might be?
2. Assuming the speaker is female, what is the significance of comparing her life to a loaded gun. How does
   she view herself? Does the speaker have any autonomy
   or independence?

3. What is implied about the relationship of men to women? Who has the power? What kind of power?

4. What is the source of the speaker's pleasure, do you think?

5. How would the poem change if the speaker were assumed to be male? How would the central metaphor, for instance, be affected?

6. How does the final stanza reinforce conventional or archaic ideas about women and their relationship to men?

7. Does the speaker have any autonomy or independence?

CHAPTER
8

INVESTIGATING THE WORK
Research and Documentation

But the whole thing, after all,
may be put very simply. I
believe that it is better to tell
the truth than to lie. I believe
that it is better to be free than
to be a slave. And I believe
that it is better to know than
to be ignorant.

—H. L. Mencken

You are free to walk into any one of thousands of libraries, seeking the truth about whatever you wish, dispelling the mists and fogs of ignorance. In the history of civilization, at no time or place, have so many people had such a freedom and privilege.

To help students learn how to use the resources of modern libraries, introductory literature courses often include a research paper, requiring you to investigate secondary materials and incorporate them into a paper. No matter what theoretical stance you employ, even a New Critical or a subjective reader-response stance, research can enrich your reading and indeed your life. So, although some strategies of documentation and research have appeared previously in this book, this chapter focuses directly on research papers, offering advice on how to do them, taking you through the process of writing one.

To help you focus on the techniques and conventions involved, I've decided to have the sample paper deal with Yeats's "Sailing to Byzantium," which was discussed in the chapter on deconstruction above. (You might want to refresh your memory of Yeats's poem at this point.) The topic of the model paper deals with a variety of critical theories, so again you'll be getting some reinforcement here. What is different about this chapter, then, is simply the explicit coverage of how to bring research and documentation into your writing about literature.

THE PURPOSES OF RESEARCH

If Yeats's poem is the focus of your essay, then it is the "primary source." That's the work that is the object of attention, and for most research papers the primary source will be a literary work—a poem, a story, a play, or perhaps an essay. But the primary source could conceivably be anything—a biography, a history, a work of science, an advertisement, even a critical work. Secondary sources are the materials consulted to shed light on the primary source. The secondary sources, in other words, are what other people have said about the work, along with any other documents you think useful and relevant. And how will you determine which secondary sources are useful and relevant? By thinking about your purpose. There are two reasons for using secondary sources: to evolve and support your argument, and to suggest the significance of your argument.

Evolving and Supporting Your Argument

Whether you are assigned a topic, or develop one yourself, a research essay will involve you in an argument. You may do research in order to discover what the issues are and where you stand; but even if the assignment essentially asks you to amass information on a particular topic, your discussion is implicitly an argument because you are claiming that *this* is the relevant information, and that you have organized and reported it accurately. Even an informational essay, in other words, will be held together by a controlling idea.

For instance, say you're given this (pretty awful) assignment:

> In a formal research paper, using at least five different sources, provide your classmates with information about Yeats's life around the time he is writing "Sailing to Byzantium." Limit your paper to about eight pages, including documentation.

The assignment doesn't ask you to relate the biographical information to the poem, only to provide information about Yeats's life around the time of the poem. You could argue that the assignment implies the facts should relate somehow to the poem. But it would be best with such an assignment to ask for clarification. Certainly you can't present every fact we know about Yeats's life and time. Where would you stop? Is the architecture of his home relevant? Is his diet significant? What about world events? Was Yeats even interested in world events?

Often (fortunately) the assignment for a research paper will be more like this:

> In a formal research paper, using at least five different sources, discuss how Yeats's life helps us to understand "Sailing to Byzantium."

Here of course you're being asked to do biographical criticism, interpreting the poem using secondary sources. Not only must you locate and organize and present relevant facts, you've got to use them to read the poem.

Suggesting the Significance of Your Argument

If there is published criticism on the primary work, you'll want to consult as much as possible (I'll cover in a moment how you can find such criticism). For some works, like "Sailing," you probably won't be able to read more than a fraction of what has been said. But the more you read, the more you will know even about those secondary works you haven't read. Critical discussion of a work is like a conversation. You can often listen carefully at various points and have a pretty good idea what has already been said. In the conversation some sources are mentioned again and again, and so these clearly are things you'll most want to try to see.

Getting some idea what has already been said does two things. Ideas of your own may be sparked; and you can also place your ideas within the context of what others have said. The reader will be interested in knowing if your interpretation of the poem is totally different from what anyone has said, or if it is similar to the mainstream reading, or if it falls into one of several camps. In the process, you'll be convincing your readers that you're informed.

Thus, in any case, your research paper is not simply a string of quotations and paraphrases: it is an argument, and your voice, your posture, and your presentation are very important. The critics and documents that you bring on stage are there to support and illuminate *your* discussion. It's absolutely crucial, then, that your reader is able instantly to sort out which ideas are yours and which have some other source.

To illustrate appropriate referencing, I'm going to show you some examples. First, let's imagine that you notice and copy the following passage from pages 171–72 of a secondary source, Albert Ketcheman's *William Butler Yeats:*

> And the poems, even the most crucial one, "Sailing to Byzantium," are clear enough. The reader's only real problem in that poem is to see why Byzantium itself was so attractive to Yeats.

You also copy down another passage, this one from page 199 of Clark's *Yeats:*

> The movement of "Sailing to Byzantium" is quite clear, and so are its essential terms. The poem begins with the familiar lament for lost bodily vigor and sexuality, a regret not overcome by the compensating

> sense of increased wisdom, a Yeatsian obsession which, in the earlier fragment, is exceedingly blunt.

Now, imagine that you write the following sentence in your paper:

> 1. Some critics might think that "Sailing to Byzantium" is quite clear, but at least three terms in the poem are ambiguous.

In this passage the critical context is vaguely presented, and it is not clear that the assertion of ambiguity is your own idea. This isn't a very fair or helpful reference. So you revise the sentence, coming up with this more explicit statement:

> 2. Ketcheman says "Sailing to Byzantium" is "clear enough" (171), and Clark says its "movement" and "essential terms" are "quite clear" (199), but at least three terms in the poem are ambiguous.

This version is better, but the significance of your assertion is still not directly stated. It's not really clear who says that three terms are ambiguous. Here's another revision:

> 3. Typical opinions are offered by Ketcheman, who says "Sailing to Byzantium" is "clear enough" (171), and by Clark, who says its "movement" and "essential terms" are "quite clear" (199). I find, however, at least three terms that these critics explain in contradictory terms, and which remain ambiguous and puzzling.

In this version both the critical context and your place within that context are made clear. There's no question who's saying what.

HOW TO DO RESEARCH

Selecting (or Being Selected by) the Topic

What resources you will need depends on your topic. What task are you trying to accomplish? If you're generating your own topic, the invention strategies for a research paper are pretty much the same as for an undocumented essay. In other words, your best route to a good topic is writing: asking yourself questions, adopting any of the various critical stances, looking at various elements of the work. The difference is that you have resources to consult, and reading the published criticism and other secondary sources will certainly help you refine your topic.

Whatever you do, if you have a choice in the matter, don't (as some guides suggest) settle firmly on your topic before you start your research. Instead, stay flexible and let your topic evolve as you work. Likewise, as you draft your essay, you want your topic to be focused, but I don't believe you necessarily have to "narrow" your topic. The scope of the topic should depend on the resources and your ambition. You probably can't do an analysis of all of Yeats's works, but you could take a poem from the beginning, middle, and end, and offer some speculations about his career. You probably can't provide a survey of all the scholarship on Yeats, but you could select three different articles and suggest some of the variety of the work.

The best guide to whether the topic is workable is your teacher. Seek out his or her feedback early on and throughout the process.

Into the Library

It's absolutely crucial that you get to the library as soon as possible. Some students put off going to the library because they're afraid they'll get lost or won't know how to find things. But that's the whole point: of course you'll get lost, and of course you don't know how to find things. I've spent many hours prowling the stacks of many libraries, and I've yet to see the bleached bones of a lost student. You will get lost but you'll find your way around eventually, and you'll run into who knows what adventures in the meantime; you won't know where things are, but you'll find them, if they can be found. The sooner you get started, the more time you'll have to process the materials you do find, and to track down those you can't immediately locate.

After you get yourself to the library (the most important step), the next most important thing to remember is this: the reference librarian can walk on water, see into the future, and tell you how to find anything. Reference librarians are paid to help patrons find things, so ask them whenever you need help. Obviously they can't do your research; but you'll likely be amazed by the search strategies they can recommend.

Strategic Browsing

My own favorite research strategy at the beginning of a project is what I think of as strategic browsing. First I go to the card catalogue (which may be on computer) and find out the call numbers for a few books about the author or subject I'm working on. Then I go into "the stacks" and find those books. They'll be shelved with similar books, and so I can start browsing. I look for extremely worn books, which means they're probably important, and for rather new books, which means the references to other works should be fairly up-to-date. I look at the tables of contents and in the indexes of the books I've picked up, and I skim material that seems promising. I carry notecards with me, and I make a card for the most promising sources I turn up.

Sometimes I don't put down all the information on a particular source, and this omission usually causes me aggravation later. So, when you turn up a source, make a card that will allow you not only to find it, but also to use the card to make your bibliography (in case you return the book before you do the bibliography). For a book, list the author, title, publisher, place of publication, date, and page numbers (if appropriate). For a journal article, list the author, title, name of the journal, date of publication, volume number, and page numbers. An example of each appears on the following page.

Background Sources

Another good first step is to do some focused background reading. Encyclopaedias can provide you with basic information. The *Encyclopaedia Brittanica* is especially helpful, and *The Reader's Encyclopedia* has information on characters,

Jay, Gregory. <u>America
the Scrivener.</u>
Ithaca: Cornell
UP, 1990.

Thesing, William. "The
Inevitable Demise of
Victorian Scholarship."
<u>Victorian Studies</u> 87
(May 1990): 43-113.

authors, books, and terms. You can also find useful introductions to authors and works in *The Oxford Companion to English Literature* and *The Oxford Companion to American Literature*. These and other works will be in the reference area of your library. You won't want to cite general sources in your paper usually: they're just part of your preliminary research, providing you with whatever is common knowledge. (And as a rule, "common knowledge" does not require documentation, even if it's news to you, unless you use the words or phrasing of the original. When in doubt, ask your teacher or do the documentation.)

Bibliographies and Indexes

I'll mention here just some of the lists of books and articles. One of the most valuable is the *MLA International Bibliography*, which appears annually, providing a comprehensive list of scholarship for the preceding year. It lists the articles and books published on a particular author or subject during the indexed year. (Authors are listed by country and by the time period in which they wrote.) *The Reader's Guide to Periodical Literature* is another valuable resource, similar in scope to the MLA guide. By beginning with the most current year, and working backwards, you can get a wealth of materials to consult. Usually you'll be able to tell from the title whether the citation will be relevant to your topic. You should also know that *The Essay and General Literature Index* has the particular virtue of including references to essays published in collections.

You can also consult specialized bibliographies. For a major author, it's likely that that someone has published a bibliography devoted to that author and related matters. There are also bibliographies on particular subjects and (my favorite) even a bibliography of bibliographies. Check the publication date of these books. Some will be more current than others.

Consider also generating your own bibliography by doing a computer search of the topic. Check with the reference librarian about the cost and feasibility of this strategy.

Finally, two other resources out of the many available must be mentioned: *Poetry Explication: A Checklist of Interpretation since 1925 of British and American Poems Past and Present* and *Twentieth-Century Short Story Explication: Interpretations 1900-1975, of Short Fiction Since 1800*. These bibliographies are extremely useful for finding criticism on poems and short fiction.

Practical Tips

You may find, of course, that the book you want is checked out. If the card catalogue you're using is computerized, you'll probably be able to find out immediately if the book is available. The circulation desk of the library will likely have some procedure for recalling the book. If your library doesn't own the book you need, see about inter-library loan. It may take time, and it may cost a little, but most libraries can get books on loan from a system of other libraries (here's another reason to start as soon as possible).

Journal articles will ordinarily be available, if your library subscribes to the journal (check the card catalogue or database). That's because journals ordinarily can't be checked out. (Faculty usually can check out journals for brief periods.) If you don't have time to read the journal article, you can photocopy it. Whatever you do, don't ever tear an article or a page out of journal. There is, I'm certain, a special place in the lowest circle of Hades for journal mutilators, who have deprived their fellow human beings of the opportunity to learn. And there is probably no sin, except for stealing a book, that librarians and scholars loathe more.

In any event, with a little patience and industry you should be able to find ample materials on almost any topic.

THE WRITING PROCESS: THE RESEARCH PAPER

I'm going to trace here the process of writing a research paper in such a way that various critical approaches are reviewed. Here is the assignment:

> Briefly discuss at least two different interpretations of Yeats's "Sailing to Byzantium" and compare these readings to your own.

And here is how one student, Ann Loudermilk, proceeded.

Getting Ideas

First Source. By browsing through various sources, Ann notices that Cleanth Brooks's study of this poem is often mentioned. So she locates *The Well-Wrought Urn* and makes a "Works Cited" entry for it in a computer file.

```
Brooks, Cleanth.
    The Well-Wrought Urn. New York: Holt, 1947.
```

She then reads through the essay, making the following notes:

```
Brooks 178-91
    The tension for Brooks:

    nature vs. art
    becoming vs. being
    sensual vs. intellectual
    here vs. Byzantium
    aging vs. timelessness
```

Ann doesn't put any quotation marks here because this set of oppositions is her own interpretation of Brooks's argument. She has noticed that he repeatedly identifies oppositions in the poem, and so she lists them. Can you see these oppositions? In the first stanza, for instance, Yeats discusses the world of nature ("fish, flesh, or fowl," "sensual music"), and he concludes that those in the world of nature neglect art ("monuments of unageing intellect").

Ann puts the page numbers where this discussion occurs at the beginning of her note. This is a good idea because she might forget to put down the page number after she's made the note. Then she'd have to hunt around to find the material.

```
Brooks 188-89: "artifice" and unity

"The word 'artifice' fits the prayer at one level
after another; the fact that he is to be taken out
of nature; that his body is to be an artifice ham-
mered out of gold; that it will not age but will
have the finality of a work of art."

Brooks thus believes Yeats favors the latter items in
the list of elements in tension.
```

You'll notice that Ann uses quotation marks for part of the note: these are Brooks's words. It's crucial to keep straight what is your summary of the criticism, and what is quoted. Otherwise, you may use the critic's phrasing, thinking it's your own. Ann has also put a tag word at the top to suggest what the note is about. As her computer notes pile up, these tags will allow her to sort them and move them around more easily. As she understands how her paper is going to develop, she may add to or alter these tags.

```
Brooks 189: "artifice" and irony

"But 'artifice' unquestionably carries an ironic
qualification too. The prayer, for all its passion,
is a modest one. He does not ask that he be gath-
ered into the 'artifice of eternity.' The qualifi-
cation does not turn the prayer into mockery, but
it is all-important: it limits as well as defines
the power of the sages to whom the poet appeals."
```

Brooks's focus on irony in the next quotation should suggest that his stance is indeed New Critical:

```
Brooks 186-87: thesis

"To which world is Yeats committed? Which does he
choose?

"The question is idle—as idle as / the question
which the earnest schoolmarm puts to the little
girl reading for the first time 'L'Allegro—Il
Penseroso': which does Milton really prefer, mirth
or melancholy. . . .

"Yeats chooses both and neither."
```

On this note, Ann has a slash after "as" to let her know where the page break comes in Brooks's essay. If she needs to quote only a part of this passage, she'll know which page(s) to cite. She has also left out material, indicated by the ellipsis.

Brooks's point in the next passage noted suggests the complexity of Yeats's poem, refusing easy categorization into one thing or the other:

> Brooks 189-90: irony of the golden bird—both natural
> and supernatural
>
> > "The irony [of the poem] is directed, it seems to
> > me, not at our yearning to transcend the world of
> > nature, but at the human situation itself in which
> > supernatural and natural are intermixed—the human
> > situation which is inevitably caught between the
> > claims of both natural and supernatural. The golden
> > bird whose bodily form the speaker will take in
> > Byzantium will be withdrawn from the flux of the
> > world of becoming. But so withdrawn, it will sing
> > of the world of becoming—'Of what is past, or pass-
> > ing, or to come.'"

Brooks's New Critical stance is clear here, as he finds irony, unity, complexity.

Thus, using her notes, Ann sketches out what she might say about Brooks:

> Operating as a New Critic, Cleanth Brooks identifies a
> number of tensions in Yeats's poem—between nature and
> art, becoming and being, the sensual and intellectual,
> "here" and Byzantium, aging and timelessness (178-91).
> How Yeats manages to unify these tensions is epito-
> mized for Brooks by the word "artifice" in the third
> stanza. The word suggests that Yeats's speaker will be
> taken out of nature (188-89), but it occurs in a
> phrase that ironically qualifies this suggestion: the
> speaker will become an "artifice of eternity," rather
> than genuinely a part of eternity (189). Thus, Brooks
> says, of the oppositions set up by the poem, Yeats
> "chooses both and neither" (187). The poem is unified
> by the idea that the golden bird, like "the human sit-

> uation," is "inevitably caught between the claims of
> both natural and supernatural" (189-90).

You'll notice that Ann names the source, Brooks, and simply
puts the page reference where the quotation or reference
ends. She is following the new MLA style of documentation.
The "works cited" page, at the end of her essay, will give the
reader the bibliographical information needed to track the
source down.

    <u>Second Source</u>. In the card catalogue, Ann comes across a
work by Brenda Webster, *Yeats: A Psychoanalytic Study*—
obviously a distinctive approach. Here are the notes she
makes while reading Webster, which turns out to be a difficult work to understand:

> Webster, Brenda.
>> *Yeats: A Psychoanalytic Study*. New York: MacMillan,
>> 1973.

Here are some of the few sentences Ann thinks she understands:

> Webster 213-14: bird as defense
>> "The bird functions as a defense against anxieties
>> unconsciously raised by the poem—not just the fear
>> of aging and thwarted sexuality . . . but the over-
>> arching fear of a loss of integrity."

> Webster 214: Yeats's operation
>> "Sailing" was written before Yeats had a "Steinach
>> operation, which increased his sense of sexual
>> vitality."

Ann makes a note to see what a Steinach operation is.

> Webster 214: union with the mother
>> "The old man's frustrated sexual desire is the vis-
>> ible strand of what we shall see is a submerged
>> theme or fantasy of union with the mother." A few
>> sentences later: "in the works by Yeats that

embody incestuous fantasies, the hero is often symbolically castrated or mutilated by the mother figure before he can be loved. In "Sailing" Yeats
endows the aging process itself with the threatening qualities of a cruel mother. Now it is age that
sexually frustrates the old man and threatens him
with disintegration and loss of self."

Then she sketches out what she might say about Webster:

According to Brenda Webster, Yeats's speaker wants
to become a golden bird as "a defense against anxieties unconsciously raised by the poem" (113). Yeats's
fears included, Webster says, aging and thwarted sexuality; soon after writing the poem Yeats would have a
Steinach operation, increasing his sexual vitality
(Webster 214). But the most important anxiety, Webster
believes, was Yeats's fear of "a loss of integrity"
(214). Yeats dreams of becoming a golden bird so that
he might have an ageless body. But this desire is part
of a deeper one: he wants to reunite with his mother,
and removing his manhood by becoming a golden bird is,
so Webster says, part of that process.

But I don't see how a golden bird can join with the
mother any more easily than a grown man, or a wooden
pig, or a crystal do-do bird.

Third Source. Ann's teacher has mentioned one source in
class, "The Practice of Theory" by Lawrence Lipking. Ann gets
this essay and finds (as we have seen above) that Lipking
examines Yeats's poem from a deconstructive perspective in
order to show what is wrong with deconstruction. For the
essay itself she makes a card:

Lipking, Lawrence. "The Practice of Theory." In
    Literary Theories in Praxis. Ed. Shirley Staton.
    Philadelphia: U of Pennsylvania P, 1987, 426-40.
    Rpt. from *College Forum* 14: 23-29.

Then for each point that she thinks she might use, Ann also makes a note:

> Lipking 431: Singing—pro or con?
>
> > Lipking asks why should soul "louder sing / For every tatter in its mortal dress"? He sees two possibilities. 1) The soul is singing to distract itself from the tatters of its mortal dress (for example, sore throats, hemorrhoids, arthritis). 2) The soul is singing in celebration of its body falling apart because the tatters bring the soul closer to eternity and separation from the body. Lipking concludes there is no way to tell which of these meanings is right, and therefore "the line does not make sense," if by "sense" we mean that a statement cannot mean one thing and the opposite thing at the same time.
>
> Lipking 431: singing school—yes or no?
>
> > Lipking asks if there is a singing school. If "Nor is there singing school" means there isn't one, then how come the speaker wants some singing masters in the next verse? The lines are contradictory: the poem doesn't make sense.
>
> Lipking 432: Status of eternity?
>
> > Lipking asks if the artifice of eternity is "something permanent (an eternal artifice) or something evanescent (an illusion without any substance)." He says he can't decide based on the poem.
>
> Lipking 432: "That"
>
> > Lipking points to the uncertainty of the opening "That." Yeats himself, Lipking points out, said it "was the worst syntax he ever wrote."
>
> Lipking 432-33: the bird—obvious contradiction
>
> > Lipking finds one contradiction in the poem "so important and obvious that it is noticed by a great many students, and even some critics." Namely, the

speaker cannot claim he will "never take / My bodily form from any natural thing" because, Lipking
says, "every bodily form must be taken from nature,
whether the form of a bird or simply the golden
form embodied by an artist."

At this point, Ann tries to write a quick summary of what
she has learned. This step is useful, but too often passed over;
it allows you to work with your materials, to evolve your own
ideas before you actually start trying to write the paper itself.
Here is what Ann writes:

In "The Practice of Theory" Lawrence Lipking simply
says what nearly every student who has read Yeats's
poem carefully thinks: the poem does not make sense.
The reference of the opening "That" is never made
clear, as Lipking says (432). Nor can the reader tell
if there is a singing school or not: as Lipking notes,
"Nor is there singing school" seems to say there is no
singing school, but then the speaker immediately
desires to have singing masters in the next verse
(431). The lines are thus contradictory.

Lipking also points to the uncertainty involved in
the assertion that the soul should "louder sing / For
every tatter in its mortal dress." Does this statement
mean that the soul should sing to distract itself from
the decay of the body, its "mortal dress"? Or does it
mean that the soul should sing in celebration of its
body falling apart, since such disintegration brings
the soul closer to eternity and separation from the
body? Lipking concludes there is no way to tell which
of these meanings is right, and therefore "the line
does not make sense," if by "sense" we mean that a
statement cannot mean one thing and the opposite thing
at the same time (431). Likewise, Lipking notes that
the speaker cannot carry out his declaration to "never
take / My bodily form from any natural thing" because
"every bodily form must be taken from nature, whether
the form of a bird or simply the golden form embodied
by an artist" (432-33).

In pointing out these problems in the poem,
Lipking's point is not that Yeats's poem is a poor
one. The problem, Lipking says, is that when we adopt
a deconstructive stance, we are inevitably committed
to seeing how a work fails to make sense. Language
always, if we read closely enough, fails to make
sense.

Organizing

At this point Ann determines she's got plenty of secondary
sources to satisfy the assignment. Now she needs to work on
her own reading. Her first reaction to "Sailing" was quite different from any of the critics she has read. She did not find
the speaker of the poem to be appealing. Yeats, or his
spokesman, strikes Ann as self-absorbed, fretful, whining, and
even a bit pompous. She decides that her view is so different
that it should be interesting to her readers, and she determines after looking over the poem again that her reading can
be supported. So she writes the following shaping draft of her
reading:

1. I'd like to see what a feminist critic would do
   with this poem. Women appear only as the imaginary
   "ladies of Byzantium" who no doubt drop grapes and
   cherries into the mouths of the lords of Byzantium.
   Women are conspicuous by their absence. Yeats
   doesn't even consider whether "That" country, whatever it is, is a place for old women or even old
   people. It's just no country for old men. An "aged
   man" is "a paltry thing," but an aged woman apparently isn't worth considering.

2. Why is Yeats so self-absorbed and depressed that he
   desires the ridiculous transformation into a
   singing golden bird?(Is this the best paradise he
   can come up with?) Given three wishes, he wants to
   be a bird? And not even a real bird?
   Yeats frets because he is obsessed with aging.
   But what aspect of aging? Sex appeal, it seems. He

focuses on "The young / In one another's arms," and the other images relate to sexuality: salmon struggling upstream to reproduce and die; mackerel crowded together to mate. The "birds in the trees" are linked in our culture to romance. The reference to "dying generations" compresses the problem: he is dying while generations continue to be produced.

3. When he perceives his sexual appeal is waning, an older man today might buy a Porsche and chase younger women. Yeats's solution is even more desperate and absurd. He aims to do away with the physical altogether. Yeats changes sex into music: the transition is the reference to "sensual music." So he wants to leave the world of the sensual, passing from sensual music to music alone. As a golden bird, his sensual music will be outside nature. He will avoid the male horror of aging. Why can't our culture be more comfortable with life's natural processes?

Drafting

Now Ann is ready to put it all together. With this much preparation, she simply needs to introduce the critical statements, refine them and link them together. How can these statements be related?

She could simply describe how they relate to one another and contrast them to her own position. A more ambitious approach would be to present the other positions in some sort of sequence leading up to her ideas. What kind of sequence could there be? Brooks's New Critical reading sees some oppositions, and he argues that they are unified by the ironic status of the golden bird, both within and without nature. Lipking's deconstructive reading, however, refuses to allow such a resolution, identifying logical problems that cannot be explained away. And Webster's psychological study suggests why Yeats's logic should fail: he is attempting to deal with an impossible desire, the Oedipal impulse to rejoin his mother. Ann's point is a variation of Webster's position: the poem's problems do stem from Yeats's psychological distress, but that distress is not so convoluted as an Oedipal obsession. It is simply the fear of growing old and sexually unattractive.

After a draft or two and a close revision, the following paper emerges:

Ann Loudermilk
Professor Jane Taylor
March 24, 1992

FOUR VIEWS OF YEATS'S
"SAILING TO BYZANTIUM"

W. B. Yeats's "Sailing to Byzantium," one of the most-read poems in the English language, is also one of the most challenging. Yeats scholars keep insisting that the poem is clear, yet various interpretations keep appearing.[1] The syntax of the poem can be difficult. Yeats, in fact, said the opening line was "the worst syntax he ever wrote" (qtd. in Lipking 432). But even after the reader has determined what the lines mean, certain difficulties remain. Perhaps the most crucial question is how the poem resolves the opposing forces it sets up. Every reader perceives that nature and art, youth and age, and a number of other elements are opposed. But how does Yeats's desire to become a golden bird, an "artifice of eternity," resolve the poem's tensions?

A persuasive discussion of how the poem's oppositions are resolved occurs in Cleanth Brooks's New

The introduction sets up the problem: critics say the poem is clear, but conflicting interpretations continue to appear.

The focus for conflicting interpretations: the golden bird.

Brooks's reading.

From the notes
on Brooks.

Webster's reading.

From the notes
on Webster.

Critical reading. Brooks argues that
they are unified by the ironic status of the golden bird. He means
that the bird is, as Yeats puts it,
an "artifice," and it is therefore
outside of nature. His body will not
age, but will have "the finality of
a work of art" (189). Brooks reveals
here his adherence to the New
Critical idea that the work of art
has a stable presence and perma-
nence. But "artifice," as Brooks
recognizes, is qualified by Yeats,
who wants to become an "artifice of
eternity." About this qualification,
Brooks says the following:

> The qualification does not turn
> the prayer into mockery, but it
> is all-important: it limits as
> well as defines the power of the
> sages to whom the poet appeals.
> (189)

Thus Brooks believes the poem is
unified by this balancing of its
various oppositions.

But Brenda Webster strives to
discover why such a complex process
of unifying opposites would appeal
to Yeats, and her Freudian reading
finds the answer in, of course, the
Oedipus complex. For Webster, the
golden bird is not an ironically
unifying device, it is rather "a
defense against anxieties unconsciously raised by the poem—not just
the fear of aging and thwarted sexuality . . . but the overarching fear

of a loss of integrity" (213-14).
Yeats overcomes this fear of self-
loss, Webster argues, by desiring a
union with his mother, a kind of
return to the womb. The symbol of
the golden bird is part of this
desire, Webster says, because in
Yeats's other works involving
"incestuous fantasies, the hero is
often symbolically castrated or
mutilated by the mother figure
before he can be loved" (214). But,
Webster tells us:

> In "Sailing" Yeats endows the
> aging process itself with the
> threatening qualities of a cruel
> mother. Now it is age that sexu-
> ally frustrates the old man and
> threatens him with disintegration
> and loss of self. (214)

Lipking's reading.

For Lawrence Lipking, and I must
confess for me, such psychoanalyti-
cal explanations are not satisfying.
Lipking simply admits that crucial
lines in the poem do not make sense
(431). Lipking sees two possible
answers to the question of why the
soul should "louder sing / For every
tatter in its mortal dress." On the
one hand, perhaps the soul is
singing to distract itself from the
tatters of its mortal dress. On the

From the notes
on Lipking.

other hand, perhaps the soul is
singing in celebration of its body
falling apart because the tatters
bring the soul closer to eternity
and separation from the body.
Lipking concludes there is no way to

tell which of these meanings is right, and therefore "the line does not make sense," if by "sense" we mean that a statement cannot mean one thing and the opposite thing at the same time (431).

Lipking likewise considers whether there is a singing school in the poem. The line "Nor is there singing school" seems to say there is no such school, but the speaker desires some singing masters in the next verse. Rather than attempting some ingenious explanation, Lipking simply acknowledges that the lines are contradictory and the poem at every point deconstructs itself. Brooks's unification of the poem, Lipking would say, simply overlooks the evidence, engaging in wishful thinking. The golden bird, rather than being the key to the poem's unity, involves it in an obvious contradiction "so important and obvious that it is noticed by a great many students, and even some critics" (432). Namely, the speaker cannot claim he will "never take / My bodily form from any natural thing" because, Lipking says, "every bodily form must be taken from nature, whether the form of a bird or simply the golden form embodied by an artist" (433).

Here Ann places her own ideas in the context of these critics.

I agree with Webster and Lipking that this much-honored poem contains hopeless contradictions, but I think the explanation is less hidden than

From Ann's
freewriting.

an Oedipus complex and less shocking
than the deconstructive idea that
all language is contradictory.
Instead, Yeats is undergoing the
sort of crisis many older men under-
go when they perceive themselves to
be aging and growing unattractive.
He wants to become a golden bird
because he wants to be beautiful,
but he does not want to engage in
sexual competition for women.

This retreat from sexuality is
prepared for in the first stanza,
where Yeats focuses on "The young /
In one another's arms." Other images
also relate to sexuality: salmon
struggling upstream to reproduce and
die; mackerel crowded together to
mate. And the "birds in the trees"
are linked in our culture to
romance. The problem Yeats faces is
compressed into the reference to
"dying generations": he is dying
while generations continue to be
produced.

Conclusion: Ann
emphasizes the con-
cern with aging and
unatttractiveness in
the poem.

Yeats is so intent on escaping
the sexual that he cannot even consider whether "That" country,
whichever it is, is a place for old
women or even old people. All he can
consider is that it is no country
for old men—really, for one old man
in particular. An "aged man" is "a
paltry thing," but an aged woman
apparently is not worth considering.
Thus, Yeats aims to do away with the
physical altogether. He combines sex
and music in the "sensual music,"

and in becoming the golden bird he
will make the transformation complete, turning his sexual being into
music alone. As a golden bird, his
sensual music will be outside
nature, and he will avoid the horror—which is for him, strictly masculine, strictly his own—of aging.

NOTE

[1] See for instance Ketcheman, who says "Sailing to
Byzantium" is "clear enough" (171), and Clark, who says its
"movement" and "essential terms" are "quite clear" (199).
They disagree however on several points.

WORKS CITED

Brooks, Cleanth. *The Well-Wrought Urn*. New York:
    Holt, 1947.
Clark, Donald. *Yeats*. New York: Basic Books, 1962.
Ketcheman, Albert. *William Butler Yeats: A Life*. New
    York: Harper, 1958.
Lipking, Lawrence. "The Practice of Theory." In
    Literary Theories in Praxis. Ed. Shirley Staton.
    Philadelphia: U of Pennsylvania P, 1987, 426-40.
    Rpt. from *College Forum* 14: 23-29.
Webster, Brenda. *Yeats: A Psychoanalytic Study*. New
    York: MacMillan, 1973.

Works Cited and Recommended

Chapter One: Critical Worlds

Derrida, Jacques. *Of Grammatology*. Trans. G. C. Spivak. Baltimore: Johns Hopkins UP, 1976.

Gill, Brendan. *Here at The New Yorker*. New York: Random House, 1975.

———. *A New York Life*. New York: Poseidon, 1990.

Chapter Two: New Criticism

Berman, Art. "The New Criticism." *From the New Criticism to Deconstruction*. Urbana: U of Illinois P, 1988. 26–59.

Brooks, Cleanth. *The Well-Wrought Urn*. New York: Harcourt, 1947.

Brooks, Cleanth, and Robert Penn Warren. *Understanding Poetry*. New York: Holt, 1938.

Coleridge, Samuel Taylor. *Biographia Literaria*. 1817. New York: Dutton, 1960.

Eliot, T. S. *Selected Essays*. New York: Harcourt, 1932.

Graff, Gerald. *Professing Literature: An Institutional History*. Chicago: U of Chicago P, 1987.

Keats, John. *The Letters of John Keats, 1814–1821.* 2 vols. Cambridge: Harvard UP, 1958.

Lynn, Steven. "René Wellek." *Modern American Critics.* Ed. Gregory Jay. Detroit: Gale Research, 1988. 290–303.

Ransom, John Crowe. *The New Criticism.* New York: New Directions, 1941.

Richards, I. A. *Practical Criticism.* New York: Harcourt, 1929.

Sosnoski, James. "Cleanth Brooks." *Modern American Critics.* Ed. Gregory Jay. Detroit: Gale Research, 1988. 33-42.

Wellek, René, and Austin Warren. *Theory of Literature.* 1942. New York: Harcourt, 1977.

Willingham, John. "The New Criticism: Then and Now." *Contemporary Literary Theory.* Ed. Douglas Atkins and Laura Morrow. Amherst: U of Massachusetts, 1989.

Wimsatt, W. K, Jr., "The Affective Fallacy." In Wimsatt.

Wimsatt, W. K., Jr., ed. *The Verbal Icon: Studies in the Meaning of Poetry.* Lexington: U of Kentucky P, 1954.

Wimsatt, W. K., Jr., and Monroe Beardsley. "The Intentional Fallacy." Wimsatt 3–18.

Chapter Three: Reader-Response Criticism

Berg, Temma. "Psychologies of Reading." *Tracing Literary Theory.* Ed. Joseph Natoli. Urbana: U of Illinois P, 1987. 248–77.

Bleich, David. *Readings and Feelings: An Introduction to Subjective Criticism.* Urbana, Illinois: National Council of Teachers of English, 1975.

———. *Subjective Criticism.* Baltimore: Johns Hopkins UP, 1978.

Crosman, Robert. "How Readers Make Meaning." *College Literature* 9 (1982): 207–15. Rpt. in *Literary Theories in Praxis*. Ed. Shirley Staton. Philadelphia: U of Pennsylvania P, 1987. 357–66.

Fish, Stanley. *Doing What Comes Naturally: Change, Rhetoric, and the Practice of Theory in Literary and Legal Studies*. Durham, N.C.: Duke UP, 1989.

———. *Is There a Text in This Class? The Authority of Interpretive Communities*. Cambridge: Harvard UP, 1980.

———. "Rhetoric." *Critical Terms for Literary Study*. Ed. Frank Lentricchia and Thomas McLaughlin. Chicago: U of Chicago P, 1990. 203–222.

———. *Self-Consuming Artifacts: The Experience of Seventeenth-Century Literature*. Berkeley: U of California P, 1972.

———. *Surprised By Sin: The Reader in Paradise Lost*. Berkeley: U of California P, 1967.

Holland, Norman. "*Hamlet*—My Greatest Creation." *Journal of the American Academy of Psychoanalysis* 3 (1975): 419–27.

———. *Poems in Persons: An Introduction to the Psychoanalysis of Literature*. New York: Norton, 1973.

Iser, Wolfgang. *The Implied Reader: Patterns of Communication in Prose Fiction from Bunyan to Beckett*. Baltimore: Johns Hopkins UP, 1974.

Jauss, Hans Robert. "Literary History as a Challenge to Literary Theory." *Toward an Aesthetic of Reception*. Trans. Timothy Bahti. Brighton, Eng: Harvester Press, 1982. 18–45.

Kuhn, Thomas. *The Structure of Scientific Revolutions*. 2nd ed. Chicago: U of Chicago P, 1970.

Lynn, Steven. "Reader-Response Criticism." *Encyclopedia of English Studies*. Ed. Charles Moren et. al. Urbana, Ill.: NCTE, forthcoming.

Mailloux, Steven. *Interpretive Conventions: The Reader in the Study of American Fiction.* Ithaca: Cornell UP, 1982.

———. "The Turns of Reader-Response Criticism." *Conversations: Contemporary Critical Theory and the Teaching of Literature.* Ed. Charles Moran and Elizabeth Penfield. Urbana, Illinois: NCTE, 1990.

Peckham, Morse. "The Problem of Interpretation." *College Literature* 6 (1979): 1–17.

Rosenblatt, Louise. *Literature as Exploration.* 1938. Rev. ed. New York: Noble and Noble, 1968.

———. *The Reader, the Text, the Poem: The Transactional Theory of the Literary Work.* Carbondale: Southern Illinois UP, 1978.

Scholes, Robert. *Semiotics and Interpretation.* New Haven: Yale UP, 1982.

Tompkins, Jane P. "The Reader in History: The Changing Shape of Literary Response." *Reader-Response Criticism.* Ed. Jane Tompkins. Baltimore: Johns Hopkins UP, 1980.

Wellek, René, and Austin Warren. *Theory of Literature.* 1942. New York: Harcourt, 1977.

Chapter Four: Deconstruction

Bannet, Eve Tavor. *Structuralism and the Logic of Dissent.* Urbana: U of Illinois P, 1989.

Brooks, Cleanth. *The Well-Wrought Urn.* New York: Harcourt, 1947.

Crowley, Sharon. *A Teacher's Introduction to Deconstruction.* Urbana, Ill.: NCTE, 1989.

Culler, Jonathan. *On Deconstruction: Theory and Criticism after Structuralism.* Ithaca: Cornell UP, 1982.

————. *The Pursuit of Signs: Semiotics, Literature, Deconstruction.* Ithaca: Cornell UP, 1981.

Derrida, Jacques. "Différance." *Margins of Philosophy.* Trans. Alan Bass. Chicago: U of Chicago P, 1982. 1–29.

————. "Structure, Sign, and Play in the Discourse of the Human Sciences." *The Structuralist Controversy.* Ed. Richard Macksey and Eugenio Donato. Baltimore: Johns Hopkins UP, 1972. 247–72.

————. *Writing and Difference.* Trans. Alan Bass. Chicago: U of Chicago P, 1978.

De Man, Paul. "Semiology and Rhetoric." *Allegories of Reading.* New Haven: Yale UP, 1979. 3–20.

Eagleton, Terry. "Post-Structuralism." *Literary Theory: An Introduction.* Minneapolis: U of Minnesota P, 1983. 127–50.

Jay, Gregory. *America the Scrivener.* Ithaca: U of Cornell P, 1991.

Johnson, Barbara. *The Critical Difference.* Baltimore: Johns Hopkins UP, 1980.

Lipking, Lawrence. "The Practice of Theory." *Profession* 83 (1983): 21–28. Rpt. in *Literary Theories in Praxis.* Ed. Shirley Staton. Philadelphia: U of Pennsylvania P, 1987. 426–40.

Lynn, Steven. *Samuel Johnson after Deconstruction.* Carbondale: Southern Illinois UP, 1992.

Norris, Christopher. *Deconstruction: Theory and Practice.* New York: Methuen, 1982.

Selden, Raman. "Poststructuralist Theories." *A Reader's Guide to Contemporary Literary Theory.* 2nd ed. Lexington: U of Kentucky P, 1989. 70–113.

Tompkins, Jane. "A Short Course in Post-Structuralism." *Conversations: Contemporary Critical Theory and the Teaching of Literature.* Ed. Charles Moran and Elizabeth Penfield. Urbana, Ill.: NCTE, 1990. 19–37.

Chapter Five: Biographical, Historical, and New Historical Criticism

Auerbach, Erich. *Mimesis: The Representation of Reality in Western Literature.* Princeton: Princeton UP, 1953.

Bannet, Eve Tavor. *Structuralism and the Logic of Dissent: Barthes, Derrida, Foucault, Lacan.* Urbana: U of Illinois P, 1989.

Cheever, John. *The Brigadier and the Golf Widow.* New York: Harper, 1964.

———. *The Journals of John Cheever.* Ed. Robert Gottlieb. New York: Knopf, 1991.

———. *The Letters of John Cheever.* Ed. Benjamin Cheever. New York: Simon and Schuster, 1988.

Cheever, Susan. *Home Before Dark.* Boston: Houghton, 1984.

Coale, Samuel. *John Cheever.* New York: Frederick Ungar, 1977.

Donaldson, Scott. *John Cheever.* New York: Random, 1988.

Foucault, Michel. *Discipline and Punish: The Birth of the Prison.* Trans. Alan Sheridan. New York: Pantheon, 1977.

———. *The History of Sexuality.* Vol. 1. Trans. R. Hurley. New York: Pantheon, 1978.

Greenblatt, Stephen. *Renaissance Self-Fashioning: From More to Shakespeare.* Chicago: U of Chicago P, 1980.

———. *Shakespearean Negotiations: The Circulation of Social Energy in Renaissance England.* Berkeley: U of California P, 1988.

Griffith, Kelley, Jr. *Writing Essays About Literature.* San Diego: Harcourt, 1986.

Howard, Jean. "The New Historicism in Renaissance Studies." *ELR* 16 (1986): 13–43.

"Milton, John." *The Oxford Companion to English Literature.* 5th ed. 1985.

Montrose, Louis. "Of Gentlemen and Shepherds: The Politics of Elizabethan Pastoral Form." *ELH* 50 (1983): 415–59.

Patterson, Annabel. "Historical Scholarship." *An Introduction to Scholarship in Modern Languages and Literatures.* Ed. Joseph Gibaldi. 2nd ed. New York: MLA, 1992. 183–200.

Racevskis, Karlis. "Genealogical Critique: Michel Foucault and the Systems of Thought." *Contemporary Literary Theory.* Ed. G. Douglas Atkins and Laura Morrow. Amherst: U of Massachusetts P, 1989. 229–46.

Thomas, Brooks. "The Historical Necessity for—and Difficulties with—New Historical Analysis in Introductory Literature Courses." *College English* 49 (1987): 509–22.

Tillyard, E. M. W. *The Elizabethan World Picture.* New York: MacMillan, 1944.

Veeser, H. Aram, ed. *The New Historicism.* New York: Routledge, 1989.

Waldeland, Lynne. *John Cheever.* Boston: Twayne, 1979.

White, Hayden. *Tropics of Discourse: Essays in Cultural Criticism.* Baltimore: Johns Hopkins UP, 1978.

Woodhouse, A. S. P. "The Historical Criticism of Milton." *PMLA* 66 (1951): 1033–44.

Chapter Six: Psychological Criticism

Adler, Alfred. *The Individual Psychology of Alfred Adler.* Ed. Heinz and Rowena R. Ansbacher. New York: Anchor Books, 1978.

Eagleton, Terry. "Psychoanalysis." *Literary Theory: An Introduction.* Minneapolis: U of Minnesota P, 1983. 151–93.

Freud, Sigmund. "Creative Writers and Day-Dreaming." Gay 436–42.

———. "The Ego and the Id." Gay 629–58.

———. *New Introductory Lectures on Psychoanalysis.* Trans. and ed. James Strachey. New York: Norton, 1966.

Gay, Peter, ed. *The Freud Reader.* New York: Norton, 1989.

Holland, Norman. *The Brain of Robert Frost: A Cognitive Approach to Literature.* New York: Routledge, 1988.

———. *Holland's Guide to Psychoanalytic Psychology and Literature-and-Psychology.* New York: Oxford UP, 1990.

Jones, Judy, and William Wilson. *An Incomplete Education.* New York: Ballantine, 1987.

Marshall, Donald G. "Literary Interpretation." *Introduction to Scholarship in Modern Languages and Literatures.* Ed. Joseph Gibaldi. New York: MLA, 1992. 159–82.

Meltzer, Françoise. "Unconscious." *Critical Terms for Literary Study.* Ed. Frank Lentricchia and Thomas McLaughlin. Chicago: U of Chicago P, 1990. 147–62.

Willbern, David. "Reading after Freud." *Contemporary Literary Theory.* Ed. G. Douglas Atkins and Laura Morrow. Amherst: U of Massachusetts, 1989. 158–179.

Chapter Seven: Feminist Criticism

Astell, Mary. *A Serious Proposal to the Ladies.* London, 1692. Excerpt rpt. in *The Norton Anthology of Literature by Women.* Ed. Gilbert and Gubar. New York: Norton, 1985. 113–17.

Atkins, Douglas. *Reading Deconstruction, Deconstructive Reading.* Lexington: UP of Kentucky, 1983.

Beauvoir, Simone de. *The Second Sex.* Trans. H. M. Parshley. New York: Vintage, 1974. Trans. of *Le deuxième sexe.* 2 vols. Paris: Gallimard, 1949.

Crewe, Louie, and Rictor Norton. "The Homophobic Imagination: An Editorial." *College English* 36 (1974): 272–90.

Culler, Jonathan. "Reading as a Woman." *On Deconstruction: Theory and Criticism after Structuralism.* Ithaca: Cornell UP, 1982. 43–64.

Eighteenth-Century Women Poets: An Oxford Anthology. New York: Oxford UP, 1989.

Gibbs, Nancy. "The War Against Feminism." *Time* 9 March 1992: 50–55.

Gilbert, Sandra, and Susan Gubar. *The Madwoman in the Attic.* New Haven: Yale UP, 1979.

———, ed. *The Norton Anthology of Literature by Women.* New York: Norton, 1985.

Gorman, Christine. "Sizing Up the Sexes." *Time* 20 January 1992: 42–51.

Jehlen, Myra. "Gender." *Critical Terms for Literary Study.* Ed. Frank Lentricchia and Thomas McLaughlin. Chicago: U of Chicago P, 1990.

Laqueur, Thomas. *Making Sex: Body and Gender from the Greeks to Freud.* Cambridge: Harvard UP, 1992.

Lynn, Steven. "Sexual Difference and Johnson's Brain." *Fresh Views of Samuel Johnson.* Ed. Prem Nath. Troy, N.Y.: Whitston, 1987. 123–49.

Millet, Kate. *Sexual Politics.* Garden City, N.Y.: Doubleday, 1970.

Mahoney, John, ed. *The Enlightenment and English Literature.* Lexington, Mass.: Heath, 1980.

Rich, Adrienne. "Compulsory Heterosexuality and Lesbian Existence." *The Powers of Desire: The Politics of*

Sexuality. Ed. Ann Snitow et al. New York: Monthly Review, 1983. 177–205.

Ruthven, K. K. *Feminist Literary Studies: An Introduction.* Cambridge: Cambridge UP, 1984.

Schor, Naomi A. "Feminist and Gender Studies." *Introduction to Scholarship in Modern Languages and Literatures.* 2nd ed. Ed. Joseph Gibaldi. New York: Modern Language Association, 1992. 262–87.

Sedgwick, Eve. *Epistemology of the Closet.* Berkeley: U of Cal P, 1991.

Selden, Raman. "Feminist Criticism." *A Reader's Guide to Contemporary Literary Theory.* 2nd ed. Lexington: UP of Kentucky, 1989. 134–54.

Showalter, Elaine. A *Literature of Their Own: British Women Novelists from Bronte to Lessing.* Princeton, N.J.: Princeton UP, 1977.

Smith, Barbara. "Toward Black Feminist Criticism." *New Feminist Criticism.* Ed. Elaine Showalter. New York: Pantheon, 1985. 168–85.

Torsney, Cheryl. "The Critical Quilt: Alternative Authority in Feminist Criticism." *Contemporary Literary Theory.* Ed. G. Douglas Atkins and Laura Morrow. Amherst: U of Massachusetts P, 1989. 180–99.

Tillotson, Geoffrey, Paul Fussell, and Marshall Waingrow. *Eighteenth-Century English Literature.* New York: Harcourt, Brace & World, 1969.

Uphaus, Robert, and Gretchen Foster, eds. *The 'Other' Eighteenth Century: English Women of Letters.* East Lansing, Mich.: Colleagues Press, 1991.

Webster, Roger. *Studying Literary Theory: An Introduction.* London: Edward Arnold, 1990. 71–79.

Woolf, Virginia. *A Room of One's Own.* New York: Harcourt, 1981.

INDEX